Rehabilitation for Mental Health Problems
An Introductory Handbook

Clephane Hume
Lecturer, Queen Margaret College,
Edinburgh

Ian Pullen
Consultant Psychiatrist,
Royal Edinburgh Hospital;
Honorary Senior Lecturer,
University of Edinburgh

SECOND EDITION

CHURCHILL LIVINGSTONE
EDINBURGH LONDON MADRID MELBOURNE NEW YORK
AND TOKYO 1994

CHURCHILL LIVINGSTONE
Medical Division of Longman Group UK Limited

Distributed in the United States of America by Churchill
Livingstone Inc., 650 Avenue of the Americas, New York, N.Y.
10011, and by associated companies, branches and
representatives throughout the world.

First edition 1986
Second edition 1994

ISBN 0-443-04554-2

British Library of Cataloguing in Publication Data
A catalogue record for this book is available from the
British Library.

Library of Congress Cataloging in Publication Data
Hume, Clephane.
    Rehabilitation for mental health problems: an introduction handbook/
Clephane A. Hume, Ian Pullen. – 2nd ed.
        p. cm.
    Rev. ed of: Rehabilitation in psychiatry/[edited by] Clephane Hume, Ian Pullen,
1986.
    Includes bibliographical references and index.
    ISBN 0-443-04554-2
    1. Mentally ill–Rehabilitation. 2. Rehabilitation. I. Pullen, Ian M.
II. Rehabilitation in psychiatry. III. Title.
    [DNLM: 1. Mental Disorders–rehabilitation. WM 29.1 H921r 1993]
RC439.5.R425   1993
616.89' 16–dc20
DNLM/DLC
for Library of Congress   93–18261

Produced by Longman Singapore Publishers (Pte) Ltd.
Printed in Singapore

Contents

Contributors   vii

Preface to the second edition   ix

Preface to the first edition   xi

1. What is rehabilitation?   1
    Clephane Hume

2. The task   17
    Ian Pullen

3. The development of rehabilitation and community care   35
    Ian Pullen

4. Community care—motivation and evaluation   45
    Ian Pullen

5. Assessment and evaluation   61
    Clephane Hume

6. Management options   75
    Ian Pullen

7. Planning a care package   97
    Clephane Hume

8. Teamwork   113
    Ben Thomas

9. The family and rehabilitation   133
    Colin Elliot

10. Transcultural aspects of rehabilitation   145
    David Mumford

11. Substance abuse 159
Ben Thomas

12. Old age 181
Ian Pullen

13. Physical handicap 205
Clephane Hume, Nicola Stuckey

14. Mental handicap/learning disability 233
Ros Lyall

15. The future 259
Clephane Hume, Ian Pullen

Index 263

Contributors

Colin Elliot RMN Dip.Social Work MBA
Practice Team Manager (Community Care), Lothian Regional
Council Social Work Department, Edinburgh

Clephane A. Hume BA DipCOT CertFE
Lecturer, Queen Margaret College, Edinburgh

Rosalind H. Lyall MBChB MPhil MRCPsych
Consultant Psychiatrist in Learning Disabilities, Gogarburn
Hospital and City of Edinburgh Community Learning Disability
Services, Edinburgh

David B. Mumford MD MPhil MRCPsych
Consultant Psychiatrist, Barrow Hospital, Bristol

Ian M. Pullen FRCPsych
Consultant Psychiatrist, Royal Edinburgh Hospital; Honorary
Senior Lecturer, University of Edinburgh

Nicola Stuckey BA(Hons) MSc
Principal Clinical Psychologist, Robert Fergusson Unit, Royal
Edinburgh Hospital, Edinburgh

Ben L. Thomas MSc BSc RGN RMN DipN RNT
Chief Nurse Advisor/Director of Quality, Bethlem Royal Hospital
and Maudsley Hospital Special Health Authority; Honorary
Lecturer, Institute of Psychiatry, London

Preface to the second edition

Although it is only six years since the first edition of this book appeared, a second edition is already necessary. The pace of change has accelerated as much in the field of mental health as in any other. After decades of paying lipservice to the ideals of Community Care, change is happening. Old mental hospitals are closing and the diversity of services for people with mental health problems in the community is increasing. This new edition reflects these changes.

This edition, like its predecessor, has been written as a basic handbook for anyone wishing to obtain an up to date, practical and readable overview of the field of rehabilitation. All of the chapters have been completely rewritten. Responding to readers' comments we have included two entirely new chapters — on substance abuse and practice in a multicultural society — and a wider range of disciplines is reflected amongst contributing authors. Sales of the first edition worldwide have encouraged us to be less parochial and to include more references to practices in other parts of the world.

The title of this new edition acknowledges a fundamental change of practice. Rehabilitation has ceased to be the sole preserve of the psychiatric team based in the psychiatric hospital, and has become a multi-agency activity. Voluntary organisations, such as local mental health associations, work alongside the statutory health and social services, and private providers. Above all, people with serious mental health problems and their carers are being empowered to make their own decisions and to have people or organisations act as advocates for them.

In six years much has changed. In the first edition, for simplicity, the pronoun 'he' was used throughout the book. This convention now seems outdated and chapters alternate in the use of 'he' or 'she'.

This edition has been shaped by the readers of the first edition. We hope that our new readership will prove to be as encouraging and constructive critics.

Edinburgh 1993

C.H.
I.P.

Preface to the first edition

Edinburgh has been called the 'Athens of the North' and, less charitably, the 'Reykjavik of the South'*. It is all a matter of perspective.

In many respects rehabilitation is in a similar position. What is called a 'rehabilitation unit' by one team may be described as a 'back ward' by another. In fact neither description is necessarily correct. This book attempts to set rehabilitation in perspective.

Many people will find themselves working in rehabilitation, either permanently or on placement, without any clear idea of what 'rehabilitation' means, its potential and its limitations. Others will be expected to know something about rehabilitation for examinations! Our intention has been to provide basic information in as readable a form as possible. The book should be short enough to be read from cover to cover (by the determined), but each chapter is written to be read on its own (for the selective).

While the book is written by members of different professions, we have tried to avoid the common pitfall of many multi-author books: that of presenting the doctor's, nurse's, occupational therapist's, psychologist's and social worker's views in turn. Most of the book has been written by two of us (an occupational therapist and a psychiatrist), but we invited clinical psychologists to write chapters on the psychological approach and on mental handicap. A nurse was invited to contribute a chapter on the multi-disciplinary team.

The omission of a social worker reflects our wish to limit the number of contributors.

After an historical introduction we move to chapters describing the task of rehabilitation and the arguments for and against different treatment settings. Organisation and treatment planning

* Tom Stoppard 1972 *Jumpers* Faber, London, p. 69

follow, making a clear case for careful planning of all work with patients. The multidisciplinary team has been reviewed critically with suggestions for improving teamwork. This chapter includes an important section on burnout—a particular risk in rehabilitation work.

Psychological approaches, the special problems of mental handicap and rehabilitation of the elderly and physically handicapped follow. We end with a brief look into the rehabilitation crystal ball.

For simplicity the pronoun 'he' is used throughout the book when referring to patients, staff or relatives. This convention has been followed as the English language has no single pronoun denoting both sexes, and s/he and he/she are unnecessarily clumsy.

We hope this book will be stimulating and thought-provoking, but the reader is warned that 'Reading is sometimes an ingenious device for avoiding thought'!**

This book has come through a long gestation period starting with encouragement from Dr James Affleck when we were both members of his rehabilitation team. It would not have seen the light of day without the support of our publisher Sally Morris, and the assiduous typing of Dianne Birse. We are grateful to all of them.

Edinburgh 1986   C.H.
                                                   I.P.

** Sir Arthur Helps 1847, 1853 *Friends in Council* Book 2, ch1

1. What is rehabilitation?

Clephane Hume

Any patient, however seemingly intractable the condition, retains the capacity to surprise the persistent therapist.

Wing and Brown 1970

INTRODUCTION

Rehabilitation is the process through which a person is helped to adjust to the limitations of his disability. Lost skills may be regained, or new coping strategies developed, so that the person achieves competence. The nature of the impairment dictates the particular focus of rehabilitation, but at all times the person must be treated as an individual. The complexity and variety of problems presented must never be allowed to obscure the individual's needs. Ultimately, the focus of rehabilitation must be the quality of the person's life.

The rehabilitation process requires the involvement of a number of people. Family and friends, fellow patients and hospital staff, all play a part. The location of treatment is important—the process cannot be carried out in an institutional vacuum. For those in hospital, the realities of the outside world must be considered and treatment extended into the community prior to resettlement. People already living outside hospital must be helped to improve their quality of life in accordance with the difficulties imposed by their illness. This may mean providing people with information from which to make choices, or developing skills to meet the demands of everyday living.

Rehabilitation means systematic work for clients and staff over long periods of time. Though achievements may be reached only slowly and even painfully, the results can be rewarding.

AIMS OF REHABILITATION

The principal aim of rehabilitation is to enable the individual to attain his maximum level of independence, psychologically, socially, physically and economically. In practice, this may mean helping someone to regain his former level of ability or enabling him to reach greater independence than previously.

'Maximum level' means the optimum level for that individual and therefore it is inappropriate to define a general standard of independent function. Success is a personal matter, to be judged according to achievements reached in terms of the goals for the individual. Thus, what is a realistic aim for one person may be unattainable for the next. Maintaining the client in an independent living situation within the community may be a realistic aim for one person, while the potential of a long-term patient to increase his skills may be such that to be discharged from hospital may be inappropriate for his needs. Rehabilitation therefore means empowering the person to attain his full potential within the environment in which he is living.

Handicap and the rights of the individual

In the context of psychiatry, it is necessary to consider what constitutes handicap or disability. As someone with a spinal injury uses a wheelchair to move around freely, a person who has hallucinatory experiences may be able to adjust to the demands on his life-style and be able to continue to lead an effective life. Such disabilities do not mean that the person is handicapped. Often the handicap is consequent on the reactions of others to the person's illness, rather than the illness itself. Caplan (1961) suggests that problems associated with mental illness are to a large extent 'superimposed, preventable and treatable'. It should also be remembered that the person may have difficulties which were present before the onset of the illness and which may complicate the situation, e.g. poor social skills or low intelligence.

Wing & Morris (1981) describe three factors which contribute to handicap:

- psychiatric disabilities arising from the symptoms and illness process
- social disadvantages such as poverty and unemployment
- adverse personal reaction to illness.

Physical and social environmental factors are thus crucial in determining the degree of handicap and all the above factors should be taken into account when devising a treatment programme to meet the needs of the individual.

In considering disability, it is well to remember the words of the United Nations Declaration on the Rights of Disabled Persons (1975):

'Disabled persons have the inherent right to respect for their human dignity. Disabled persons, whatever the origin, nature, and severity of their handicaps and disabilities have the same fundamental rights as their fellow citizens of the same age, which implies first and foremost the right to enjoy a decent life, as normal and full as possible.'

Helander (1984) develops this into 10 commandments for integrated living and although these are written in the context of community-based rehabilitation in developing countries, it would do no harm to question whether or not psychiatric patients living in the community enjoy such rights. It is also worth remembering the rights of any person to have basic amenities such as food and shelter, and the right to participate in the social and political structures of society.

STAGES OF REHABILITATION

These will vary according to the living situation of the person. For convenience, they are divided here into hospital and community contexts.

Hospital

1. Preparing for resettlement in another unit or in the community
2. Bridging the gap
3. Community support.

Preparing for resettlement

For someone newly admitted to hospital, rehabilitation begins with diagnosis. This does not mean that the diagnosis dictates the person's programme, but rather that, as treatment of the acute illness is initiated, general plans for future management should be discussed. As acute symptoms subside, more detailed consideration can be given to rehabilitation. The original plans may have to be modified and referral to a special ward or unit focusing on rehabilitation may be considered. For many patients, programmes will be initiated in hospital for continuation after discharge.

For those who have spent some time in hospital, the process of rehabilitation may mean following a staged programme, which is designed to reduce dependence on staff and the institution by gradually promoting independence in all aspects of behaviour. Revision of former skills will be required, together with re-education for community living. Resources for this will vary, so that the actual location of treatment may be in a ward, or the hospital may have a comprehensive transitional care system, including half-way houses, hostels and group homes attached to the hospital. As far as possible, the final stage of hospital-based rehabilitation should take place in accommodation which provides a realistic environment—ideally a flat where people can stay for fixed periods of time in order to try out their skills with minimal supervision from staff.

Bridging the gap

Rehabilitation, especially for long-term patients, does not end with discharge. On the contrary, it is intensified as the patient comes face to face with the realities and problems of life in the community. 'Going it alone' and getting readjusted is a stressful experience for most patients. Support from known and trusted people is essential during this bridging phase if the experiences gained at earlier stages of the programme are to be consolidated and augmented, and the person successfully integrated into community living.

Community support

Continuing support will be necessary to maintain progress, provide help at times of crisis and prevent deterioration. For some people day care will be required, while for others regular contact with a community psychiatric nurse will be indicated. In some instances, attendance at a medication clinic may suffice. Long-term patients will benefit from support which can promote the confidence required to cope with unexpected events in a rather unstructured existence. This will help to prevent the person clinging to routines established in hospital and which are inappropriate for life in the community.

People should be encouraged to make full use of the services and community resources available. They must understand the roles of members of the primary health care team, including the general practitioner, and how to obtain help. Attention will be required in order to build up social networks so that the additional problem of the loneliness experienced by many chronic patients can be reduced. The use of lunch clubs and community leisure facilities should have been commenced during hospitalisation and continuing use of these will facilitate the development of skills and encourage integration rather than isolation.

While it is recognised that support for the client is essential, it must also be remembered that support for carers should be considered. This is as important for relatives of those experiencing illness for the first time as for those who have a chronic condition (see Ch. 9).

Community

1. Identifying problems
2. Implementing strategies to overcome these problems
3. Support in maintaining changes.

Identifying problems

Ways of assessing difficulties are described in Chapter 5. It is always essential to determine what the problems are, as a basis for designing intervention. Problems may be primarily due to the illness, the environment, or a combination of both and it is important to discover the real cause.

People will be helped to identify difficulties and to discuss ways in which these may be overcome through the use of community resources, in order to prevent admission.

Implementing strategies

Increasing the person's knowledge of community resources, teaching alternative methods of coping, or developing skills may all be utilised in overcoming problems. Supportive counselling of the individual, involving significant others as appropriate, may be of particular importance.

Support

Community support for patients leaving hospital has been described above and those already in the community may have similar needs. With the increased focus on care in the community, many people will have only brief admissions to hospital, or may remain at home.

For some people day hospital attendance may be indicated; for others, contact with a member of a community psychiatric/mental health team will provide the support necessary to enable them to cope.

PRINCIPLES OF REHABILITATION

There is nothing particularly complicated about the concepts involved in rehabilitation. Applying them is perhaps not so easy, but experience is part of any learning process, including rehabilitation itself.

In essence, rehabilitation involves compensation and education. Through building on the person's abilities, using compensatory measures where abilities are limited, and by educating the person about day-to-day life skills and different ways of coping, it is possible to help someone achieve a reasonable quality of life. An essential component of rehabilitation is teamwork (see Ch. 8). *The team is the cornerstone of the rehabilitation process.* Without effective teamwork, communication and co-operation, the concepts described below are of little use. Co-ordination may appear time-consuming, but it is time well invested, and can avoid duplication of effort. Much time can be wasted if someone is unaware of what a colleague is doing. Efficient and effective organisation and communication go a long way towards achieving results. The concept of teamwork is not idealistic or unattainable and is worth working for.

The simple concepts below provide a framework and general approach — the bricks with which to create structures of any complexity.

Four basic principles are:

1. Listen to the client
2. Know the community
3. Pay attention to detail
4. Remember how the world has changed.

Listen to the client

But of course you do! Remember that it is necessary to listen very carefully and to watch the non-verbal messages in order to identify the real problem. It is important to avoid imposing one's own view of the problem onto the person, and to avoid 'jumping in' with comments when reflective silence is required. Careful open-ended questioning will help the individual to talk about problems which might not have been apparent at first. Other people may have identified all sorts of problems, but it is the individual himself who will tell you what his difficulties really are. However, he may need help separating the core problems from those of lesser importance.

Know the community

It is essential to be familiar with the community to which patients are returning if they are to be prepared adequately for the transition. Likewise, a care package for someone already living in the community cannot be planned without knowledge of the resources which are locally available. This means knowing where to find important local facilities (e.g. health centre, community centre, post office, church, job centre), and also how to discover what is available. Members of the rehabilitation team should be aware of directories and resource lists compiled by local councils of social services or mental health groups.

As well as practical information, an understanding of cultural norms is necessary. The catchment area may include exclusive residential areas, deprived inner-city housing schemes and minority ethnic groups. It is necessary to be aware of 'what goes' in each. Patients moving into unfamiliar surroundings will need guidance about what is expected of them.

There is now increased awareness of transcultural problems, the difficulties experienced by people moving from one country to another (see Ch. 10). This is not, however, the prerogative of immigrants as moving from a rural community to a city can be just as difficult.

Pay attention to detail

Absolutely nothing is too small or too obvious to be taken for granted. An apparently trivial setback may prove to be an enormous stumbling block for some people. Similarly, routine tasks which most people perform without much thought, will, for some, assume a significance out of all proportion.

Even if someone has no difficulty with some aspects of daily living, it is not safe to assume competence in others. It is important to check that he can carry out a specific task, and to record the result of the observations.

Pat could cook, generally look after himself and cope well at his job in the hospital. A hostel place was found for him on the other side of town. 'No good', he said, 'it's too far to walk.' 'But you can get a bus to the end of the road.' It wasn't just a lack of familiarity with the complications of pay-as-you-enter buses, but a hitherto unvoiced fear of using public transport which had to be considered. Meanwhile, someone else took the bed in the hostel...

Remember how the world has changed

For some patients, leaving hospital, or becoming ill, is like moving to a foreign country with all the anxieties such a change arouses. The feeling of *dis-ease* experienced if one is not *au fait* with social conventions may be shared by a patient who returns home on a weekend pass as a virtual stranger visiting his own home.

Changes will be particularly noticeable for long-term patients. They may not even recognise where they used to live with all the new buildings or the bypass cutting across town. However, this also has relevance for others. Patterns and norms of society are constantly changing. It does not take long for shops to alter or businesses to move. Even the reorganisation of the layout of the supermarket can be unsettling. As microchip technology and other developments occur at a bewildering rate, so the adjustments required of clients multiply. The speed of progress may seem to have alarming dimensions.

The rate of inflation may be a complaint for everyone but it can pose a real problem for patients.

Betty just could not accept that she would have to pay 60 pence for a pudding to go with the rest of the meal she had so painstakingly selected at the supermarket. She felt she could not possibly justify spending the equivalent of twelve shillings in 'old money'. Indeed, the total of her purchases almost caused her to walk out of the shop empty-handed. Hunger and her escort prevailed upon her to do otherwise!

If all this seems obvious—good! If not, perhaps it has raised questions about your own practice. If you are tempted to bypass the remainder of the list, go back to point 3! Further points to consider are:

5. Graded programmes
6. Timing
7. Education and re-education
8. Re-orientation
9. Staff attitudes
10. Consistency
11. Security
12. Attitudes to medication.

Graded programmes

The grading and staging of programmes allow the person to progress at an individual rate through a series of tasks, towards the achievement of the eventual objective. A goal which seems remote may leave him unmotivated, through lack of conviction that such a task can ever be accomplished. Success in small stages, appropriate to the individual, promotes confidence and will encourage further effort.

Compare the person's skills to a pile of bricks. To build the wall, bricks are systematically placed in layers to achieve a tall, stable structure. Each brick might be small, but contributes to the finished product. The person's skills also need to be well integrated and held together on firm foundations.

Timing

One step at a time is enough. The individual needs time to consolidate each new experience before embarking on the next. If for example, someone has a change of occupation, wait, and give him time to adjust to this new routine before making a change in accommodation (unless, of course, circumstances mean that this is impossible or the goals are well within his capabilities). Likewise, medication should not be altered just before someone moves to a new unit as he will have enough stress to contend with in the move itself.

Education and re-education

Some people have never had the opportunity to learn basic living skills. Others will have forgotten them, or they may have atrophied through lack of use due to illness. Essential skills for each individual will depend on the accommodation anticipated. Someone who aims to live in a hostel may not need to be domestically self-sufficient, whereas no group home resident can survive and co-operate with fellow residents without competence in household tasks. If someone is unable to reach a safe level of performance, it will be necessary to consider alternative arrangements.

Re-orientation

This is closely linked to the points made above. Dormant skills may be renewed in the light of modern requirements. Detailed knowledge of local resources and facilities must be acquired. Some people have been known to ride a bus from terminus to terminus in order to gain an impression of their new surroundings. Imagine how you would feel moving to a strange town.

Staff attitudes

Attitudes are of paramount importance. The role of staff is in some ways similar to that of parent. They provide a secure base from which to experiment and to which to return when in need of support: but not a dominating influence. Too little intervention may mean lack of structure and the balance may be difficult to achieve.

Staff may have to learn to stand back and watch a person struggle to do things for himself. Clark (1984) suggests that 'challenges can be more valuable than tender loving care'. It is by no means easy to resist the temptation to intervene but allowing impending disaster to materialise may permit valuable learning. We all learn from making mistakes. Needless to say, success is also necessary and achievements should be reinforced in a way that is not patronising.

Consistency

This is really self-explanatory but conflicting messages and changing attitudes are confusing for both clients and colleagues. Firm encouragement one day will be undermined if followed by a laissez-faire approach the next. Uncertainty about the reaction likely to be received from staff is bound to reduce confidence. Consistency of personnel is as important as consistency of approach. It is inevitable that staff will change and in teaching hospitals, the turnover may be rapid. Newcomers, both staff and patients, take time to settle into the ways of a new unit, and may feel that they are just getting to know the situation when they are moved on again. For the sake of continuity, and to provide a sense of security, it is essential to have a core of permanent staff. This is particularly important in rehabilitation of long-term patients where change may be slow to occur and consistency may be required over several years.

Security

Being able to try something out is the most effective way to learn, though not all learning is painless. People need an environment in which failure is accepted as just part of life, rather than being regarded as a major disaster. They must feel able to accept support and try again.

Attitude to medication

Many people would place this much higher up the list. If a person cannot appreciate and accept the need for necessary prescribed medication, the entire treatment programme may be placed in jeopardy. Most people are aware of the problems of becoming dependent upon medication and are consequently reluctant to expose themselves to the possibility. It can be very hard for some people to understand the need to take pills, especially when they feel well and have little insight into the fact that they have ever been ill. They may be prepared to swallow medication when supervised, but not when left to their own devices. The need to take a tablet to suppress undesirable side-effects may be more readily understood.

The prospect of taking medication on a long-term basis can be hard to come to terms with and the idea of long-term psychotropic medication may lead to the same sort of reactions as are produced by the prospect of daily insulin injections or thyroid replacement therapy.

On the other hand, some people learn to recognise changes in their illness and adjust their medication accordingly.

Applying the principles of rehabilitation

To turn the rehabilitation process into a working model, the concepts require to be applied throughout all stages of the person's programme. Caplan (1964) stated that 'Rehabilitation begins with diagnosis' and the sooner the process can be started, the greater the chance of prevention of handicap.

These principles can be applied to different aspects of daily life:

- personal independence
- domestic skills and household management
- leisure and social skills
- work/occupation.

These are broad categories and it is obvious that there will be overlaps between them (Hume 1990). In planning a programme, it may be relevant to focus on for example, domestic skills and personal independence, omitting work.

It will also be necessary to consider what treatment approaches may be used within the overall rehabilitation process. The compensatory aspects of the rehabilitative approach will only be implemented after other approaches have been used. Initial treatment may involve a humanistic approach to restore the person's self-esteem and motivate him towards future goals, or it might be relevant to use a behavioural approach with very specific targets to be achieved and rewards contingent on these. A cognitive approach may alter someone's faulty self-perceptions, thus making it possible to continue to tackle other aspects of rehabilitation (see Ch. 7).

FACTORS INFLUENCING THE REHABILITATION PROCESS

Principles and concepts are not enough. Staff must be aware of the dynamics of the therapeutic relationship and the factors that will influence this.

Communication

It is crucial to a therapeutic relationship that patients, staff and relatives are clear about the targets to be aimed at and the methods by which they may be achieved. People involved may have different ideas and yet assume that everyone agrees with their viewpoint.

Good communication with regular review of goals and reinforcement of achievements will lead to increased motivation on all sides. It is worth considering our own individual styles of communication. Is the language we use fully understood by the person we are talking to ? This does not just mean do we speak the same language, but is the pattern of speech too complex, are the words used unfamiliar in the social and educational background from which the person comes? If he is familiar with psychiatric terminology, is his use of words based on genuine understanding or mere repetition of jargon? We may falsely assume that he understands more than he does. Use of straightforward and concise language without abstract concepts will be of benefit to most people.

All this may sound obvious, but how many people leave their doctor's surgery sure that they know what has been said, only to wonder some time later what was really meant? Are you both using the same agenda? Consider whether or not communication has been two-way. (Try reading *The Telephone* in *Prayers of Life* by Michel Quoist 1963.)

The client

'You can only rehabilitate a volunteer' was the observation of one experienced practitioner. But how is motivation achieved? There is no simple answer. Motivation comes from within, but it is also determined by external factors. Good communication, which enhances understanding of personal goals, may facilitate motivation and the person's level of self-confidence should also be considered. Of equal importance is the recognition of the person's hopes and ambitions. Reconciling people's limitations with their ambitions may mean helping them to recognise their abilities and to gain confidence in trying out their skills.

Is discharge for a long-term patient an idea which is too remote to be contemplated, or a suggestion which is too threatening at present? Where does the person want to live? Does he have ideas of sharing accommodation? Is there a realistic possibility of someone newly diagnosed as having a major illness returning to his former occupation and if so, are his employers supportive or should he be seeking alternatives?

It may also be necessary to consider goals which are not directly in line with the individual's wishes. If this is the case, the reasons must be discussed; for example, helping a person come to terms with the unpleasant reality that a family relationship is over, and he has been finally excluded. How can he be helped to adjust to the change or motivated to work towards a different goal?

The staff —knowledge, skills, attitudes

Knowledge

All members of the multidisciplinary hospital treatment team will already have some knowledge of psychiatric disorders, consequent problems and their management. In addition to the recognition of illness and its management (physical, medical and social), team members should be aware of the factors contributing to institutionalisation and its prevention.

The extent and range of any team member's knowledge will depend on the level of training and professional experience. The strength of a clinical team depends on the depth and breadth of experience, both personal and professional, that individuals contribute to the team as a whole. Mutual respect (which must be earned) and the recognition of each team member's particular areas of knowledge and expertise are vital to the most effective functioning of the team. Which team member knows most about voluntary resources? Who enjoys encouraging patients to participate in social activities?

Rehabilitation teams in the community or in voluntary organisations will likewise be composed of people with different levels of knowledge and experience and team members should be aware of each other's particular areas of expertise.

Skills

Each team member will contribute the skills specific to his own professional training—conceptual, diagnostic, organisational, caring and administrative. Some skills will be shared by many, others will be core skills of a particular profession. Listening and observing, interpersonal relationship skills and the ability to facilitate therapeutic intervention will be common to all. Of special importance are the skills of the counsellor—the ability to listen, to provide acceptance, warmth and accurate empathy together with consistency. The focus should be on helping the person to work through problems and identify solutions—a client centred focus. It is a necessary part of rehabilitation for the person to develop decision-making skills rather than to be told what to do. The temptation to advise or even to dictate may be great at times, but in the long run it is counterproductive. Life, particularly in hospital, may not offer many opportunities for making choices, even in mundane matters, but the everyday world demands the ability to do so.

Attitudes

Not everyone is suited to the demands of working in rehabilitation. The pace is often slow, with change occurring over years rather than weeks. Staff must be able to maintain a positive, patient and consistent approach over long periods of time. They must be empathetic, being able to understand just what the individual is going through, and must be able to communicate this to the patient, without becoming over-involved. Many health care workers are very caring people and it is difficult for them to maintain a balance between caring and over-protection.

Above all, a commonsense approach is required. For much of the time, psychiatry will have to be forgotten and all those involved in treatment will have to turn their attention to such practical subjects as how to help the person undertake a shopping expedition or look after his personal hygiene.

At times of frustration, disappointment or failure, it can be hard to maintain therapeutic optimism. It is then that the team must offer each other mutual support and encouragement to avoid being overwhelmed by a sense of hopelessness.

Social, economic and other external influences

Changes in society inevitably affect the task of rehabilitation both directly and indirectly. Economic recession and financial constraints can lead to reduced staffing levels and cut-backs which can affect morale.

Introduction of new legislation and implementation of policies arising from it can result in resistance to change and initial frustrations. Learning to operate within a new system always requires adjustments while the 'teething problems' are sorted out. Frequent change is unsettling for everyone, but even apparently unattractive options may prove their worth in the long-term.

Faced with the prospect of fewer staff—and therefore less time to spend with clients—and little prospect of new resources being provided, there is a danger that people 'give up' and rehabilitation slows down. Yet the response can be more creative. If it is not possible to provide the same service as before, the existing structure must be evaluated to determine which parts are most effective, and where there are overlaps with other services. It is then possible to decide whether or not there is a new way of providing something rather different.

In times of high unemployment, the focus of rehabilitation must change. There may seem to be little point in rehabilitating people for a return to work if no jobs are available. This view, however, eliminates the idea of devising alternatives, such as co-operative schemes or self-employment, either of which may be quite realistic. Only if these options are not feasible should the emphasis shift to ensuring a good quality of life by providing interests and occupational opportunities other than remunerative work.

Finally, the fact remains that there is a stigma attached to psychiatric illness both for sufferers and those involved in caring for them. This will not change without better public understanding of psychiatric disorder and it is the responsibility of all concerned to promote this.

CONCLUSION

Rehabilitation is a potentially long-term and ever-changing task. The work may be tedious at times, frustrating at others, but the rewards of seeing people living their lives to the full cannot be underestimated.

REFERENCES AND FURTHER READING

Anthony W 1980 The principles of psychiatric rehabilitation. University Park Press, Baltimore
Caplan G 1961 An approach to community mental health. Tavistock, London
Caplan G 1964 Principles of preventive psychiatry. Basic Books, New York
Clark D H 1984 The development of a psychiatric rehabilitation service. Lancet 2: 625–627
Dyer J 1988 Rehabilitation. In: Kendell R E, Zealley A K (eds) Companion to psychiatric studies, 4th edn. Churchill Livingstone, Edinburgh, chapter 41
Helander 1984 On prejudice and dignity. World Health, May. WHO, Geneva
Hume C 1990 Rehabilitation. In: Creek J (ed) Occupational therapy and mental health. Churchill Livingstone, Edinburgh, chapter 25
Patmore C 1987 Living after mental illness. Croom Helm, London
Quoist M 1963 Prayers of life. Gill and Son, Dublin
United Nations 1975 Declaration on the rights of disabled persons.
Watts F & Bennett D (eds) 1983 Principles of psychiatric rehabilitation. Wiley, Chichester
Wing J & Morris B 1981 (eds) Handbook of psychiatric rehabilitation practice. Oxford University Press, Oxford

2. The task

Ian Pullen

The enormous disability associated with mental illness is to a large extent superimposed, preventable and treatable.

Gerald Caplan 1961

If any single factor was responsible for the decline in standards in the large asylums, it was the sheer size of the task set for them — the colossal number of patients requiring care. Yet what are the true dimensions of the problem? What proportion of the population is mentally ill, and of this number how many are in need of rehabilitation or long-term care?

Epidemiological sophistication came late to psychiatry. A hundred years ago, the increased availability of asylum beds led to an increase in the number of people being identified as mentally ill. This was interpreted, mistakenly, by some as meaning that mental illness was increasing and provoked *The Times* in 1877 to argue 'If lunacy continues to increase as at present, the insane will be in the majority and, freeing themselves, will put the sane in asylums'.

PREVALENCE

Early attempts to measure the extent of psychiatric morbidity in the community presented an alarming picture. The two best known American surveys of the post-war period suggested that psychiatric symptoms were very common. The Midtown Manhattan Survey (Stole et al 1962) reported that 815 out of every 1000 New Yorkers had psychiatric symptoms. The Stirling County Study (Leighton et al 1963) concluded that 690 per 1000 of an unidentified town were 'genuine psychiatric cases'. Neither study used clinicians to assess the 'cases'. Later surveys, using clinical criteria, report much lower rates.

A New Haven study reported that 'although psychiatric disorders were common, they were not ubiquitous. Over 80% of subjects had no psychiatric diagnosis, either probably or definitely, including any type of personality disorder, anxiety reaction or minor depression' (Goldberg & Huxley 1980).

Random population studies in Britain using more rigorous criteria for defining 'a case' (such as a particular score on the General Health Questionnaire or Present State Examination which are both standardised research tools) have tended to produce lower results. Goldberg & Huxley (1992) estimate a one-year prevalence rate of between 260 and 315 per 1000 population. That is, in any year, over a quarter of the population can expect to suffer from a 'mental disorder' (i.e. to have experienced more than a critical number of a particular constellation of symptoms for more than a critical time). Most of these disorders will be mild and short-lived, but others will be more severe and may become chronic.

PATHWAYS TO PSYCHIATRIC CARE

So, starting with the estimate that in any one year 260–315 people out of every 1000 will have a mental disorder, Goldberg & Huxley (1980, 1992) describe the 'Pathway to Psychiatric Care' (Table 2.1). They propose a series of 'filters' through which people have to pass if they are to get to the next level of care. 230 will pass through the first filter by presenting themselves to their general practitioner. They will do this by exhibiting illness behaviour. The GP will detect only about 100 as 'psychiatric cases' (second filter depending on the doctor's ability to detect mental disorder). The remainder, presenting mainly with physical symptoms will be treated as though physically ill.

Table 2.1 The pathway to psychiatric care — five levels and four filters. Adapted from Goldberg and Huxley (1992) Common Mental Disorders: a bio-social model

Level 1	The community	260–315/1000/year
		(1st filter)
Level 2	Total mental morbidity — attenders in primary care	230/1000/year
		(2nd filter)
Level 3	Mental disorders identified by general practitioners	102/1000/year
		(3rd filter)
Level 4	Total morbidity referred to mental illness services	24/1000/year
		(4th filter)
Level 5	Psychiatric in-patients	5.7/1000/year

The general practitioner will treat most of the psychiatric problems he identifies with simple counselling, reassurance and medication (minor tranquillisers and antidepressants). He will refer only a fifth of the patients he identifies to the psychiatric services (third filter). Depending on the psychiatric condition, the attitude of the psychiatrist and the availability of community resources and hospital beds, less than 6 per 1000 will find their way through the fourth filter into a psychiatric bed.

These studies show that the vast majority of people suffering from psychiatric conditions never come near the psychiatric services. For those who do stray into psychiatric territory, rehabilitation should be involved, not only in the management of severe handicap, but with prevention.

PREVENTION

Prevention has been divided into primary, secondary and tertiary prevention.

Primary prevention — prevention of illness

An example might be bereavement counselling. Grief is a normal, healthy reaction to loss, which occasionally leads on to a depressive illness or other pathological condition. Counselling, available at the times of this life crisis, might prevent this pathological change occurring.

It is unlikely that common disorders can ever be completely prevented: there will always be vulnerable people, and the kinds of life events that release episodes of illness are part of being alive (Goldberg & Huxley 1992).

It would seem sensible to target such help at high-risk groups such as individuals who have become depressed after a previous bereavement.

Secondary prevention — effective treatment

This is the active treatment of an episode of illness in order to reduce symptoms to a minimum and return the patient to normality in the shortest possible time.

The key to secondary prevention is early case recognition so that effective help or treatment can be started as quickly as possible. The use by health visitors of routine screening questionnaires to detect post-natal depression is a good example of secondary prevention in action.

Tertiary prevention—minimising handicap

This is the prevention (or minimising) of the handicap that occurs as a result of illness.

Rehabilitation focuses on secondary and tertiary prevention. To achieve this effectively, the notion of handicap must be understood.

HANDICAP

Most patients who suffer from long-term mental illness are handicapped in three basic ways (identified by Wing 1963):

1. They may have difficulties which were present even before the onset of the illness, such as a lack of social skills or low intelligence.

2. They have disabilities which arise as part of their illness, such as hallucinations or apathy.

3. They have secondary handicaps as a result of having been ill, and because of their own or other people's reactions to the illness.

Numbers 2 and 3 may merge to produce the picture of 'institutionalisation' which is described in Chapter 4.

ILLNESS

So far in this chapter 'illness' has not been defined. The American community surveys quoted earlier demonstrate that the number of people identified as being mentally ill will depend on how illness is defined. If we accept too broad a definition, then the majority of the population will be found to be suffering from 'mental illness'. That situation is not only of little practical use, but makes psychiatry look rather foolish.

In the 1960s, public attention was drawn to psychiatry by a group called the 'anti-psychiatrists' (Laing, Cooper, Basaglia, Szasz and others). It was a period of challenges to traditional authority and they sought to make psychiatry a political issue. The anti-psychiatrists, a heterogeneous group, considered psychiatry to be an enforcer of social control, through which patients were made to conform. They stated that there was no such thing as schizophrenia. Moreover, not only did schizophrenia not exist, but it was created by psychiatrists.

Kendell pointed out that it was true that schizophrenia is a concept, but that the same is equally true of other concepts such as tuberculosis or migraine. The fact that tuberculosis does not exist in a material sense does not stop people dying when their lungs have been destroyed by the tubercle bacillus (Kendell 1975).

It is also true that part of the disability accompanying conditions such as schizophrenia is as a result of having been labelled and treated as 'schizophrenic' by other people (Scheff 1963). But does this invalidate schizophrenia as a concept? The only question should be: Is it a useful concept?

Much of the impetus behind the anti-psychiatry movement came from its attack on the mental hospital as a place of segregation, confinement and degradation. But since the 1960s, patterns of care for the mentally ill have undergone some changes.

In the 1970s, the idea of 'critical psychiatry' appeared. Critical psychiatrists believe that mental illnesses, whatever their correct interpretation and their political significance may be, do exist and that they do call for specialised understanding and help. They are 'critical' because they think that psychiatry should examine itself to see to what extent the insights of recent sociology and philosophy can offer benefits to society (Ingleby 1981).

DIAGNOSIS

In view of these criticisms, it is necessary to justify the use of diagnosis and classification of psychiatric disorders, especially since the diagnostic categories may not represent disease entities *per se*, and they may be applied in a fashion that brings reliability into question. But all those working within the mental health field should be able to understand and justify the system that they use.

There are three aspects to every human being:

1. those shared with all mankind
2. those shared with some others, but not all
3. those which are unique to him.

The value of classification depends on the size of the second relative to the other two (Kendell 1975).

SCHIZOPHRENIA—THE CONCEPT

As much of the work of rehabilitation is concerned with schizophrenia, it is perhaps useful to consider the development of the

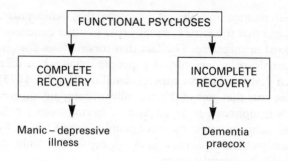

Fig. 2.1 Kraepelin's classification, i.e. diagnosis by prognosis.

concept of schizophrenia as an example of the evolution of diagnoses.

The term schizophrenia (or rather the schizophrenias) was coined by Bleuler in 1911 and was a refinement of the work published 15 years earlier by Kraepelin.

In 1896, Kraepelin divided the functional psychoses (then considered to be the type of insanity not caused by physical or organic disease) into two groups: those that always recovered, however long the recovery might be delayed; and those where recovery was never complete. This latter group he called dementia praecox. This was *diagnosis by prognosis* (outcome), the two groups being distinguished by whether or not they recovered completely (Fig. 2.1).

Bleuler widened the concept of dementia praecox by adding a group of patients who showed a similar deterioration, but without ever becoming overtly psychotic (hallucinated or deluded). These patients, now diagnosed as schizophrenic, all shared four fundamental symptoms: (1) loosening of association (lack of coherent train of thought); (2) autism (failure of social communication); (3) ambivalence; and (4) disturbances of mood (blunting/incongruity). This was *diagnosis by symptomatology*. Unfortunately, these four main symptoms are impossible to define and all-embracing, and so attempts have been made to specify precisely which symptoms to use. One example is Schneider's Symptoms of the First Rank (1959).

First rank symptoms of schizophrenia:

- thought insertion (experience of thoughts being put into one's mind)

- thought withdrawal (experience of thoughts being taken out of one's mind)
- thought broadcasting (experience of one's thoughts being known to others)
- feelings of passivity (experience of emotions, specific bodily movements or specific sensations being caused by an external agency or being under some external control)
- voices discussing one's thoughts or behaviour, as they occur, sometimes forming a running commentary
- voices discussing or arguing about one, referring to 'he'
- voices repeating one's thoughts out loud or anticipating one's thoughts
- primary delusions, arising from perceptions which in themselves are normal (e.g. 'I know that I am God because the traffic lights changed to green').

Although Schneider's symptoms correspond fairly well to the existing concept of schizophrenia in Britain, they were not the result of research and only about 70% of patients diagnosed as having a schizophrenic illness in Britain will have first-rank symptoms.

The American Psychiatric Association's classification (1987) (DSM-III-R, see later) is more specific about which symptoms must be present before a diagnosis of schizophrenia should be made. This system is more reliable, but perhaps no more valid.

Few contemporary psychiatrists are entirely happy with our present classification, because of the diversity of presentation, features and prognoses under each diagnostic category. Even fewer would regard either manic-depressive disorder or schizophrenia as disease entities, but rather as clusters of symptoms. We continue to use the system, if only because it is familiar and we have nothing better to put in its place (Kendell 1975).

DIAGNOSIS

It may be helpful at this stage to think about the need for diagnosis, especially as the diagnostic categories may not represent disease entities *per se*, and they may be applied in a fashion that brings their reliability into question. But all those working within the field of rehabilitation should be able to understand and justify the system that they use. What therefore are the advantages and disadvantages of diagnosis?

Disadvantages

The disadvantages of diagnosis are:

1. *False sense of security.* We may quickly forget that it was quite difficult to assign the patient to a particular diagnosis, so that 'a possible case of schizophrenia' may soon be referred to as 'this schizophrenic'.

2. *Labelling.* Once a diagnostic label is applied, it alters the patient's expectations, as well as those of his relatives, employer and not least the clinical team.

3. *Inadequacy.* Every individual is unique and the diagnosis is pitifully inadequate when faced with conveying the complexity of a person's predicament.

4. *Pejorative.* Some diagnoses imply value judgements such as 'personality disorder'.

Menninger (1963) called for the abandonment of diagnosis and 'using no names at all for the conditions of mental illness'. Instead there should be a lengthy formulation of each person's predicament.

These dangers and shortcomings of diagnosis must be balanced against the advantages, if a diagnosis is to be made.

Advantages

The advantages of diagnosis are:

1. *Predictive.* It will give some indication of the natural history of the condition so that a prognosis can be given. It will predict which treatment is likely to be beneficial and, of equal importance, where no treatment will be helpful or should be offered.

2. *Confidence.* Even a serious diagnosis gives the patient and his relatives a feeling of relief that there is an explanation for what has been happening, that this condition is shared with other people. They are not alone and unique, and the clinical team knows what is wrong.

3. *Research, progress and planning.* Research depends on identifying groups of people with the same condition to be allocated to different methods of treatment or management. Without diagnostic groups, no logical progress can be made. Similarly, epidemiological research depends on studying people with different groups of diagnoses to establish common aetiological factors in the hope of prevention, and for planning the services they require.

4. *Communication.* A diagnosis is a short-hand way of communicating quite complex information about an individual.

So, despite all the shortcomings and reservations, for the foreseeable future, classification of diagnoses is inescapable. Without it, no progress can be made, no treatment logically given, nor realistic expectations and rehabilitation plans made.

CLASSIFICATION

As this book is intended for all members of the extended multidisciplinary team (non-medical and medical, voluntary and statutory), it is worth reviewing the classification in some detail to ensure that, when diagnosis is used in discussion, all those involved are talking about the same concept.

It was a salutary lesson to learn that there were not many more people with schizophrenia in the USA than in Britain, but that American psychiatrists meant something different when using the same term. The US/UK Diagnostic Project clearly demonstrated, using standard diagnostic criteria (the Present State Examination), that the same patient might receive a different label, not only on opposite sides of the Atlantic, but also on different sides of the United States (Cooper et al 1972). There is much room for confusion and this must be recognised if communication is to be effective.

Some basic definitions

Neurosis

The symptoms are only quantitatively different from normality in that they differ from normal experience only in degree. Thus someone suffering from an anxiety neurosis will have symptoms indistinguishable from normal anxiety, the sort of feelings anyone would experience in an anxiety-provoking situation such as a job interview. However, these symptoms occur out of context, or are more prolonged or severe than the situation warrants. It is therefore not difficult for us to empathise (fully understand the patient's experience). The patient usually retains insight and has unimpaired reality testing; that is he knows that his experiences are abnormal, even though he might not be able to do anything about them.

Neurosis: quantitatively different
            insight
            in touch with reality
            empathy possible

Examples: anxiety neurosis
               depressive neurosis
               obsessional neurosis
               phobic neurosis

Psychosis

The symptoms of psychosis are qualitatively quite different from normal experience. Hallucinations and delusions (unshakeable false beliefs) are so different from normal experience that it is very difficult for us to appreciate just what it must be like to be hallucinated. Empathy is therefore limited. People suffering from acute psychosis do not recognise that they are ill, or that their experiences are part of illness. That is, they do not have insight (into the fact that they are ill) and have lost touch with reality.

Psychosis: qualitatively different
               lack insight
               lose touch with reality
               empathy difficult

Examples: schizophrenia
               manic-depressive illness
               organic states (e.g. dementia)

The distinction between psychosis and neurosis is not as simple or clear cut as the summary above might suggest. A young woman suffering from anorexia nervosa (usually classified as a neurotic disorder) may see a very distorted image of herself in a mirror (i.e. loss of touch with reality). A young man suffering from chronic schizophrenia may recognise that the 'voices' are hallucinations (have insight).

It also begs the question raised earlier of 'caseness'. Assuming that every person could be placed on a continuum from total lack of anxiety at one end to the greatest possible level of anxiety at the other extreme, how far along this continuum must an individual progress before he is considered to be 'ill'? The standard answer is when his symptoms significantly interfere with his normal, everyday life—a very imprecise definition to use.

Nevertheless, neuroses and psychoses have one thing in common: they are both 'illnesses'. Illnesses (physical or mental) have a beginning, then run their course, but, most important of all, there was a time before which the illness was not present (Fig. 2.2).

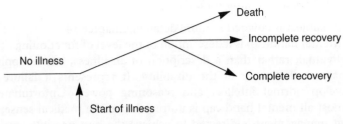

Fig. 2.2 The course of an illness.

Illness is therefore superimposed on whatever personality the individual has.

Personality is that unique combination of qualities that distinguishes each of us from our fellows. This includes predominant mood, how we react to stress, the sort of relationships we make, our moral values, sensitiveness, stability of mood, personal sense of security and so on. While these characteristics develop and mature over time, from our early 20s these features remain relatively stable. So the way we react to certain circumstances now will be very similar to the way we will respond in 5 or 10 years' time.

Personality disorder

Personality is said to be disordered when it differs significantly from what is accepted as 'normal', either in the balance of its components, their quality and expression or in its total aspect. If this definition appears unduly vague and therefore of little use, this is precisely what it is. This diagnosis depends on a mixture of objective evidence from the case history, such as pattern of relationships and behaviour, plus a subjective response of the psychiatrist (or other) to the individual at interview. It is, therefore, a most unreliable diagnostic entity and its use is severely limited. The label of personality disorder carries pejorative connotations, often involving value judgements. As there is little evidence that anything other than time alters personality, a diagnosis of personality disorder often appears to be a means of depriving someone of help.

Personality disorder: persistent pattern since 'maturity', not 'ill'

Examples: paranoid
schizoid
explosive
obsessional
inadequate

Mental handicap (learning disability)

This subject is covered in more detail in Chapter 14.

Mental handicap is a description of the level of functioning of an individual, rather than a description of an illness, and is applied whatever the cause of the disability. It represents a failure to develop normal intellect and reasoning power. Unfortunately, almost all mental handicap is untreatable in the medical sense, so that management is directed to achieve the best possible level of functioning for each individual.

THE RELIABILITY OF DIAGNOSIS

Some diagnostic categories appear to be considerably more reliable than others. Kreitman and his colleagues in Chichester set out to study the reliability of diagnoses made by six psychiatrists. The study was important in that the interviews were held under ordinary NHS working conditions. The consultants obtained 75% agreement for organic diagnoses (e.g. dementia) and 61% for functional psychoses (e.g. manic-depressive illness and schizophrenia) but only 28% agreement for neurotic disorders. In other words, reliability, particularly for non-psychotic conditions, is low (Kreitman 1961).

The reliability in research situations has been improved by the use of standardised research tools such as the Present State Examination (PSE), with which the level of agreement for diagnoses such as schizophrenia can rise above 90% (Wing et al 1974). However, the PSE is too cumbersome to use in normal clinical practice.

Thus there is a need for a classification that is not only reliable, but also useable in normal practice. The World Health Organisation produces an International Classification of Diseases (ICD-10) for use worldwide (WHO 1992). This contains a glossary of conditions, each being succinctly described allowing individual patients to be matched with a diagnostic group which is given a unique number. The principal use of the ICD is in the classification of morbidity and mortality for statistical purposes. In most countries, national statistics will be gathered using ICD codings. This allows for comparisons between countries and for the studies of the management of patients with specific conditions.

The American Psychiatric Association has also produced a series of Diagnostic and Statistical Manuals (DSM) over the past 40 years. The latest version, DSM-III-R, (American Psychiatric

Association 1987) has some advantages over the ICD system. In addition to describing the range of symptoms or behaviours likely to occur in a particular condition, it specifies which of the symptoms must have been present for a minimum specified time to justify that diagnosis (see Ch. 6). Being more specific it should be more reliable. Second, it uses a multiaxial system which ensures that certain information that may be of value in planning treatment and predicting outcome for each person is recorded on each of five axes. Axes I and II comprise mental disorders; axis III, physical disorders; and axes IV and V, severity of psychological stressors and a global assessment of functioning.

A community survey of 576 Edinburgh women which compared the ICD and DSM diagnoses, found that only 56% of depressives and only 17% of cases of anxiety were labelled the same way by both systems (Surtees et al 1983). The results of a survey in psychiatric outpatients produced a 58% agreement between the two systems for depressives and 48% for cases of anxiety (Van den Brink et al 1989). Thus the more severe the case, the more reliable the diagnosis.

THE OUTCOME OF ILLNESS

Many aetiological factors are thought to be involved in the production of psychiatric illness and its maintenance once it has become established. Although for many conditions these factors are imperfectly understood, it appears that the functional psychoses (schizophrenia and manic-depressive illness) have a genetic (inherited) component, approximately 10–15% of first-degree relatives having a similar illness. Other aetiological factors include psychological and physical stresses, physical illness and other insults such as drug and alcohol abuse and withdrawal. Goldberg & Huxley (1992) have brought these ideas together in a bio-social model.

A wide range of factors, from physiological to social adversity, make people more vulnerable to the onset of common mental illness, and this effect is observed most clearly after severe and life-threatening events occur.

The eventual outcome of any illness will depend upon the nature of the condition, the extent to which precipitating factors such as family stresses can be relieved, the benefits for the patient of retaining the 'sick role', and to what extent the illness process can be modified by treatment.

Goldberg & Huxley (1992) have proposed the term 'restitution' to describe the process of losing symptoms. The factors that determine restitution are therefore concerned with the duration of symptoms and the process of recovery. There are interesting differences between the factors which promote restitution in different settings. A positive attitude of subjective social support appears to be important for people being treated in primary care, whereas for people who reach the psychiatric services, the actual level of social support is a more important factor in restitution. By the time a person reaches psychiatric care, long-term outcome is heavily influenced by long-term factors, such as length of previous history, personality and constitutional factors, and long-standing social difficulties in work and social relationships (Goldberg & Huxley 1992).

Different diagnostic groups carry different natural histories. For example, the neuroses tend to improve spontaneously over time, two-thirds having recovered or considerably improved within two years. On the other hand, some neuroses will continue to plague patients for the rest of their lives. Some conditions, such as manic-depressive disorder, may produce periods of illness interspersed with periods of complete recovery, while only a minority of people developing schizophrenia will recover completely from their first bout of illness.

This variety of outcomes was well known to the ancient Greeks who described the possibilities outlined in Figure 2.2.

PROBLEMS OF RECURRENT ILLNESS

Partial, or even complete recovery from an episode of psychiatric illness brings in its wake a number of stresses related to coming to terms with the idea of having been ill, coping with other people's changed attitudes to the 'ex-patient' and facing the uncertainty of whether and when the condition might return. With recurrent illness, it is this latter factor which assumes greatest importance.

An employer might tolerate one spell of illness sympathetically, but begin to consider retirement 'on health grounds' if the illness returns. Planning, at work or for the family at home, becomes difficult when a person is faced with uncertainty about the future. The stress will also be felt by those most closely involved emotionally, and this may completely alter the marital relationship.

For all these reasons, it is vital to start treatment as soon as possible in a new episode of illness, and to consider the merits of keeping the patient away from work to avoid a period of poor performance or disturbance that might make return to work more difficult. Those closest to the patient should be involved in the treatment planning and offered practical help and support.

'NEW CHRONIC PATIENTS'

A generation of psychiatric patients has now been exposed to 'community care' of which an important feature is the avoidance, wherever possible, of long-term in-patient care. The decline in the number of non-geriatric long-term NHS beds has meant that many patients who would previously have been resident in hospital are out in the community. However, much psychiatric illness runs a chronic course and inevitably some patients still need to remain in hospital for long periods of time (McCreadie et al 1983).

The 'new chronic patients' (a rather unfortunate, though concise term) are defined as patients aged 18–64 who have been in hospital for more than one but less than six years. Recent surveys in England and Wales (Mann & Cree 1976) and Scotland (1983) show the bed occupancy for these patients to be about 20 per 100 000 of the general population. Although for the whole group schizophrenia was the most common diagnosis, the majority of first admissions had a diagnosis of organic brain disease (pre-senile dementia and alcoholic psychosis) even though this was for the pre-geriatric age group.

Those people who during their first hospital admission, stay long enough to be termed a 'new chronic patient' are usually found to be so disabled as to be considered well placed in hospital (5.8 beds per 100 000 population). The reasons for remaining in hospital are not always medical. Of the 'new chronic patients' surveyed, it was thought that 38% did not need care in hospital and could have been discharged if other supported places had been available, and 20% could have been accommodated in staffed hostels.

'GRADUATE PATIENTS'

We live in an ageing population. The reasons for this are covered in more detail in Chapter 12. Many patients who came into hospital as young people are now growing old within the system. When they reach the age of 65, they may be called 'graduates'.

As a group, 'graduates' tend to be treated separately from 'psychogeriatric' patients of the same age, many of whom will be suffering from dementia. However, increased age brings increased frailty and the probability of physical illness. Staffing levels and expectations will have to match the needs of this particular group.

Over recent years, there has been a growth in the amount of supported accommodation available, much of it provided by the voluntary sector (housing associations and other charities). It is as yet unclear just what the final lowest reasonable number of long-stay hospital beds will be, but this final irreducible number should depend on the quality, range and extent of accommodation provided in the community. It is salutary to note that much of the reduction in bed numbers has been achieved not so much by the discharge of large numbers of chronic patients as by the death of residents in hospital. During the period 1976–86, twice as many long-stay mental hospital patients had died in hospital, as were discharged (Mahoney 1988).

CONCLUSIONS: CLASSIFICATION OR CONFUSION?

Although over a quarter of the adult population will experience psychiatric disorder in any given year, very few develop serious mental illnesses. Despite the shortcomings of the present classification systems, it is necessary to arrive at a diagnosis before any logical treatment or management plans can be made. Schizophrenia, the most common diagnosis in rehabilitation work, is one of the more reliable diagnostic entities. The main lesson is that a diagnosis, once made, is not applied for life, but should be reviewed critically from time to time.

REFERENCES

American Psychiatric Association 1987 Diagnostic and statistical manual of mental disorders—DSM-III-R. APA, Washington
Caplan G 1961 An approach to community mental health. Tavistock, London
Cooper J E, Kendell R E, Gurland B J et al 1972 Maudsley Monograph No. 20. Oxford University Press, London
Goldberg D, Huxley P 1980 Mental illness in the community: the pathway to psychiatric care. Tavistock, London
Goldberg D, Huxley P 1992 Common mental disorders: a bio-social model. Routledge, London
Ingleby D 1981 Critical psychiatry: the politics of mental health. Penguin, London
Kendell R E 1975 The role of diagnosis in psychiatry. Blackwell, Oxford
Kreitman N 1961 The reliability of psychiatric diagnosis. Journal of Mental Science 107: 876–886
Leighton D C, Harding J C, Macklin D M, Macmillan A M, Leighton A H 1963 The character of danger [Stirling County]. Basic Books, New York

McCreadie R G, Oliver A, Wilson A, Burton L L 1983 The Scottish survey of 'new chronic' inpatients. British Journal of Psychiatry 143: 564–571

Mahoney J 1988 Finance and government policy. In: Lavender A, Holloway F (eds) Community care in practice. Wiley, Chichester

Mann S A, Cree W 1976 The 'new long-stay' in mental hospitals. British Journal of Hospital Medicine 56–63 (July)

Menninger K 1963 The vital balance. Viking press, New York

Scheff T J 1963 The role of the mentally ill and the dynamics of mental disorder: a research framework. Sociometry 26: 436–453

Schneider K 1959 Clinical psychopathology. Grune and Stratton, New York

Stole L, Langer T, Michael S, Opiler M, Rennie T 1962 Mental health in the metropolis [Manhattan]. McGraw-Hill, New York

Surtees P G, Dean C, Ingham J G, Kreitman N, Miller P, Sashidharan S P 1983 Psychiatric disorders in women from an Edinburgh community. British Journal of Psychiatry 142: 238–246

Van den Brink W et al 1989 Archives of General Psychiatry 46: 369–372

Wing J K 1963 Rehabilitation of psychiatric patients. British Journal of Psychiatry 109: 635–641

Wing J K, Cooper J E, Sartorius N 1974 Description and classification of psychiatric symptoms. Cambridge University Press, Cambridge

World Health Organisation (1992) International Classification of Diseases — 10th revision. WHO, Geneva

3. The development of rehabilitation and community care

Ian Pullen

The past is a foreign country: they do things differently there.
L P Hartley, **The Go-Between**

THE TURN OF A TIDE

Four decades ago, a tide turned. For two centuries, the number of beds in Britain occupied by the mentally ill steadily increased. Then, in 1954, the peak was reached and numbers began to fall. At first the fall was rapid, but after 1970 the trend slowed, only to accelerate again in the mid 1980s. In the past 40 years, psychiatric beds have been reduced by two thirds. This change has not been confined to Britain, but has occurred at different rates throughout the West, being most dramatic in the United States.

Deinstitutionalisation, the discharge of patients from hospital and their resettlement in the community, came about largely as a result of changing attitudes to care and was helped by the discovery and introduction of effective drugs. However, the major precipitant, both in Britain and the United States, appears to have been severe overcrowding in the large Victorian mental hospitals. The achievement of deinstitutionalisation has not been without problems. There has been a huge increase in the number of readmissions to hospital, a higher turnover of patients and a rise in the number of discharged but disturbed former patients. In many areas, the development of effective community services has lagged behind the rundown of in-patient facilities. As a result, many of these discharged former patients face bleak lives in bed and breakfast accommodation or common lodging houses.

OUR ASYLUM HERITAGE

A persisting question is why the asylums, which began with great

35

optimism and high discharge rates, should over time have become so overwhelmed by the increasing chronicity of their patients that they had to be constantly enlarged and supplemented by new institutions (Freeman & Bennett 1991). Successive Lunacy Acts throughout the 19th century first gave permission, and later compelled counties to build asylums. Admission procedures were tightened up and asylums were only to take certified patients. There is no simple explanation. Certainly many patients suffered from serious physical conditions in addition to mental illness. One author has suggested that schizophrenia did increase in 19th century Britain, although this opinion is contested (Hare 1983).

The original idea had been for small institutions 'where the patients could be known', but by 1900, the average asylum contained 961 patients and by 1930, this number had risen to 1221. Patients worked on hospital farms and in the gardens, but their work was organised for the maintenance of the institution, not for their own benefit. They moved from place to place in groups and were counted in and out of wards by nurses who often could not remember their names (Jones 1960).

Between the wars conditions began to improve: 1920 brought the opening of the Maudsley Hospital for voluntary patients in London, a change that required a special Act of Parliament. The Royal Commission (1924–6) suggested that a special officer should be appointed in each hospital to direct patients' activities. In 1925, the first trained occupational therapist was employed in Aberdeen and more followed during the 1930s. In 1928, it was recommended that British mental hospitals should employ someone similar to the almoners of the large voluntary (general) hospitals 'to allay the patients' anxieties about home conditions during treatment and to help with employment and any domestic difficulties after discharge'. The first British social workers were American trained, but in 1929 a training course was started at the London School of Economics.

The Mental Treatment Act, 1930, introduced voluntary treatment: however, a voluntary patient had to give 72 hours' notice in writing if he wanted to discharge himself. The Act also gave local authorities the power to provide psychiatric out-patient facilities staffed by mental hospital doctors.

The economic depression of the 1930s was the catalyst for the development of the first Home Treatment Service in Amsterdam. Querido was hired by the city authorities at a time of financial stringency to save money by reducing the number of psychiatric patients in hospital. He found that it was much more effective to intervene before a patient was admitted, rather than to try to discharge established patients (Querido 1968). This was a proto-type for the Family Crisis Teams that were set up in both the United States and Britain in the 1960s.

The immediate post-war period brought administrative and therapeutic changes. The first British day hospital was opened in 1946 under the title Social Psychotherapy Centre, but was later renamed the Marlborough Day Hospital, introducing the concept of 'part-time' hospital care. In 1947, Maxwell Jones moved to the Henderson Hospital in London, taking with him the community and group methods he had developed during the war. The Henderson was the start of the therapeutic community movement which was to have so much influence on the running of the mental hospitals and other institutions caring for people over succeeding decades.

THE NATIONAL HEALTH SERVICE

The inception of the National Health Service (NHS) in Britain in 1948 allowed psychiatry to develop as a salaried medical service undiluted by the demands of private practice. Out-patient facilities were expanded; a variety of stepping stones were placed between community and hospital, adding hostels to day hospitals. Domiciliary visits strengthened links with general practitioners. In the United States, on the other hand, the more usual way of providing psychiatric care was by office-based private practice. This allowed for more intensive and prolonged psychotherapy to take place and consequently dynamic psychotherapy and psycho-analysis flourished.

Elsewhere new models of service were being developed. In the 13th Arrondissement of Paris, a novel sectorised service was set up in the 1950s. A multidisciplinary team working in each sector catchment area assumed responsibility for a patient throughout his contact with the psychiatric service, whether he was being supported at home or in hospital (Chick 1967). Although this model was not replicated elsewhere in France, it was similar to the model that was to develop in Britain two decades later.

The decade from 1952 to 1962 saw the introduction of many of the drugs that are used in psychiatry today. Reserpine, the first of the group of antipsychotic drugs, was soon superseded by chlor-promazine (Largactil) which was introduced in 1954. Chlordiazepoxide (Librium) heralded the benzodiazepine minor tranquillisers in 1960, to be followed by the tricyclic anti-depressants, to complete the triad.

The rapid reduction of psychiatric hospital patient numbers started before the widespread introduction of drugs, suggesting that it was a change in attitude to hospital and community treatment that was responsible, a change that was reflected in the Mental Health Acts of 1959 (England and Wales) and 1960 (Scotland). These Acts, in addition to providing for the safe protection of the patient and the public, introduced two new principles: first, that the arrangements for the treatment of mental illness should as far as possible parallel those for the treatment of physical illness; second, that provision should be made for the treatment of the mentally ill in the community rather than in hospital. The most important provision was contained in a small sub-section which stated that nothing in the Act should be construed as preventing a patient who required treatment from being admitted to any hospital without formality. In other words, as many patients as possible should be treated in the community, and those requiring hospital treatment should wherever possible be treated as voluntary patients.

The psychiatric services were becoming more aware of the need to assess and evaluate the treatment they were offering. The 'Worthing Experiment' in 1958 was the first systematic attempt to evaluate community care. Sainsbury concluded that 'a community service promotes the earlier referral of patients, thereby reducing the long period during which families suffer considerable hardship, and it can be as effective as hospital care' (Sainsbury 1969).

Much impetus was given to the community psychiatry movement by the revelations about the conditions inside some mental hospitals. Barton described institutional neurosis in 1959 and two years later Goffman, a sociologist, published *Asylums—A Study of Total Institutions based on studies of North American State Hospitals.* Two other important works were published in 1961. Wing & Brown described three different mental hospitals where patients' behaviour was correlated with different hospital and ward regimes. The same year Tooth & Brooke predicted that, if the steep decline in the hospital population continued, the large mental hospitals could be closed by the mid 1970s.

The 1960s proved a time of social change throughout the West, culminating in the student riots in several countries in 1968. It was also a time of therapeutic optimism. Caplan pioneered the theme of preventive psychiatry and the idea was promulgated that if only psychiatrists could become involved in everything from education to town planning, a more psychologically healthy society would be created. These wild claims raised expectations far in excess of what realistically could be delivered. The Group for the Advancement of Psychiatry (GAP) in 1967 declared community psychiatry to be the third psychiatric revolution.*

The 1960s also saw the emergence of the antipsychiatry movement. The concept of mental illness was challenged (e.g. Szasz) and others proposed that psychosis was a 'healthy' way of coping with the stresses of modern society (e.g. Laing).

The 1970s brought a new realism. It was clear that the earlier estimates of the speed of decline of hospital populations were far from correct, and public inquiries into hospital scandals publicised the inhumane treatment of patients in some rundown mental hospitals.

Hospital Services for the Mentally Ill (DHSS 1971) proposed an integrated hospital and community service based on a psychiatric department in a district general hospital. In-patient, day patient, out-patient, GP and local authority services in an area were to be used as flexibly as possible. There should be an emphasis on rehabilitation and on the preservation of the patient's personal relationships and his contacts with the local community. Thus, there would be a gradual phasing out of the old mental hospitals in England and Wales. Local authorities were to provide adequate community services, and social services would have the responsibility for finding suitable residential accommodation for patients discharged from hospital.

The Seebohm Committee Report (1968) led to a radical reorganisation of social services in the early 1970s in England and Wales. Psychiatric social workers were to be transferred to local authority teams and the notion of 'specialist' social workers was to be replaced by 'generic' social work. Community psychiatric nurses (CPNs), who had been developing their role over the previous decade, were used by many services to fill this gap. Their role was made more distinct by the introduction of long-acting depot injections of antipsychotic drugs.

Throughout the 1970s, there was a growth in the voluntary (non-statutory) sector. National and local mental health associations (e.g. MIND in England and Wales, SAMH in Scotland) were formed as pressure groups to campaign for better care for the

---

* The first psychiatric revolution was Pinel unchaining patients; the second was Freud's discovery of psychoanalysis.

mentally ill. Support groups for specific conditions also appeared (e.g. National Schizophrenia Fellowship) to raise money for research and to provide support for relatives and sufferers. Other organisations (e.g. Richmond Fellowship) set out to provide a direct service, such as the provision of hostels.

But, slowly, critics of the move towards community care were emerging. In the United States, Hawks (1975) asked if this was not merely another distraction from the care of the chronically ill. In Britain, it became clear that local authorities were not providing the hostels and other support services that were required. This was acknowledged in a further White Paper entitled Better Services for the Mentally Ill (DHSS 1975). In addition to the objective of increased staffing (especially social workers), there was to be a radical shift of resources away from in-patient care to fund increased out-patient, day patient and community residential facilities. The district general hospital was to be the base for a specialist team consisting of psychiatrists, nurses, social workers, clinical psychologists and occupational therapists.

Whereas the initial decline in psychiatric beds appears to have come from an attitudinal change amongst the staff providing the service, since 1980 there has been political pressure to close beds rapidly, despite the obvious lack of community resources. A series of consultative documents were issued in an attempt to remove a serious log jam: the reluctance of the two separate organisations, health authorities and local authorities, to fund community resources which each felt the other should be providing. The concepts of 'joint finance' and the provision of 'dowries' to move with the patient discharged from hospital were two attempts to improve the situation.

In 1983, a further GAP report, entitled Community Care: A Reappraisal, questioned the assumptions upon which community care was based and commented on the paucity of good research to justify these assumptions. Bennett (1978) had already pointed out that the effectiveness of hospital care had never been properly evaluated either.

Twenty years or so after the last mental health legislation, further Mental Health Acts were introduced in England and Wales (1983) and Scotland (1984). The basic tenets of the previous Acts remain unchanged, but additional rights were introduced including the right to be legally represented to contest detention and the right to refuse treatment and to have a second opinion. With the decreased average length of treatment, the period of time between reviews of detention orders is reduced.

RECENT CHANGES

The mid 1980s saw two reports that were critical of the way deinstitutionalisation was being carried out. The Short Report (the report of a Select Committee of the House of Commons 1985) was critical of the way in which the removal of hospital facilities had preceded the provision of services in the community stating 'Any fool can close a long term hospital: it takes time and trouble to do it properly and compassionately'. The notion that the move towards the community could be 'cost-neutral' was challenged and the committee recommended increased funding. The following year the independent Audit Commission (1986), reiterating that the rundown of hospital facilities had outstripped the development of community services, disagreed with the argument for increased funding, citing examples of successful implementation where agencies were working together. The committee also highlighted the problems of bridging finance—the funding that was required to set up alternatives to hospital care before patients could be discharged and the money realised from the sale of the hospital.

The government commissioned Sir Roy Griffiths to review community care. The Griffiths Report (1988) proposed that the mentally ill, mentally handicapped and the elderly should become the responsibility of local authorities. Social services departments would have responsibility for assessing the needs of individuals, devising and purchasing care packages and identifying a care manager.

The government's response, Caring for People: Community care in the Next Decade and Beyond (DHSS 1989) and the subsequent legislation, the NHS and Community Care Act (1990), implemented many of Griffiths' proposals. Local authorities were to be given the 'lead' role for buying appropriate care, and further hospital discharges were not to be allowed until adequate care was available. The implementation date was postponed for two years (to 1993) because of the political sensitivity surrounding the increasingly unpopular 'community charge' (poll tax). It was feared that introduction would increase community charge bills by an unacceptable amount.

The overall NHS reforms outlined in Working for Patients (DHSS 1989) are also expected to have an impact on mental health services. The separation of 'purchaser' and 'provider' roles, encourages the purchaser (health authority) to buy the services it requires for the population it serves from the mental health services, or the voluntary or private sectors. The introduction of 'capital charging' for all NHS hospitals means that from 1991 there will be a charge levied on all hospital property reflecting its value. So mental hospitals occupying expensive sites will attract very substantial charges, perhaps encouraging closure.

HISTORY—LEARNING FROM THE PAST

This review of the development of our present way of working is necessarily selective. Some changes and developments are, perhaps, given undue prominence, while other important events are only briefly mentioned, if at all. It is a personal view which aims to highlight some issues which all those interested and involved in rehabilitation might note, and be stimulated to enquire further.

It is now difficult to understand how, in the name of helping the mentally ill, doctors and others came to treat so badly the patients entrusted to their care. The torture and privation carried out prior to the 19th century, and even the tens of thousands of leucotomies carried out in the 1950s, are difficult to justify. The lesson that must be learned is that the impression that a particular form of treatment or management is effective is not enough. Each method of treatment must be objectively tested and assessed. It is only by evaluating our services that progress will be made and mistaken treatments avoided.

The 'ideal' service may not be ideal for a different population or culture, or if tried on a different scale. The ideal small institutions developed into the impersonal destructive asylums, partly as a result of size. Similarly, blind allegiance to a philosophy may result in suffering. While no one could dispute that life in a caring family is better than life in an uncaring institution, the mass discharge of the chronically disabled into a community with few provisions for their care seems to be cruelty carried out with the best of ideals, but naively.

History catalogues the fluctuations in the quality of services for the mentally ill with the changes in the economic and social climate. Not all of these variations were predictable. Unemployment may improve the quality of staff being recruited into the mental health field, but recession brings financial stringency and the risk of falling standards. Reduced nursing levels on wards may lead to doors being locked through lack of staff to observe suicidal patients. Cutbacks in local authority budgets (highlighted following the non-payment of the community charge, especially in Scotland) may lead to delays in discharge through lack of personnel to support families, or scarcity of hostel places. The voluntary sector is not immune from cuts in grants received from the statutory authorities.

Throughout history, the mental health services have suffered from the stigma associated with mental illness. Mental health does not attract much public or political interest. Some politically determined policies, such as the move towards community care, may be attributable more to a naive belief that they will save money than to the pursuit of some ideal. It remains to be seen whether the NHS reforms prove to be the way forward for the purchase of the right care package for individual patients, or the disintegration of a planned development of local services. Mental health charities attract just 3% of all money raised in Britain by medical charities.

Above all, psychiatry has suffered from poor communication. The jargon of psychiatry (psychology and social work) has all too often been unintelligible to patients, their families and the general public alike. It is to be hoped that initiatives such as the Royal College of Psychiatrists' public education exercise on depression will raise the profile of mental health issues.

REFERENCES

Audit Commission 1986 Making a reality of community care. HMSO, London
Barton R 1959 Institutional neurosis. Wright, Bristol
Bennett D H 1978 Community psychiatry. British Journal of Psychiatry 132: 209–220
Chick J 1967 In: Freeman H L, Farndale J (eds) New aspects of the mental health services. Pergamon, Oxford
DHSS 1971 Hospital services for the mentally ill. HMSO, London
DHSS 1975 Better services for the mentally ill. HMSO, London
DHSS 1989 Caring for people: community care in the next decade and beyond. HMSO, London
DHSS 1989 Working for patients. HMSO, London
Freeman H L, Bennett D H 1991 Introduction. In: Bennett D H, Freeman H L (eds) Community psychiatry. Churchill Livingstone, Edinburgh
Goffman E 1961 Asylums—a study of total institutions. Doubleday, New York reprinted 1970 by Penguin Books, London
Group for the Advancement of Psychiatry 1967 Education for community psychiatry, Report No. 64. Mental Health Materials Centre, New York
Group for the Advancement of Psychiatry 1983 Community psychiatry: a reappraisal, Report No. 113. Mental Health Materials Center, New York
Hare E 1983 Was insanity on the increase? British Journal of Psychiatry 142: 439–455
Hawks D 1975 Community care: an analysis of assumptions. British Journal of Psychiatry 127: 176–185
Jones K 1960 Mental health and social policy 1845–1959. Routledge and Kegan Paul, London

Querido A 1968 The development of socio-medical care in the Netherlands. Routledge and Kegan Paul, London

Report from the Social Services Committee Session 1984/5 on Community Care (Short Report) 1985. HMSO, London

Report of the Committee on Local Authority and Allied Personal Social Services 1968 (The Seebohm Report) Command 3703. HMSO, London

Report to the Secretary of State for Social Services by Sir Roy Griffiths 1988 Community care: agenda for action. HMSO, London

Sainsbury P 1969 Social and community psychiatry. American Journal of Psychiatry 125: 1226–1231

Tooth G C, Brooke E M 1961 Trends in the mental hospital population. Lancet 1: 710–713

Wing J K, Brown G W 1961 Social treatment of schizophrenia: a comparative survey of three mental hospitals. Journal of Mental Science 107: 847–861

4. Community care – motivation and evaluation

Ian Pullen

Home is home, though it be never so homely.

John Clare 1630

The shift from hospital to community care, which began in the mid 1950s, brought about a questioning of the long-term effects of hospital stay on the patient. Barton (1959) spelled out, more explicitly, the undesirable effects of institutions.

HOME VERSUS HOSPITAL

In 1964, community psychiatry was proclaimed the third psychiatric revolution (the first two being Pinel's unchaining of the insane and Freud's discovery of psychoanalysis). The concept of community psychiatry involved psychiatrists accepting responsibility for a catchment area population, promoting mental health, prevention, earlier involvement with patients and earlier treatment and, above all, the idea of treating people wherever possible in their own surroundings and keeping the length of time in hospital to a minimum.

There were strong advocates of the new system, and in 1967 the American Group for the Advancement of Psychiatry enthusiastically supported 'this emerging sub-specialty of psychiatry'. But not everyone shared this enthusiasm. Kubie (1968), in America, feared that community psychiatry would 'suffer the fate of all good intentions not guided by mature judgement and experience'. Dunham (1965) called it the 'newest therapeutic bandwagon' while in Britain, Hawks considered it 'another distraction from the care of the chronically ill' (Hawks 1975), and feared it would attract resources and interest away from psychiatry's main task of treating and caring for those with 'genuine mental illness'.

In other words, critics feared (and many continue to fear) that the untested ideals of community care would lead not to better community mental health, but instead divert resources away from the treatment of those who were chronically ill.

THEORY OF COMMUNITY PSYCHIATRY

The Group for the Advancement of Psychiatry summarised community psychiatry as 'the application and practice of psychiatry in non-institutional and relatively non-traditional settings'. It has the following characteristics:

1. It is based on the assumption that socio-cultural conditions significantly influence the manifestations and course of psychiatric illness.

2. It studies the role of social environment in psychiatric illness.

3. It is concerned with the organisation and delivery of mental health services.

4. It uses social and environmental measures to prevent psychiatric illness and to treat and care for those who develop psychiatric disorders.

5. It supplies treatment and care as close as possible to the patient's home or work place.

6. It uses community resources to extend services beyond the more conventional psychiatric treatment settings.

In short, it sets out to provide care for the psychiatrically ill as close to their homes as possible and to direct efforts towards prevention of psychiatric illness.

The decision to admit

In the past, the decision to admit a patient to hospital was a more or less automatic response to certain diagnoses. So, a diagnosis of schizophrenia or psychosis with the presence of hallucinations and delusions meant certain admission. In some British hospitals, within the past 20 years, the family doctor, whose knowledge of psychiatry might be rudimentary, had the right to admit patients direct to the wards.

Well, what is wrong with that? As we shall see later, the decision to admit should *not* be taken lightly as it carries serious implications for the patient's future.

The presence of hallucinations will have a very different significance depending on whether they started last week or have been present for years. In general, it is not the number or even the severity of symptoms that is important, but rather how much of the healthy person is functioning *in spite of the symptoms*, and what stresses and supports are present if we are to make a sensible decision about how and where best to provide treatment.

Debilitating effect of institutions

The problems are of two kinds:

1. long-stay institutions appear to lead to the development of an 'institutional syndrome', which makes the patient less fit for life outside the institution;
2. mere admission to a psychiatric unit stigmatises the patient.

The attitudes and expectations of the patient, as well as those of people about him, change as a result of being in hospital. This affects the chances of successful adjustment back into the community.

THE 'INSTITUTIONAL SYNDROME'

Barton (1959) and Goffman (1961) described the institutional syndrome, which is characterised by:

- apathy
- lack of initiative
- loss of interest (in things or events not immediately personal or present)
- submissiveness
- lack of expression of feeling or resentment of harsh or unfair orders from staff
- loss of individuality
- deterioration in personal habits, toilet and general standards.

There is a resigned acceptance that things will go on as they are 'unchangingly, inevitably and indefinitely'.

How does this state of acceptance, passivity and apathy arise? It appears to be a result of at least three factors including the disease process itself, a restricted life-style prior to admission and the effects of institutional life. Hospital admission not only separates the patient from the world outside, but also takes over virtually all decision-making and functions for self-preservation. Wing (1961), studying a group of patients who had spent more than two years in hospital, found that the longer the stay in hospital, the more unfavourable the patient's attitude to discharge.

Barton suggested eight aetiological factors associated with the institutional syndrome:

1. loss of contact with the outside world
2. enforced idleness
3. brutality, brow-beating and teasing
4. bossiness of the staff
5. loss of personal friends, possessions and personal events (e.g. birthdays)
6. drugs
7. ward atmosphere
8. loss of prospects outside the institution.

If Barton's suggestions are correct, and remember that they have not been specifically tested, then it would suggest that the institutional syndrome should be reduced by altering these factors, or should be less likely to occur if patients are treated in the community. Presumably, the more the patient is in touch with the community, the less likely he is to lose contact with the 'real' world, personal friends, possessions and personal events. The prevailing ward atmosphere, domineering, or even cruel ward staff, should be looked for and where possible changed.

But changing systems is not as simple as might at first appear. Firstly, people in institutions tend to resist change and, even when identified, undesirable attitudes might prove very difficult to change. Secondly, even where there is a desire to change, the precise changes brought about might not be what one had anticipated.

A recent study in a Scottish psychiatric hospital monitored staff and patient activity in a ward for the care of the elderly during several thousand 30-second time intervals. The first measurements were taken in an old ward of poor design with toilets and dining room situated at a distance from the sitting room. Over 60% of the patients' time was spent in total inactivity. 30% of their time was devoted to self-care (dressing, toileting) and eating.

The measurements were repeated after a move to a purpose-built unit of compact design and with increased nurse staffing levels. Time spent in total inactivity increased to 75%, and self-care reduced to 15%. Although 10% of the time was spent in staff–patient contact (including medical staff and an occupational therapist), the time nurses spent in contact with patients, except when they were giving instructions, dispensing medication or applying dressings, was only 1.5% of the patient's day. Thus nurses were only spending 20 seconds per hour talking to an individual patient. The compact design of the ward meant that nurses spent less time taking patients to and from the toilet and meals. The increased nursing levels paradoxically reduced their contact with patients. For example, in under-staffed wards where one nurse would help a patient to dress, the nurse talked to the patient. If two nurses dressed a patient, the nurses tended to talk to each other.

But it is not only prolonged spells in hospital that produce problems. *Any* hospital admission may have adverse effects. These adverse effects include:

- crisis of admission (the stress of going into hospital)
- stigma
- changes of attitude, lowered expectations
- increased risk of readmission
- poorer social adjustment, financial costs to the family
- crisis of discharge.

For many people, admission to a psychiatric unit is a terrifying experience. This results partly from ignorance and fantasies about 'madness'. But part of the fear is based in reality. The 'revolving door' policy propels patients out of hospital at an earlier stage in their recovery. As soon as people show signs of improvement they are discharged. Also, alternatives to admission, such as acute day units, now cope with many patients who only a few years ago would have been treated in hospital. Acute wards tend to contain a concentration of bizarre and disturbed behaviour that previously would have been diluted by a larger number of recovering patients and those with minor conditions. Thus many psychiatric wards are disturbed and disturbing.

Hospital admission affects the attitude and expectations of the patient, his family and other important people such as his employer. Doctors are not immune from this influence. Mendel & Rapport (1970) showed that a history of previous admission greatly influenced the doctor towards a decision to readmit the patient. So the decision to admit a patient for the first time may affect the rest of his life. Under stress, the patient's expectations may well be that he will not cope, and in the event of being seen by a psychiatrist, he is more likely to end up in hospital again.

Attempts to combat the institutional syndrome

What can be done to modify the effect of the institution on a patient? Barton suggested the following:

1. Re-establishment of patient's contacts —with ward/hospital functions, patient's home and locality.
2. Provision of a daily sequence of useful occupations, recreations and social events 14 hours a day, 7 days a week: ward programmes, shaving, grooming, toilet, dressing and self-care; redevelopment of social skills and graces; cooking and household management; recreation; physical exercise; work.
3. Eradication of brutality, brow-beating and teasing.
4. Alteration of the attitude of professional staff.
5. Encouragement (and possibility) for a patient to have friends, possessions and to enjoy personal events.
6. Reduction of drugs.
7. Provision of a homely, friendly, permissive ward atmosphere.
8. Making the patient aware of prospects of accommodation, work and friends outside hospital.

How do Barton's suggestions stand up to scrutiny three decades after they were first proposed? Undoubtedly, the attitude of professional staff and their contact with patients must at all times be monitored and attempts made, where necessary, to modify the way they relate to people in their care. Provision must be made for patients to spend more time out of the ward or hospital and among people in 'normal' surroundings. Links must be maintained with friends and family, and in many cases links will have to be re-made. The illness and its associated behaviour might have alienated family and friends, and contact lost. It is not just hospital or home visits that should be suggested, but the reinclusion of the patient in normal family events and activities. For many chronically handicapped people, the ward will remain their home for many months or years. They have a right to live in a homely atmosphere with adequate privacy and to be surrounded by their personal possessions.

Perhaps the two suggestions which, in the light of current experience, might seem inappropriate are numbers 2 and 6. The idea of anyone (ourselves included!) devoting 14 hours a day, 7 days a week to 'useful occupations, recreations and social events' is daunting. There is a danger that any attempt to provide this amount of stimulation and structure would lead to the provision of large group activities and the re-creation of institutional behaviour. While, at first glance, the idea of every patient joining in for a keep-fit routine first thing in the morning might seem healthy, dealing with a group *en masse* reduces staff–patient interaction and allows the patient to 'switch off'. Less activity, but tailored to the needs of the individual, is more appropriate. The reduction of drugs, usually antipsychotics, is only appropriate where over-prescribing is the practice. Many patients may be less able to take part in rehabilitation activities if they are under-medicated (see Ch. 6).

Research evidence

Stein & Test (1978) drew attention to the research evaluating the effect of more humane, pleasant hospital environments. While such treatment does appear to be correlated with adjustment in hospital, it is unrelated to discharge rates or post-hospital adjustment. Wing & Brown (1961) surveyed three British mental hospitals identified by the letters A, B and C. The subjects were female patients under the age of 60, with a diagnosis of schizophrenia, who had spent more than two years in hospital. The patient's mental state, behaviour in the ward and attitude to discharge were assessed, as was the ward (ward restrictiveness scores). A consistent pattern emerged. At hospital A, where the main emphasis of care was on the long-stay patients, there was least clinical disturbance and most personal freedom, useful occupation and optimism among the nursing staff. At hospital C, where progress had been slower, there was most clinical disturbance among patients and least personal freedom, useful occupation and optimism. Hospital B was intermediate.

This was good preliminary evidence that social conditions in psychiatric hospitals do influence the mental state of patients with schizophrenia. The longer-term study (Wing & Brown 1970) concluded that a substantial proportion, though by no means all, of the morbidity shown by long-stay schizophrenic patients in hospital is produced by their environment. A comparison with a fourth hospital 30 years later replicated many of the findings except that the association between social and clinical poverty was much weaker than in 1960 (Curson et al 1992).

Poverty of social environment (fewest personal possessions, little contact with the world outside and pessimistic nurses) was very highly correlated with the clinical poverty syndrome (institutionalism). It appears that people with schizophrenia may be vulnerable to under-stimulating environments wherever they occur, in hospital *or* the community.

That the rehabilitation process precipitated relapse of florid symptoms could not be ruled out by the studies and should be borne in mind.

Clearly the most important single factor associated with clinical improvement (primary handicap) was a reduction in the amount of time spent doing nothing. The only important category distinguishing patients who improved clinically from those who did not was work and occupational therapy.

This work has been quoted extensively because of its great importance for the field of rehabilitation. It is the only systematic study of different hospitals and different social environments over a period of years, and it has answered many basic questions.

Linn (1970) went further by looking at a wider range of variables, and found that discharge rates were unrelated to 'humane treatment' (hospital atmosphere, good facilities, humanistic policies). These findings are similar to those for other types of in-patient treatment such as therapeutic communities and token economy wards, both of which have been shown to improve behaviour and change attitudes within the institution, but this progress is seldom maintained after discharge.

These negative findings should not detract from the very real need to improve standards of care and humanity within institutions. If there are doubts about the effects that institutions have on patients, then what attempts have been made to reduce the amount of time patients spend in hospital?

ATTEMPTS TO REDUCE THE LENGTH OF HOSPITAL STAY

In 1978, researchers in Edinburgh and London were tackling this problem. Noting trends towards shorter hospital admissions in British psychiatric hospitals, both teams set out to assess the effects of very short stays in hospital. They randomly allocated patients to a 'short stay' or 'normal stay' ward. The 'short stay' patients spent less than half the length of time in hospital compared with the normal patients (Kennedy & Hird 1980, Hirsch et al 1979). It appears that patients often get better in time for discharge!

In the United States, Caffey and colleagues (1968) randomly allocated newly admitted schizophrenic patients to one of three treatments: (1) normal hospital care with usual after-care; (2) brief intensive treatment with special after-care; and (3) normal hospital care with special after-care. The brief treatment lasted an average of 29 days compared with 83 for the other two forms, but the readmission rate was not significantly different and overall the 'brief group' spent less time in hospital.

In summary, these studies show that brief hospital admission is as effective as longer admission. Although these patients spent less time in hospital, the total amount of time spent in contact with the hospital (for example, as day patients) may be longer. Although the relapse rate was identical to that of the longer stay patients, it has been shown that as hospital admissions get shorter, in some cases readmission rates increase.

ATTEMPTS TO MANAGE WITHOUT HOSPITAL ADMISSION

A further step in the attempt to avoid the debilitating effects of hospital admission is to try to avoid hospital admission altogether. In Denver, Langsley et al (1971) studied a group of patients for whom it had been decided that hospital admission was necessary. Providing they lived within one hour's travelling time from the hospital, lived with their family and were not homicidal, they were randomly allocated to normal hospital admission or sent home to be treated by the Family Crisis Therapy (FCT) Team. The FCT group of patients were in touch with the crisis team for an average of 24 days. The control group who had been admitted to hospital as usual spent an average of 29 days in hospital (Table 4.1).

During the study period, none of the patients allocated to FCT needed to be admitted (remember all of these patients had been thought to require hospital admission at the time they entered the

Table 4.1   Family Crisis Therapy (Langsley et al 1971)

Family Crisis Therapy group	Normal hospital admission (control group)
24.2 Days average contact	28.6 Days average contact
4.2 Clinic visits	
1.3 Home visits	
5.4 Telephone calls	
1.2 Contacts with other agencies	

study). During the six months after the study, fewer of the FCT patients required readmission (13% compared with 29% of those treated in hospital).

Although patients treated at home got better at the same rate as those in hospital—no faster but no slower—on social adjustment scores, those treated at home seemed to have fewer problems as a result of the illness. Finally, it was calculated that treatment at home cost one sixth of that of hospital treatment.

This work was replicated by Fenton in Montreal with similar conclusions (Fenton et al 1982). More recently, a longer study has been reported from London (Muijen et al 1992). Using a similar design over three years (of which the final 18 months were evaluated), home care provided by the daily living programme (DLP) reduced hospital use by 80%, with patients being admitted for an average of 14 days compared with 72 days. It is of interest to note that the trial hospital (Maudsley Hospital) has an exceptionally long average length of stay. However, the DLP was expensive with concentrated use of staff on relatively few patients, so there was no reduction of direct treatment costs, although the treatment was 'individualised'.

So it appears that a wide range of patients with serious mental illness can be treated as effectively at home as they are in hospital providing they have a supportive family who are prepared to shoulder this burden. But many of our patients have lost contact with their families, have no surviving family or, as is often the case, have no family who are prepared to look after them. For this group, we have to fall back on day hospital, group homes, hostels and other forms of supported accommodation.

Day versus in-patient care

Day hospitals have been used both as a transition between in-patient care and the community, and as an alternative to 24-hour care. Although descriptive studies of day hospital treatment are enthusiastic, 'controlled studies comparing the effectiveness of day versus in-patient treatment are scarce' (Stein & Test 1978). One early study (Herz et al 1971) randomly allocated patients to either day or in-patient treatment. They reported that the day patients spent significantly less time in contact with the hospital, had a lower readmission rate than the in-patients and scored lower on several measures of symptomatology. However, such research has several limitations. The studies performed so far have excluded from day hospitals a large number of patients regarded as being too disturbed, and readmission rates following day hospital treatment remain high.

Hostels ('Half-way houses')

Hostels are another possibility for the treatment of the chronically disturbed or impaired patient. These facilities, with an emphasis on re-socialisation and resettlement, have been used mainly as a transition from hospital to community. There have been few attempts at controlled research in this area, but descriptive reports have been encouraging. A major problem is again the high hospital readmission rate, in part due to the fact that many patients have a recurrence of severe symptoms when pushed to 'move on' to a more independent life (Stein & Test 1978). This has led to the realisation that it is unrealistic for all hostels to be transitional, and that there is a need for some long-stay hostel places.

In Manchester, Douglas House, a new type of hostel ward for chronic psychotic patients was described (Goldberg et al 1985). To be effective, the authors considered it should cater for no more than 12 residents. Their description of the hostel and its programme are well worth studying.

The principle of 'normalisation' is increasingly being used in the planning of residential services. It has been argued that services provided in the community for people with psychiatric disability have tended to segregate them from others and emphasise the way in which they are different. Thus many community residential settings may continue to provide a stigmatising, impoverished environment, offering few opportunities for self-development and participation in community life (Morris 1981). There is also the danger of falling into the trap of believing that community care must be better than hospital care. The provision of inadequately financed or managed supported accommodation manned by untrained staff of low status will not provide an adequate level of care. The Wagner Report (1988) advocated improved training, supervision and managerial support, and recommended that more staff obtain formal qualifications.

ATTEMPTS TO TREAT CHRONIC PATIENTS IN THE COMMUNITY

Marx et al (1973) decided to try community treatment for a group of patients still in hospital and who were not considered to be capable of 'sustained community living'. The patients were randomly allocated to an experimental group and a control group. The experimental group of patients spent up to eight days in the research ward for assessment before being sent out into the community regardless of their symptoms. The control group patients either stayed on their wards or were sent to a research ward for five months' training before being discharged.

As chronic patients are prone to drop out of treatment if they have to attend a clinic, the experimental treatment involved staff going out to the patients. Staff spent much of the day and evening alongside the patients, teaching coping skills and helping them to acquire skills of daily living such as cooking and self-care. The treatment lasted five months after which the patients were linked in with the usual community services. These unselected chronically symptomatic patients managed well in the community. Only one out of 21 experimental patients required hospital admission during the five month period, and then only for one day. During the two years of follow-up, the group gained a significantly higher level of independent living than the control group, although over time the difference between the two groups diminished.

CLOSURE OF MENTAL HOSPITALS

The closure of large mental hospitals is, according to some, occurring decades too late, while others contend that it represents a step in the dark. Fortunately some of the closures are being closely monitored. Powick Hospital closed in 1978 to be replaced by a psychiatric unit in Kidderminster's District General Hospital. Reviewing the first seven years of the new unit, Lawrence and colleagues (1991) reported that there had been a marked increase in the number of admissions per head of population, but more of the admissions lasted less than one week.

In north London, the TAPS project has been monitoring the rundown of two of the largest hospitals in the region, Claybury and Friern Barnet. Prior to the decision of the regional health authority to close the hospital (taken in 1983), most of the reduction in bed numbers had been as a result of deaths. Since the change of policy, it has been demonstrated that the cost of care in the community is not lower just for the first wave of patients to leave (i.e. the patients with least handicap), but also for the whole of the hospital population (Leff et al 1990).

HAZARDS OF COMMUNITY CARE

Concern has been expressed by the National Schizophrenia Fellowship and MENCAP that the rundown of hospital beds may make it more difficult for sufferers to obtain in-patient care when required. This problem would be exacerbated where closure of beds preceded the provision of community facilities. One measure of the success or failure of community care would be the suicide rate.

Morgan (1992) was invited to review the delivery of mental health care in one health authority in the Southwest of England following a spate of suicides. His investigation drew attention to the hazards of what he called 'fast lane community care'. There was a risk of fragmentation of the service, conflicting ideologies and difficulty monitoring and evaluating dispersed resources.

The suicide rate, especially among young people, is rising. The aetiology is multifactorial and must include the current high level of unemployment. Nevertheless, approximately half of suicides have had contact with the mental health services at some time in their life, and of those, approximately half will have been seen within the previous two months. Suicide should remain a topic for regular clinical audit.

LIMITATIONS OF THESE STUDIES

A great deal of time and effort has gone into all the experimental evaluations described above. Undoubtedly they tell us more about what might be achieved, but caution must be exercised when trying to apply these results to 'real' services.

The short-stay experiments described by Kennedy & Hird (1980) and Hirsch et al (1979) only ran for a limited period (1–2 years) and the earlier studies of home treatment (Langsley et al 1971, Fenton et al 1982) ran for an even shorter time (1 year). What can be achieved by a determined team for a time-limited study cannot and should not be taken as indicative of what could be achieved by an average service over many years. The level of stress and hours of work that could be tolerated in order to 'prove' the test service effective, would not be acceptable or reasonable for permanent service provision. None of these models of service was continued after the experimental period even though they demonstrated that their models all saved money!

Recent studies have lasted longer (e.g. the DLP: 3 years in total) but remain, in many ways, unrealistic. The Maudsley Hospital provides a unique and therefore unrepresentative service. The length of time spent by the experimental group in hospital was greater than that of the patients in the short-stay studies of two decades earlier. Evaluation of novel, but sustainable, services must be preferable. One such home treatment service has been described by Dean & Gadd (1990).

DOES IT SAVE MONEY?

It was thought that closing expensive mental hospitals and caring for patients in the community would prove cheaper, and hence the idea was very popular with politicians. Langsley et al (1971) calculated that FCT treatment for his patients cost only one sixth of that of hospital admission. Weisbrod et al (1980) carried out a more extensive cost/benefit analysis of their community care service in Wisconsin and found that the cost of patient care in either hospital or community setting was very high. The hospital-based programme was about 10% cheaper per patient, but taking all benefits and costs into account, the community programme provided some benefits to patients not supplied by the hospital service. The TAPS monitoring of a real service change supports the notion of community care costs being lower.

Further research is required for clarification. But it is clear that the massive savings that had been anticipated will not materialise. The challenge for service planners is to provide as high a quality of care as possible, within a limited budget, while safeguarding the benefits of independence and normality in the community for the patient. There is a grave danger of recreating institutions in the community. Life in an inadequately supervised and unstimulating lodging house may reproduce all the faults of the old mental hospital. This means that priorities must be addressed. As Hawks (1975) observed in the 1970s, services for people with serious and chronic mental illness and disability must remain a priority.

'At a time when the traditional pattern of psychiatric services is being challenged all over Europe, there is an opportunity for research to inform planning' (Wing 1990). It remains to be seen whether political dogma or evaluative research will have the greater impact on the shape of future mental health services.

REFERENCES

Barton R 1959 Institutional neurosis. Wright, Bristol
Caffey E M, Jones R B, Diamond L S et al 1968 Brief hospital treatment of
  schizophrenia: early results of a multiple hospital study. Hospital and
  Community Psychiatry 19: 282–287
Curson D A, Pantelis C, Ward J, Barnes T R E 1992 Institutionalism and
  schizophrenia 30 years on. British Journal of Psychiatry 160: 230–241
Dean C, Gadd E M 1990 Home treatment for acute psychiatric illness. British
  Medical Journal 310: 1021–1022
Dunham H W 1965 Community psychiatry, the newest therapeutic bandwagon.
  Archives of General Psychiatry 12: 303–313
Fenton F R, Tessier L, Struening E L, Smith F A, Benoit C 1982 Home and
  hospital psychiatric treatment. Croom Helm, London
Goffman E 1961 Asylums — a study of total institutions. Doubleday, New York
  reprinted 1970 by Penguin Books, London
Goldberg D P, Bridges K, Cooper W, Hyde C, Sterling C, Wyatt R 1985
  Douglas House: a new type of hostel ward for chronic psychotic patients.
  British Journal of Psychiatry 147: 383–388
Group for the Advancement of Psychiatry 1967 Education for community
  psychiatry, Report No. 64. Mental Health Materials Center, New York
Group for the Advancement of Psychiatry 1983 Community psychiatry: a
  reappraisal, Report No. 113. Mental Health Materials Center, New York
Hawks D 1975 Community care: an analysis of assumptions. British Journal of
  Psychiatry 127: 176–185
Herz M I, Endicott J, Spitzer R L, Mesnikoff A 1971 Day versus in-patient
  hospitalisation: a controlled study. American Journal of Psychiatry
  127: 1371–1381
Hirsch S R, Platt S, Knights A, Weyman A 1979 Shortening hospital stay for
  psychiatric care: effect on patients and their families. British Medical Journal
  1: 442–446
Kennedy P, Hird F 1980 Description and evaluation of a short-stay admission
  ward. British Journal of Psychiatry 136: 205–215
Kubie L 1968 Pitfalls of community psychiatry. Archives of General Psychiatry
  18: 257–266
Langsley D G, Machotka P, Flomenhaft M S W 1971 Avoiding mental hospital
  admission: a follow-up study. American Journal of Psychiatry 127: 1391–1394
Lawrence R E, Copas J B, Cooper P W 1991 Community care—does it reduce the
  need for psychiatric beds? British Journal of Psychiatry 159: 334–340
Leff J P 1990 The TAPS project 3: predicting the community cost of closing
  psychiatric hospitals. British Journal of Psychiatry 157: 661–670
Linn L S 1970 State hospital environments and rates of patient discharge. Archives
  of General Psychiatry 23: 346–351
Marx A J, Test M A, Stein L I Extrahospital management of severe mental illness.
  Archives of General Psychiatry 29: 205–211
Mendel W M, Rapport S 1970 Determinants of the decision for psychiatric
  hospitalisation. Archives of General Psychiatry 20: 321–328
Morgan H G 1992 Suicide prevention: hazards in the fast lane to community care.
  British Journal of Psychiatry 160: 149–153
Morris B 1981 Residential units. In: Wing J K, Morris B (eds) Handbook of
  psychiatric rehabilitation practice. Oxford University Press, Oxford
Muijen M, Marks I M, Audini B, McNamee G 1992 The daily living programme:
  preliminary comparison of community versus hospital-based treatment for the
  seriously mentally ill emergency admission. British Journal of Psychiatry 160:
  379–384

Stein L I, Test M A 1978 Alternatives to mental hospital treatment. Plenum Press, New York

Stein L I, Test M A 1980 Alternatives to mental hospital treatment. Archives of General Psychiatry 37: 392–397

Wagner G 1988 A positive choice. HMSO, London

Weisbrod B A, Test M A, Stein L I 1980 Alternative to mental hospital II: economic cost-benefit analysis. Archives of General Psychiatry 37: 400–405

Wing J K 1961 A simple and reliable subclassification of chronic schizophrenia. Journal of Mental Science 107: 862–875

Wing J K 1990 Planning services for long-term psychiatric disorder. In: Goldberg D, Tantam D (eds) The public health impact of mental disorder. Hogrefe and Huber Publishers, Toronto

Wing J K, Brown G W 1961 Social treatment of schizophrenia: a comparative survey of three mental hospitals. Journal of Mental Science 107: 847–861

Wing J K, Brown G W 1970 Institutionalism and schizophrenia: a comparative study of three mental hospitals 1960–68. Cambridge University Press, London

5. Assessment and evaluation

Clephane Hume

The beginning of an acquaintance whether with persons or things is to get a definite outline for our ignorance.

George Eliot, **Daniel Deronda**

ASSESSMENT AND EVALUATION

Assessment is the foundation of any treatment regime or intervention. If the problems are not identified, potential solutions cannot be suggested. Evaluation is an equally important aspect of rehabilitation, since careful consideration of the programmes provided forms the basis for improving services.

Assessment

The purpose of assessment is to provide:

1. objective rather than anecdotal information
2. a measure of skills, achievement, deficits, problems
3. a baseline from which to monitor change
4. selection of patients for specific programmes
5. standard information, so that groups of patients can be compared for evaluation
6. assessment of need, so that appropriate services can be provided.

Observations must be carefully recorded so that the information collected is readily available to all those concerned with treatment.

METHODS OF ASSESSMENT

Various methods are used and may include observational procedures or interviews, tests, rating scales and self-assessment questionnaires. The focus in rehabilitation is on functional performance and the ability to cope with the practicalities of day-to-day living.

Most assessments involve observation of patients performing particular tasks. The context may be formal, in that the person is instructed to carry out specific tasks in order to rate performance, or informal, where he is observed over a longer period of time, carrying out routine tasks rather than following special instructions. Recent technological advances have increased the range of assessment media available so that audio or video recorders may be used to record observations, or computer tests or interviews utilised. Collation and interpretation of data may also be computerised.

The individual may also be involved in self-assessment through the use of questionnaires and inventories. Methods using biofeedback may also provide the individual with information, for example in relation to levels of anxiety.

Assessment skills are not the prerogative of any one profession and should be developed by all members of the treatment team. Many people automatically observe patients on a day-to-day basis without reflecting too much about this aspect of their work. It is easy to form clinical impressions from such observations but careful recording and analysis of data may reveal a different picture. It is not that most people lack powers of observation, but rather that the difficulty lies in interpretation. Experience and discussion with others involved in patient assessment will help to develop these skills.

Schedules, questionnaires, rating scales, inventories and check lists

These are all ways of collecting information in a systematic way. The most simple can be administered with little or no training, while the more complex will require special training (e.g. the Present State Examination—PSE) (Peck & Dean 1988). Specific rehabilitation schedules are available such as the Morningside Rehabilitation Status Scale (MRSS) (Affleck & McGuire 1984) and REHAB (Baker 1983). Both of these have been well researched and standardised, thus ensuring consistent results when used by different assessors. Such inter-rater reliability and validity of content for use with patients in rehabilitation units ensure a better quality of assessment. The Disability Assessment Schedule developed by the World Health Organization (WHO DAS) (1988) is designed to be used in different countries and this considers social factors in addition to the person's behaviour.

Particular aspects of behaviour may be assessed through specific assessments such as those which investigate social networks or social skills. Comprehensive assessments, such as the Valpar Battery for occupational skills, provide in-depth information but may be costly to obtain and time consuming to administer. The testing and interpretation of certain aspects of behaviour or function may be the province of particular professionals, e.g. IQ testing by clinical psychologists.

Check lists of skills or behaviour may be used to monitor performance and to make sure that important areas have not been overlooked.

Designing assessment forms

Although standardised schedules have the advantage of allowing comparison with established norms and other programmes, the treatment team may wish to devise its own assessment schedule to meet local requirements. Design is important. Any bias on the part of the person completing the assessment should be minimised, if not eliminated, by careful planning and testing, and the information collected must be clearly recorded without ambiguity. A team wishing to design its own schedule is advised to seek the advice of a clinical psychologist in order to avoid the pitfalls inherent in such an exercise.

The design of a form can be divided into stages:

1. Decide on the area of behaviour to be assessed, e.g. ability for independent living.
2. List the topics to be included — shopping, cooking, budgeting, etc. A factor analysis will reveal the frequency and therefore the relevance of particular tasks for inclusion in an assessment.
3. Decide how information is to be rated and recorded.
4. Draft guidelines or a protocol for use.
5. Try it out.

A small pilot study will inevitably reveal ambiguities and the fact that the criteria are not as clear as was originally thought. Modifications will be necessary! When all team members can agree on the scores for particular individuals (inter-rater reliability), the form is ready for use.

To be of use in relation to treatment planning, findings of assessments and their significance should be interpreted according to individual circumstances. For example, in a hospital assessment of domestic skills, one patient stated that he could not make his bed as the blankets were 'too difficult'. It was only later discovered that at home he used a continental quilt and so the problem was not what it originally seemed to be. When given a downie (continental quilt), he managed independently.

Observation and behavioural analysis

Assessment may be very specifically used in observing particular behaviour patterns and analysing incidents which occur within a unit. Careful observation (and recording) of repeated 'difficult' behaviour may reveal specific factors which precede or precipitate an incident, thus indicating ways of intervention and prevention. Modification of the environment may be the solution rather than treatment for the individual.

Measurement, i.e. counting the frequency of occurrence and duration of particular behaviour patterns will also give a more accurate picture of the situation. Such problems may seem greater and of longer duration than is actually the case.

Recording information

Within the ruling of the Data Protection Acts in the United Kingdom, all information recorded in patients'/clients' files must be made accessible to them on request. Material should therefore be carefully (and legibly!) recorded.

In most instances, information will be written into case notes or Kardex folders. Some places use profile folders or special files to record abilities, goals and performance and these can enhance the professional appearance of material. In other instances, information is recorded by computer, with graphic output. Checklists may be simply ticked or scores recorded on standard forms. Some information lends itself more readily to visual presentation and this may be much easier to interpret.

Graphic scales may be used (Kugler 1992), where a cross is drawn on a line to represent inclination towards two extremes of behaviour. Alternatively, the rater may have the choice of a range of descriptions (semantic differentials), picking out the one which is most applicable (Fig. 5.1).

Some forms include numeric scores which are tallied on completion of each assessment and these often give space for several assessments in order to provide easy to read comparisons. Charts,

Adjective	Inclines to	Average	Inclines to	Adjective
Sad	√			Happy
Tidy			√	Untidy

Fig. 5.1 Behaviour rating scale.

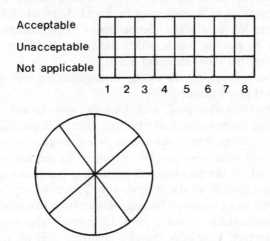

Acceptable

Unacceptable

Not applicable

1 2 3 4 5 6 7 8

Fig. 5.2 Recording charts.

such as the Gunzburg (1973) PAC (patient assessment chart) present comprehensive information in an easy to read format. A simple pie chart or histogram, which can be filled in when the person reaches a predetermined stage of rehabilitation, (e.g. after 3 months), will quickly provide information about areas of achievement and deficit, which means more to most people than particular scores or figures (Fig. 5.2).

Information which is clearly presented and easily understood, preferably typed or neatly written on one side of a piece of paper, is much more likely to be used than a dossier of information which is poorly presented and difficult to sort out.

Disadvantages of different types of assessment

Forms which are completed after discussion between team members must be carefully used in order to ensure that the results recorded are a true reflection of behaviour, not an arithmetical consensus. People do not behave in the same way in different situations, and consequently there may be considerable variations in the observations of different staff.

Rating scales may have various degrees of complexity. There is, however, the danger that the more gradations in the scale, the less reliable ratings become. Choosing between nine gradations is not recommended! Raters may also develop a fixed way of responding so that extremes of a scale may be avoided, or all ticks incline towards the left of a scale. (Some scales force changes in such behaviour by putting words which the rater would expect to be grouped together into a different order.)

Numerical scores should clearly distinguish between high and low levels of performance.

Formalised/standardised and battery assessments may be intimidating to the individual who feels that he is participating in a 'test' situation, but contrary to what might be expected, computerised interviews can be welcomed by patients who may feel relieved of the pressure of answering questions in a way which is acceptable to the interviewer. There is some evidence that people may give more honest answers to a machine than to another, potentially critical person. Computers also stick rigidly to the interview schedule, thereby ensuring that all topics are dealt with. The disadvantage is of course, that particular topics cannot be developed at will.

Self-rating forms give an impression of the person's own perception of his abilities, but it is important to remember that he may under-rate his level of performance, or be over optimistic. Care must therefore be taken in using such information.

Selection of assessments is important—a test which is standardised for one group of patients will not be reliable for use with another. Acquiring ideas from other people may thus not be the answer to another unit's need. Modifying standardised forms renders them invalid.

In conclusion, assessment procedures should be easy to complete, not too time consuming and provide the desired information. It is always important to remember that one assessment reflects ability to perform that task at a given time and will not necessarily be applicable to long-term performance.

Results should be meticulously recorded—if you were to be unexpectedly absent tomorrow, would your findings be accessible and comprehensible to your colleagues?

TIMING OF ASSESSMENTS

Given that assessment is the baseline for planning treatment, it is important to monitor and record function at all stages of a programme.

Hospital

Initial assessment

After admission to the rehabilitation unit or programme, and following a suitable interval (e.g. 2 weeks) during which the patient can be familiarised with the day to day routine, an initial assessment should be carried out. This will serve the dual purpose of recording abilities at the beginning of the rehabilitation programme and providing information for treatment planning.

Continuing assessment

Staff will be constantly observing the patient's behaviour, so that informal assessment is a continuing process. However, to ensure that any changes are documented, it is necessary to conduct formal assessments at regular intervals. This may constitute part of a routine review process which will ensure that all patients are considered and no-one gets overlooked because he is unobtrusive. In this way, improvement or deterioration can be clearly seen on the basis of measurable results rather than clinical impressions, and causes of unacceptable behaviour can be investigated.

The team may decide to do a systematic assessment of certain areas of function over a period of time, beginning for example, with personal life skills and moving through domestic and occupational skills to community living skills. Some areas of function, e.g. tests of cognition, may be the domain of the clinical psychologist. Others, such as domestic and vocational skills, are within the remit of the occupational therapist, although such assessments will draw upon the observations of other team members (see Ch. 8).

As indicated above, when carrying out specific assessments, it is important to remember that the person's ability to perform a task at the time of the test does not necessarily mean that he will be motivated to perform that task when left to his own devices. For example, under test conditions, someone may go shopping and cook a meal successfully, but remain poorly motivated to do so following discharge. Observation over a longer period of time will give more accurate information than can be gained from a single exercise. Similarly, the circumstances of assessment should be considered — someone whose domestic skills are being observed will be disadvantaged if preparing a meal in unfamiliar surroundings. A known environment, ideally the person's own home, should be used.

It may be necessary to assess someone for suitability for referral for specific treatment such as psychotherapy, or social skills training. Group leaders will have their own criteria for selection and team members should familiarise themselves with these in order to avoid unrealistic referrals and false hopes. The individual should always be included in planning treatment programmes and findings of assessments should be discussed with him, even if only in general terms. This provides a chance for reality testing and learning, as well as identifying goals for future action. Formal recognition of progress will be useful to those with low self-esteem and an accurate assessment will be of help to those who are over-confident or unrealistic in their view of their own abilities.

Pre-discharge assessment

As treatment progresses, and if discharge back to an existing living situation seems feasible, a home visit is indicated. Assessing the individual in familiar surroundings is of immense value. Home visits can provide additional social information, which may result in a picture very different from that obtained in hospital. This may result in further indications for intervention.

When discharge is imminent, the pre-discharge assessment should provide a summary of current performance. These results may be compared with the initial assessment to show general progress and to evaluate the efficacy of treatment. Alternatively, the data may be used as a part of research into the skills needed for living and surviving in the community. This may be used in relation to identification of behaviours which will predict the outcome of treatment.

Assessment in the community context

The prime purpose of all the assessments mentioned above is to help the clinical team to provide the best possible treatment and most suitable plans for a particular patient. While the focus has been on people in hospital, the pattern of the assessment process should be similar for people living in the community. The location may be the person's home or a local centre, but the same baseline information should be gathered at interview after referral. A plan is drawn up and implemented, progress monitored and notes completed when intervention is terminated. More reliance may be placed on interview methods and self-reporting than observation of behaviour or formal tests.

In the UK, there is a developing focus on assessment of need (see below).

WHAT TO ASSESS

Word of warning! Even with a key-worker system a large number of people may still be involved in the assessment process. Beware of over assessment, which will exhaust both client and staff. There is an infinite array of topics and check lists of skills may become very lengthy. In reality, it is not necessary for everyone to be able to accomplish all aspects of everyday life. It is more appropriate to know where to get help than to be able to do everything personally.

The choice of assessment must be tailored to the individual, in context. Commonsense and the requirements of the individual's situation should prevail. Some examples are given here to illustrate common topics.

1. Mental state: appearance and behaviour, speech, thoughts, mood, memory.
2. Cognitive function: comprehension, memory, orientation, decision making.
3. Personal life skills: hygiene, appearance, clothing, use of appliances (teeth, spectacles, etc.), taking medication.
4. Social skills: interpersonal relationships, non-verbal skills, assertive behaviour, communication skills (e.g. telephoning), literacy.
5. Domestic skills: laundry, meal planning and preparation, household cleaning and management, security and safety, dealing with emergencies.
6. Leisure: friends, hobbies, interests, participation in activities.
7. Work: general work habits, aptitudes, attitudes, ambitions, job seeking skills, relationships.
8. Community living skills: mobility, use of transport, road safety, local knowledge.

9. Home visit: facilities available, level of support, evidence of previous coping or non-coping.

Assessment of need

In relation to the United Kingdom National Health Service and Community Care Bill 1990, one of the requirements is the assessment of need. This is essentially consumer centred, so that clients and their carers have the opportunity to identify the difficulties which are priorities for them. Needs to be met can then be matched to services available within a given locality. Such assessments may be undertaken by a variety of people but often one key worker will be responsible for the initial assessment. This may cause overlaps and blurring of roles between professions, but it is sensible in both economic terms and in protecting clients from over assessment and duplication of investigation.

It is suggested (SSI 1991a) that assessment of need should be simple, speedy, informal and a jointly negotiated process between assessor and user. In terms of the assessor's time, the type of assessment should relate to the probable input of care, thus severely disabled people require longer, more specialised assessment.

Assessors will have a knowledge of the range of available services and potential users will require to have an understanding of the options open to them. Eligibility for assistance can then be discussed, with all those involved having a clear view of the situation, so that priorities will be established in accordance with individual wishes. It is obviously important that communication is facilitated, where appropriate, by the use of interpreters or a representative who can express the wishes of an individual (advocacy support).

Guidelines for the content of an assessment are detailed in the practitioners' guide for Care Management and Assessment, stage 3 (SSI 1991a). Inherent in these guidelines is the concept of a partnership and negotiation between assessor and user.

The needs led approach requires the practitioner/assessor to work according to the requirements of the employing agency and the client while retaining objectivity and accountability to provide quality assurance.

Linked to assessment of need of the individual is assessment of need within a given community in order to plan and implement services. It may be attractive to provide the resources which will be readily taken up by users, but care should be taken to avoid the 'soft' psychiatry approach, where those with minor illnesses and the 'worried well' receive attention at the expense of the chronically ill—the 'hard' psychiatry option. The dangers of 'medicalising' 'normal' anxieties, and thereby inflating demand, should be heeded. It is important in this context to establish how many chronically ill people are to be found in a given community and to draw up plans for services to match expressed needs such as respite care or day care, which will provide opportunities to increase social networks (see Ch. 7).

If community need is not properly assessed, well-intentioned people may offer treatment, such as courses in anxiety management, and wonder why people do not rush to participate. Obviously there will be a range of reasons, but one may be that the prevailing economic problems in an area give higher credibility to a practical topic such as budget cookery.

EVALUATION

Particularly in relation to care management, assessment procedures should be monitored for quality of service. Factors to be considered include cost, speed of response, efficiency, consumer satisfaction, collaboration/liaison with relevant agencies and effective use of resources. Identification of unmet need will reveal deficiencies in care plans.

Evaluation can be thought of in relation to two aspects—quality assurance and programme evaluation. Quality assurance assesses the outcome of specific programmes in relation to individual clients and should be routinely accomplished on a day-to-day basis through continuous (ongoing) assessment. If treatment proves to be ineffective, the reasons for this should be investigated, and alternative measures implemented. Likewise, if treatment has been successful, it is useful to know why. Responses may vary according to individuals and their circumstances, so that what helps A may be no use to B, but it may be possible to detect trends. The enthusiasm of the therapist is recognised as a potent influence, but this can be eliminated if treatment is carried out by different people.

Programme evaluation is used on a longer term basis and should take into consideration the resources utilised, the intervention process and the results. While it is relatively easy to identify the resources used, the actual treatment provided may cover a variety of procedures based on pharmaceutical, psychological or social principles and it can thus be difficult to distinguish the value of individual factors. Psychiatry often uses a multifactorial approach and it is often impossible and indeed undesirable, to attempt to separate social from medical factors since the two are tightly interwoven.

Programme evaluation is complex, for who is to judge efficacy? The consumer? The administrator or financial director? The mental health worker? Different beliefs about the causes of illness necessarily influence beliefs about treatment. Multifaceted problems require multifaceted solutions.

Careful collation of information regarding the nature of treatment, its frequency and duration can provide an objective opinion as to its efficacy. In this way, it is possible to discover if a regime used in one setting is of benefit in another, or to determine whether or not a particular 'package' is actually of much value in preparing people to cope with the situations it is aimed to deal with.

A further area for evaluation is the choice of approaches to treatment in relation to particular needs and diagnoses. For example, the use of a psychotherapeutic approach with psychotic patients is advocated by some practitioners and roundly condemned by others. It is necessary to evaluate the evidence surrounding both arguments before introducing this approach into a programme. The behavioural base as applied to token economy units is now largely rejected but its value in individual behaviour modification programmes is accepted. Using a philosophy with which one feels sympathetic is not a justification for its therapeutic use. Does it achieve results which cannot be obtained by any other means?

It is also important to consider the relevance of rehabilitation programmes by examining the social environment in which people will be required to cope. For example, social changes, such as rising unemployment, may render previous programme goals invalid. It may be more appropriate to shift the focus away from remunerative work, towards planning leisure time activities.

The treatment environment is also a target for evaluation (Moos 1974). Wing & Brown's work (1970) in the 1960s is not without lessons for present day accommodation, where resources for individuals in some places are not all that they should be.

Evaluation can form the basis of research and the shift to community care gives ideal opportunities to investigate the quality of life for individuals who have been transferred from long-term care through a process of rehabilitation. This may raise questions about the aims of treatment, as well as identifying deficiencies in provision of resources and services. Another aspect of evaluation is clinical audit, peer group evaluation in which the members of the multidisciplinary team consider their professional standards, effectiveness and efficiency.

RESEARCH

This will be closely linked to programme evaluation (Milne 1987, Ferguson et al 1992) but may have a higher profile in some places according to the interests of practitioners. Often it is staffs' fears of the research process and the perceived complexities of statistical analysis which cause them to shy away from carrying out research.

Principles of investigation are not overwhelmingly frightening and help is always available! Research data may be gathered through standardised interview schedules, such as the GHQ 30 or PSE, which can provide a standard diagnosis through the use of the Catego computer programme. Questionnaires and inventories may also be used to gather data for research and these may be completed by staff as part of a standard interview or filled in by the patient in order to obtain a subjective view of ability, or consumer opinion.

It is important not to devalue relatively simple research techniques. Recording what may seem very basic, routine information should not be under-rated since this can provide a basis for improving services—which is what this entire chapter is ultimately concerned with.

REFERENCES

Affleck J W, McGuire R S 1984 The measurement of psychiatric rehabilitation status—a review of the needs and a new scale. British Journal of Psychiatry 145: 517–525

Baker R 1983 A rating scale for long stay patients. Paper, World Congress on Behaviour Therapy, Washington DC

Ferguson B et al 1992 Clinical evaluation of a new community service based on general practitioner psychiatric clinics. British Journal of Psychiatry 160: 493–497

Gunzburg H C 1973 Social competence and mental handicap, 2nd edn. Balliere Tindall, London

Hall J 1977 The content of ward rating scales for long stay patients. British Journal of Psychiatry 130: 237–293

Kugler B T 1992 Rating scale methods: validity and reliability. In: Weller M, Eysenck M (eds) The scientific basis of psychiatry, 2nd edn. W B Saunders, London

Milne D 1987 Evaluating mental health practice. Croom Helm, London

Moos R 1974 Evaluating treatment environments. J Wiley, New York

Peck D Dean C 1988 Measurement in psychiatry. In: Kendell R, Zealley A (eds) Companion to psychiatric studies. Churchill Livingstone, Edinburgh

SSI 1991a Care management and assessment. Practitioners' guide. HMSO, London

SSI 1991b Care management and assessment. Managers' guide. HMSO, London

WHO 1988 Psychiatric Disability Assessment Schedule (WHO DAS) WHO, Geneva

Wing J K, Brown G 1970 Institutionalism and schizophrenia. Cambridge University Press, Cambridge

6. Management options

Ian Pullen

Patients may recover in spite of drugs or because of them.
J H Gaddum 1959

Constructing a care package is like designing a building. The architect of the whole scheme must have received the appropriate level of training and experience, and should possess her own vision and ideals in addition to those shared with the rest of her profession. She should be a good communicator and co-ordinator as she will have to bring together the conflicting advice and requirements of the other professions and interested parties. The purpose of the building and the needs of its users must be reconciled with the materials and finance available. This will invariably demand compromise. The agreed plan must be in place before building begins if the whole edifice is to survive. Thus, if care planning is seen as the keystone, the unifying force, the patient and the management of her underlying illness are the foundations upon which everything else depends.

Management planning is part of the standard procedure of:

1. Assessment — problem list
   — resources
2. Diagnosis — nosological
   — formulation
3. Management — physical
   — psychological
   — social
4. Review — modification of management plans.

This logical procedure should be followed in all cases. A diagnosis cannot be made without a full assessment, including a full psychiatric history and mental state examination. Where possible, information from relatives and friends should be sought.

A nosological diagnosis (assigning the patients to a particular diagnostic group, e.g. schizophrenia) and a formulation (a hypothesis to explain why this patient has developed this particular illness or has relapsed at this particular time) are required. Further assessment and information may be needed to arrive at a full problem list.

Management plans must include: whether treatment of any type is required or is likely to help; where treatment should be carried out; the form, duration and expected effects, as well as any possible side-effects; whether the patient is able to give informed consent and, if not, whether the treatment should be compulsory. Treatments may be used separately or in combination.

A review date should be set when necessary changes will be made.

CHALLENGES FOR REHABILITATION

People with long-term illnesses and disabilities present a particular challenge in terms of management. Chronic conditions require treatment over prolonged periods of time, in some cases for life. It is easy to lose sight of the treatment goals and the rationale behind the treatment chosen. In desperation, drug doses may be pushed up to unacceptable levels and unhelpful combinations of drugs used. Some people change little, if at all, despite the various treatments tried but may develop irreversible changes due to long-term exposure to medication (such as tardive dyskinesia or hypothyroidism).

Many people may benefit from a care package which leads to resettlement in the community, but still have only minimal insight into the fact that they have been ill. Their ability to understand the need for continuing treatment or contact with the care team will present a considerable challenge.

MODELS OF MENTAL ILLNESS

At our present state of knowledge, there are many different ways of conceptualising any particular patient's condition. The model chosen may depend on training, dogma, or an eclectic use of the model or models that best suit that particular situation. The significance for this discussion is that the model chosen will dictate the management plan.

The most important models are (in alphabetical order): behavioural, medical, organic, psychotherapeutic and social. Other methods include the conspiratorial, crisis, family interaction and moral models (see Clare 1980). For simplicity, the medical model will be dealt with last.

1. Behavioural model

Learning theory suggests that all behaviour is learned. Behaviour that produces pleasurable responses tends to be repeated (reinforced), while behaviour that is linked with a less pleasurable outcome is not repeated (extinguished). Behaviourists deny the existence of the 'unconscious'. Phobias, obsessions and some 'undesirable' behaviours have been treated successfully along these lines.

Cognitive-behavioural theory, a recent development, proposes that abnormal thought patterns (cognitions) may not always be the result of illness, but may produce it. Thus whilst severely depressed individuals may experience negative cognitions ('I am a failure, every decision I make leads to disaster') as part of their illness, these same thoughts occurring when not depressed may precipitate a depressive illness. This model has produced successful treatment for depression and anxiety.

2. Organic model

This model considers all psychiatric symptoms to be the result of some underlying physical condition. The acute confusional state produced by a serious infection such as pneumonia, and the mood disturbances brought about by the hormone abnormalities of thyroid and pituitary disease are such conditions. Treatment should be aimed at correcting the underlying physical cause. There is certainly a growing list of conditions for which an organic cause has been found, but few psychiatrists would claim that all psychiatric illness can be explained in this way.

3. Psychotherapeutic model

This model stresses the importance of early childhood experience in the emergence, later in life, of psychiatric symptoms. Failure to master vital developmental hurdles may lead to a re-emergence, under stress, of the emotional and relationship difficulties of an earlier stage of life. These unconscious mechanisms include fixation and regression. While these theories may aid the understanding of neuroses, there is, as yet, little objective evidence to show that psychotherapeutic measures are effective.

4. Social model

The social model widens the area of psychiatric involvement. Unlike the previous models which are concerned with the individual, this model includes the individual plus her social situation within the remit of psychiatric interest. Labelling and the concepts of primary and secondary deviance are introduced. Deviant behaviour (primary deviance) may lead to a person being labelled as mentally ill. Being treated as mentally ill and admitted to a psychiatric hospital may cause abnormal behaviour (secondary deviance). The social model of psychiatric disorder has encouraged such developments as the therapeutic community and 'normalisation' programmes.

5. Medical model

The medical model takes into account not merely the symptom, syndrome or disease, but the person who suffers, her personal and social situation, her biological, psychological and social status. The medical model, as applied to psychiatry, embodies the basic principle that every illness is the product of two factors: environment working on the organism (Clare 1980). Thus the medical model is not to be confused, as it frequently is, with the organic model.

Purists insist that only one model should be used. Yet, at present, no one model can explain all psychiatric conditions any more than any single method of treatment has been found to be universally effective.

In the rehabilitation of people with mental health problems, a flexible approach is recommended based on the medical model, but using the other models where applicable. There may well be occasions where two (or more) different management approaches, based on different models, may be used simultaneously. Thus a woman who has developed a schizophrenic illness may, on leaving hospital, receive medication (medical model) in a hostel run on therapeutic community lines (social model) while receiving social skills training (behavioural model). At the end of the day, we are all in the business of trying to produce the best possible outcome for each person rather than proving that our ideological stance is best.

Table 6.1   Choice of treatment

Illness	Problems	Treatment
Acute psychosis	? Precipitants, where to treat, medication	Likely to include short-term medication plus social intervention
Chronic psychosis	? Continuing stresses, rehabilitation, compliance and motivation	? Depot medication, behaviour therapy, social therapies
Acute relapse of chronic psychosis	? Precipitants, ? stopped medication	? Depot medication long-term, move to supported accommodation or other environmental manipulation

THE RANGE OF TREATMENTS

As most treatments can be used in any setting, the decision where to treat should be based on social, rather than strictly medical criteria.

Choice of treatment

In addition to the factors mentioned above, the duration of the illness will have to be considered. Is this an acute illness, is it chronic, or is it an acute episode in a chronic condition (Table 6.1)?

PHYSICAL METHODS OF TREATMENT

Physical methods of treatment should be used as part of an overall management plan. There are clear indications for their use in treatment rather than merely for 'patient control'.

Psychotropic drugs

A number of simple guidelines ensure the sensible and safe use of medication. These may be summarised as:

Specific indications   — e.g. diagnosis
? Suicide risk   — least toxic preparation/other
                             safeguards

Use well-tried drugs first	— the newest might not be the best
Dose	— may be crucial to be effective
	— special care with elderly people
Frequency/route of administration	— may affect compliance
?Contraindications	— drug interaction
Set date for review	— review short-term medication weekly, long-term regularly
Monitor	— response/side-effects/toxic effects
Use drugs singly	— avoid two drugs of same type
	— avoid drugs to mask side-effects
If no change	— check compliance, ? further drug justified
Who prescribes	— must be clear—GP or hospital

A cost: benefit analysis could be applied, as follows, to any form of treatment:

1. What is the risk to the patient of not treating the condition?
2. What are the benefits of treating the patient?
3. What is the risk of adverse effects of treatment?

The above recommendations represent a common-sense approach which is clear and easy to apply. However, the chronically ill, behaviourally disturbed individual, whether in hospital or supported accommodation, may provoke a muddled treatment plan. It is not unusual to find long-stay patients who are receiving a number of different drugs of the same type (perhaps three antipsychotics) in high dosage, together with a drug to counteract side-effects, despite a clear statement in the clinical case notes to the effect that 'this patient has not responded to any medication'.

Another common pattern is for a patient to receive a relatively high dose of medication, quite appropriately, during a period of relapse and acute disturbance. Then, as the condition and behaviour settles, there is a reluctance to reduce the medication 'in case she relapses'. When a further relapse does occur the drugs are increased further. The pattern repeats itself and soon the patient is receiving very high doses of medication.

Sensible prescribing requires knowledge of the mode and duration of action of drugs (half-life). Drugs should be prescribed to be taken as few times a day as possible as this will encourage compliance and also prevent accumulation of the drug. Thus some drugs must be given four hourly (droperidol) while others only four weekly (depot haloperidol).

Not only is it bad practice to give a second drug to counteract the side-effects of the first drug, in some cases it is dangerous. It is now recognised that the routine prescription of 'anti-Parkinsonian' medication with antipsychotic drugs may increase significantly the risk of the patient developing irreversible tardive dyskinesia (involuntary movements).

Good prescribing means considering carefully the short- and long-term effects of any course of action. This practice should be backed up by clinical audit—the regular peer review of clinical practice. Audit is now a requirement for all doctors practising in the British NHS. Local doctors meet regularly to set standards (e.g. to avoid the routine use of anti-Parkinsonian drugs), to monitor practice and suggest ways of ensuring that standards are achieved.

Sometimes it is difficult for non-medical workers to understand why a particular preparation has been selected from within a group of similar drugs. The choice will depend more on the doctor's familiarity with the drug rather than specific indications. In fact, there is often little to choose between most of the drugs within a group. For example, all of the tricyclic antidepressants appear to be equally effective although some may be rather more sedating (amitriptyline) than others (lofepramine) (see Table 6.2).

Finally, the names of drugs provide ample scope for confusion. Each compound is classified according to its primary function (e.g. antidepressant), the chemical grouping to which it belongs (e.g. tricyclic—literally having a three-ring chemical structure) and its own chemical or generic name (e.g. amitriptyline). Each generic compound will be given a proprietary or trade name by its manufacturer (e.g. Tryptizol), and these latter may vary from country to country.

Thus, using the above example, all of the following statements are correct:

> 'I am taking amitriptyline'
> 'I am prescribing Tryptizol'
> 'She is taking a tricyclic antidepressant'.

An added problem arises in connection with the treatment of psychotic illnesses such as schizophrenia. The family of drugs used to treat psychosis should, ideally, be referred to as 'antipsychotic drugs'. The older terminology of 'major tranquillisers' and

Table 6.2 A classification of psychotropic drugs (only a small selection of examples given—proprietary names omitted)

Antidepressants		
	Tricyclics	— amitriptyline
		— imipramine
		— lofepramine
	Tetracyclics	— mianserin
	SSRI	— fluoxetine
		— fluvoxamine
Antipsychotics		
	Phenothiazines	— chlorpromazine
		— thioridazine
		Depot preparations
		— flupenthixol decanoate
	Butyrophenones	— droperidol
		— haloperidol
		Depot preparations
		— haloperidol decanoate
	Substituted benzamides	— sulpiride
		— remoxipride
	Dibenzazepine	— clozapine
Minor tranquillisers (and night sedation)		
		— diazepam
		— temazepam

SSRI = selective serotonin re-uptake inhibitors

'neuroleptics' are inappropriate, referring to the unwanted effects (sedation and the tendency to produce neurological symptoms) rather than the desired effect!

Psychotherapy

Psychotherapy is any form of 'talking cure' (Rycroft 1972). It may be: interpretive, supportive, behavioural or cognitive; superficial or deep; individual, family or group. In Britain, psychotherapy tends to be used with people with neurotic disorders (phobic, obsessional, hysterical), depression (especially cognitive), or a lesser form of personality disorder. Its role in other conditions is contentious.

In the United States, it has been the practice to treat people with schizophrenia with both drugs and psychotherapy, and some psychiatrists consider psychotherapy the treatment of choice (Karon & Vandenbos 1981). This is discussed in detail later.

Social treatment

Many psychiatric conditions may be precipitated by stress. Some conditions (e.g. manic-depressive disorder and familial schizophrenia) are thought to result from the interplay of an inherited tendency and stress. Social interventions are aimed at reducing the level of stress in the lives of people at risk of relapse. These interventions include education and changing the behaviour of relatives, and reducing the amount of time that the vulnerable family member spends in close contact with other members of the family. These interventions have been studied by the MRC Social Psychiatry Unit for the past two decades, and their results are encouraging. They now run training courses in their methods and have recently published a practical guide (Kuipers et al 1992).

ECT (electroconvulsive therapy)

In recent years, much has been written about ECT, both for and against. Often the articles in the press have been written in emotive terms, describing the treatment as barbaric and its use as some form of punishment. The objective evidence has been presented very clearly by Clare (1980).

The generally accepted view amongst British psychiatrists is that ECT is an effective and safe treatment for severe depressive illness with biological features (early morning wakening, weight loss, delusions). It may also be used in severe mania which has proved unresponsive to drug treatment. The role of ECT in schizophrenia is much more contentious, and probably the majority of British psychiatrists would consider that it should not be used.

The patient should have the procedure explained and reasons for choosing this treatment discussed. She should then be in a position to give informed consent for treatment to proceed. Some patients may be incapable of giving informed consent, either because they are too ill to understand the discussion fully, or because their decision would be made on the basis of their delusions. In either case, a further opinion from an independent consultant psychiatrist should be sought. The situation regarding compulsory treatment is discussed below.

ECT is administered to the anaesthetised and muscle-relaxed patient once to three times per week for an average of four to eight treatments. (A brief description of how to administer ECT is given in Crammer et al 1991.) If the patient responds to ECT, continuation treatment with an antidepressant will be required for between 6 and 12 months to minimise the risk of relapse.

Psychosurgery

In 1936, Moniz described the first 20 cases treated by surgically interrupting the connections between the frontal lobes and the 'emotion regulating centres' of the subcortical areas of the brain. This treatment rapidly gained popularity and Moniz was jointly awarded the Nobel Prize for Physiology and Medicine in 1949. Reaching its peak in the mid 1950s, psychosurgery was aimed at the frontal lobes for anxiety and depression, and the cingulate gyrus for aggression and obsessional disorders.

Between 1942 and 1954, 10 365 people underwent leucotomy for serious mental illness in Britain. Two-thirds of the patients were suffering from chronic schizophrenia. The number now is probably less than 100 a year. It is sad that a treatment to which so many patients have been exposed has not been adequately investigated by the usual controlled trials. In Britain, it is now seldom considered. It has never been thought to be very effective in schizophrenia and so, except in the most exceptional circumstances, it seems unlikely that readers of this book are likely to come into contact with a patient receiving this treatment.

Although rehabilitation is required for a wide range of mental health problems, the core work for many services, be they statutory, voluntary or private, will be with people who have a schizophrenic illness. Thus, taking schizophrenia as the model, aetiology, the rationale for treatment and practical management will be discussed.

SCHIZOPHRENIA

About 1% of the population of the Western world suffers from schizophrenia, the peak incidence occurring between 25 and 30 years of age. Similar rates have been found in all cultures studied. There has, however, been an apparent decline in the number of new cases of schizophrenia in the past 15 years.

People with schizophrenia are not equally distributed throughout the country, but tend to be over-represented in run-down city centres. At first, this was thought to be due to the 'schizophrenogenic' effect of urban life (the 'breeder' theory). But now it is recognised that the illness process leads to loss of social competence and earning power, and those people not supported by their family drift into cheaper areas ('drift' theory).

Diagnosis

The diagnosis of schizophrenia relies on the clinical examination. There is no specific diagnostic test available. The ICD-10 (International Classification of Diseases — World Health Organization 1992) provides a glossary which allows the diagnosis to be made in descriptive terms. DSM-III-R (Diagnostic and Statistical Manual of Mental Disorders — American Psychiatric Association 1987) gives a more reliable check list, although it may be no more valid (see Table 6.3 and Ch. 2).

Schizophrenia affects personality, thoughts and mood. The major symptoms arise from a failure to recognise boundaries; between self and the environment, and between different thoughts. Thus a failure to recognise where she ends and the world begins means that her own thoughts appear to come from outside her (auditory hallucinations). She is also unable to distinguish one thought from the next.

Her train of speech may be interrupted by unrelated sentences being interpolated. In a more severe form of thought disorder, a series of apparently unrelated thoughts may be spoken ('knight's move thinking'). In extreme forms, a 'word salad' is produced as words from separate ideas are strung together. The flow of words will be totally unintelligible to the listener. Sudden interruptions to the flow of speech (thought blocking) may produce explanatory

Table 6.3 Summary of the DSM-III-R diagnostic criteria for schizophrenia

A. Presence of either (1), (2) or (3) for at least one week:
   (1) two of the following:
      (a) delusions
      (b) prominent hallucinations (throughout the day, several times a week for several weeks)
      (c) incoherence or marked loosening of associations
      (d) catatonic behaviour
      (e) flat or grossly inappropriate affect (mood)
   (2) bizarre delusions (e.g. thought broadcasting)
   (3) prominent hallucinations (e.g. running commentary)
B. Functioning in such areas as work, social relations and self-care is markedly below the highest level previously achieved
C. Other psychotic illnesses have been ruled out
D. Continuous signs of the disturbance for at least six months

delusions such as 'The man next door is taking away my thoughts by laser'.

Emotion is also affected. Often blunting of affect (mood) occurs with little or no emotional response and difficulty in making emotional contact or rapport with others. Sometimes the affect is incongruous, that is out of keeping with circumstances. An extreme example would be laughter when a patient was told that her mother had died. This is not a sign of callousness, but disorganisation.

The other aspect of the person to be affected by the schizophrenic process is the personality. The commonly held view of the schizophrenic 'split personality' is erroneous. The personality is shattered, altering drive to produce apathy and unpredictable behaviour.

The range of experiences described as the 'symptoms of the first rank' are given on page 22. These symptoms are only diagnostic of schizophrenia if the content of the delusions and hallucinations is not readily explainable in terms of the prevailing mood, and they occur in full consciousness. Thus a very depressed person who hears two 'voices' talking to each other about her while referring to her in the third person is not schizophrenic if they talk only about miserable and depressive things. Nor may a patient be diagnosed as schizophrenic if clouding of consciousness is present (delirium or acute confusion).

Aetiology

The causes of schizophrenia are not fully understood. The vulnerability-stress model is useful for understanding onset and relapse, especially in people who have a positive family history. This proposes a mixture of:

Inherited predisposition + environmental stress

Genetic factors

The general population risk of schizophrenia (1%) rises to 15% for the offspring of an affected parent. The risk for someone with an affected identical twin (monozygotic) is about 40% compared with 15% for non-identical (dizygotic) twins.

Stress

Acute stress is important in precipitating schizophrenia. There is a higher than average level of stressful life events in the three weeks prior to the onset of illness (Brown & Birley 1968). But more chronic stress is also important. Schizophrenic patients discharged home to relatives have a higher relapse rate than those discharged to live on their own (Brown et al 1966).

Expressed emotion (EE) is a measure of the number of critical comments made by relatives and the extent of emotional over-involvement and hostility expressed by relatives. This can be assessed by a complex interview (Camberwell Family Interview). A number of studies have found an association between relapse rate of schizophrenia and the EE of the key relative living with the patient (Brown et al 1972, Vaughn & Leff 1976). Patients returning to live with high EE relatives had a higher relapse rate (51%) than those returning to live with low EE relatives (13%). Two factors appear to lessen the effect of high EE relatives: the amount of face-to-face contact with the relative and medication. Low contact (less than 35 hours per week) and regular medication reduce the relapse rate (15%) in the high EE group, while lack of regular medication and high contact with the relative (more than 35 hours per week) greatly increase the relapse rate (92%) (Vaughn & Leff 1976).

It is interesting to note that the protective function of these interventions seems to occur even where EE is not greatly reduced. Recent studies have shown that these results are not confined to the English-speaking world, but are equally effective in Switzerland (Barrelet et al 1990) and Northern India (Leff et al 1990). This latter study also demonstrated a much lower incidence of high EE families in India. This may, in part, explain the much better prognosis in some less industrialised cultures.

Viruses

Speculation raised a decade ago (Crow 1983) about whether schizophrenia is catching has continued to provoke debate. It has long been known that people who go on to manifest a schizophrenic illness have an increased chance of being born in the last quarter of the year in the northern hemisphere and the second quarter of the year in the southern hemisphere. It has been argued that perhaps they are more vulnerable at this time to infection in the perinatal period.

Brain structure

CT scans (computer-assisted tomography) have demonstrated dilated ventricles in the brains of about 20% of schizophrenics. This change correlates most with the so-called defect state, the type of condition least responsive to drug treatment (reviewed by Crow 1983). There is growing evidence that these CT changes occur more frequently in sporadic cases of schizophrenia (i.e. where there is no family history of the condition). This surprising finding, and the evidence that the incidence of new cases of schizophrenia is declining, has led to the hypothesis that these sporadic cases of schizophrenia may result from some insult early in life such as obstetric complications or infections.

Dopamine theory

Over the years, numerous biochemical theories have been proposed to explain schizophrenia. The amine hypothesis implicates dopamine, a chemical transmitter present in the brain, as the most effective drugs (the antipsychotics) all block dopamine pathways. As yet there is no conclusive evidence.

Schizophrenogenic families

American writers in the 1950s and 60s promulgated the idea of pathological families which produced schizophrenic children, not by inheritance, but by their pathological interactions. Bateson et al (1956) produced the 'double bind' theory. This suggested that children were turned into schizophrenics by receiving continually, double and incongruous messages from their parents. They had to respond to both incompatible messages and not comment on them. The double bind is sometimes used in humour: a New York Jewish mother gave her son two ties for his birthday, one red, the other green. When next they met he was wearing the green tie. 'So you don't like the red tie', said the mother. He just couldn't win! The experimental evidence in support of the double bind is trivial.

Singer & Wynne (1965) claimed consistent abnormalities of speech in the parents of schizophrenics, but in London Hirsch & Leff (1975) in a blind controlled trial failed to confirm these findings.

As yet there has been no convincing experimental evidence to support the concept of the schizophrenogenic family.

Psychoanalytic theory

Freudian theory considers schizophrenia to be a regression to the early narcissistic level where the child does not distinguish between self and environment—that is loss of object relations. Reviewing the contribution that psychoanalysis has made towards the understanding of schizophrenia, Clare (1980) considers it to be 'far from self-evident'. He adds that it is worth noting that Freud never deliberately attempted to analyse a psychotically ill patient.

TREATMENTS

Physical

Chlorpromazine was introduced in 1953 and rapidly replaced earlier attempts at treatment. There is now overwhelming experimental evidence to support the clinical experience that antipsychotic drugs are effective, but not in all cases.

An American group (NIMH 1964) studied 463 young schizophrenics during their first or second acute illness. A double-blind study of three different phenothiazines and placebo (no active treatment) showed that the drugs were all better than placebo, but that there was nothing to choose between the three drugs.

In chronic schizophrenia, the response is less dramatic. Caffey et al (1964) studied 350 chronic schizophrenics all of whom had received phenothiazines for some years. The patients were divided into three groups: one group remained on their present medication; the second group had their medication halved; and the third group were transferred to a placebo 'treatment'. At four months, 5% of those patients left on their original medication had relapsed, compared with 15% of the patients on half medication and 45% of those on placebo. In other words, the drugs are having a considerable effect even after years, and the doses used were not excessive.

A third and interesting study was conducted in London by Leff & Wing (1971). They screened all admissions to the Maudsley hospital for a 20-month period for schizophrenia (first episode) and who were well six weeks after discharge. They started with 116, but only 35 entered the trial: 15 were considered to have been too ill to risk the possibility of placebo treatment; 11 were too well to require any treatment; 24 just dropped out. Of the 35 in the trial, the relapse rate at one year for those receiving medication was 35% compared with 80% of those on placebo. Of great interest was that the investigators also followed up those patients excluded from the trial. Those who were thought too ill did badly even though they were on treatment (67% relapse), while those considered too well did indeed do well without treatment (27% relapse). It appears that drugs are most effective in the middle spectrum of the illness.

A constant finding has been the failure of patients who experience negative symptoms (see below) to respond well to conventional antipsychotic medication. Claims have been made for a number of recently introduced antipsychotics including remoxipride and clozapine. Clozapine is said to be effective in 30–60% of otherwise treatment-resistant schizophrenics. At present in the UK and USA, it can only be prescribed by psychiatrists who undertake regular monitoring of the patient because of the risk of a reduction in the white blood cell count.

Psychotherapy

This has been commonly used for schizophrenia in the United States, but not in Britain. What is the evidence?

May (1968), in California, randomly allocated 228 schizophrenic patients to five treatment groups: phenothiazines; psychotherapy (analytic — two hours per week minimum); phenothiazine + psychotherapy; ECT; and milieu therapy (i.e. usual ward routine). The best outcome was equally divided between the phenothiazine group and phenothiazine + psychotherapy. Third was ECT followed by the psychotherapy and milieu therapy joint fourth. The effect of psychotherapy, which was the most expensive form of treatment, was undetectable.

Karon & Vandenbos (1981) still claim that psychotherapy is the treatment of choice, but their own experimental design was faulty. For example, all of the patients were 'unquestionably schizophrenic' but precise criteria for the inclusion are not given. It must be concluded that the case for the treatment of schizophrenia by psychotherapy is, at best, unproven, and probably it is not useful (see Falloon below).

Psychosocial interventions

Five controlled studies assessing the effect of psychosocial interventions with families of schizophrenic patients have been reviewed by Barrowclough & Tarrier (1984). Of these only two were considered to be well designed.

Falloon and colleagues (1982) in California randomly assigned 36 patients to 'family therapy' or 'individual therapy'. All were diagnosed as suffering from schizophrenia on Present State Examination (PSE). Most were living with high EE families. The 'family therapy' package included: education about the nature, course and treatment of schizophrenia; the teaching of problem-solving skills for coping with stress; and communication skills training. The control group received individual supportive psychotherapy. Both groups were controlled on medication and had emergency visits and help with finances and accommodation.

Only one patient relapsed in the family treatment group (6%) compared with eight relapses in the individual therapy group (44%) after nine months' treatment. After two years, only three of the individually treated group (17%) had not relapsed compared with 15 of the family group (83%).

Leff and colleagues (1982) treated 24 patients selected as being at very high risk of relapse. All had a relative rated as high EE with whom they were in contact more than 35 hours per week. All received a PSE diagnosis of schizophrenia. Half of the high EE relatives were the target of social intervention: relatives' group to which high and low EE relatives were invited and encouraged to discuss problems of coping; individual family sessions in the relatives' home aimed at reducing EE and/or family contact.

At nine months, the experimental group had a 9% relapse rate (one patient) compared with 50% in the control group (normal out-patient follow up). Despite these dramatic results, they only succeeded in lowering the EE in six out of 12 families, and reducing contact in five out of 12. Although critical comments within the family were reduced, the treatment was less successful in reducing emotional over-involvement.

Almost all of the intervention studies have focused on schizophrenic people living with parents. However, a recent study (Bennum & Lucas 1990) looked at patients who lived with their spouse. The findings were similar to other family studies. Smith & Birchwood (1990) have identified a problem encountered in putting these interventions into clinical practice. Up to a fifth of suitable families refused to participate and a further quarter dropped out of treatment.

MANAGEMENT OF SCHIZOPHRENIA

Assessment: leads to firm diagnosis; provides a baseline measure of symptoms; identifies stresses which may have precipitated the illness and may affect recovery as well as any supports; and assesses the prognosis and need for treatment. The initial assessment may be carried out at home or as an out-patient, but where there is immediate cause for concern, the assessment may be continued in hospital or in a day unit.

The main problems encountered are:

1. the positive symptoms: hallucinations and delusions
2. the negative symptoms: withdrawal, apathy, thought disorder
3. lack of insight: may not accept illness, or need of treatment
4. periods of acute disturbance
5. social, family and work stresses
6. risk of suicide: 15% lifetime risk.

Acute management

The choice between home, day or hospital care will depend on the severity of symptoms (including an assessment of the risk to the patient), the support available at home and the range of facilities available. The patient and family will require information about the illness, an explanation of the medication to be used, the reason for treatment in a particular setting and a realistic timescale.

A drug-free observation period may be suggested before treatment with an antipsychotic drug is begun. The staff will have to agree the appropriate level of observation required. The starting dose of chlorpromazine (perhaps 100 mg twice or three times a day) will be increased slowly, mental state and side-effects being regularly monitored. In very disturbed patients, the dose will have to be increased more rapidly, perhaps up to a daily dose of 1 000 mg. If side-effects appear, the dose should, if possible, be reduced. If this is impossible because of the severity of the illness, anticholinergic drugs (such as procyclidine) will be required. If the patient refuses medication and is acutely disturbed, compulsory treatment under the Mental Health Acts may be required.

The patient and family will require support. The family's reaction to the illness may be similar to that described for physical disability (Ch. 13). The patient requires personal contact with a limited number of staff in order to build up trust. In addition to individual support, discussion in groups will help prepare for the next stage of care.

Medication may be reduced slowly once a substantial improvement of symptoms has occurred. Excessive drowsiness, akathisia (motor restlessness) and marked stiffness or tremor suggest a further drug reduction. It is advisable not to change drug dosage at the same time as any other significant change (e.g. discharge from hospital, or transfer to a day unit). If the patient remains well after a first, brief illness for two to three months, drugs may be stopped completely.

The very disturbed patient

The intensity of the psychotic experience (hallucinations and delusions) and fear may lead to disturbed and potentially dangerous behaviour. The priority should be to help the patient by active treatment of the illness and attempting to reduce the fear. The safety of the patient and others must also be taken into account.

Antipsychotic drugs, given intramuscularly if necessary, may be required in very high doses: chlorpromazine 100–200 mg i.m. three to four hourly or droperidol 20 mg up to two hourly.

The patient should be nursed in quiet surroundings, preferably in bed, with a nurse in attendance. After a few days, it should be possible to replace the injections by an adequate dose of oral medication. It should be remembered that the reluctant patient might find it more difficult to hide liquid preparations than tablets. Antiparkinsonian drugs (e.g. procyclidine) may be required, especially as the patient improves.

Failure to respond to treatment

If the symptoms have failed to respond to the first treatment after three months, and staff are sure that the patient has been taking the medication, the treatment plan should be reviewed. If two or three antipsychotic drugs have been tried in adequate dosage, a full reappraisal should take place. The diagnosis should be reviewed and potential sustaining factors (such as continuing drug abuse) should be addressed. A trial of clozapine may be considered. If that too fails then there is little point in persisting with drug treatment.

Long-term management

The prognosis of schizophrenia is very variable. Probably a third of patients do very well, recovering completely. A third continue to

Table 6.4 Prognostic indicators for schizophrenia

Good prognosis
No family history of schizophrenia
Normal pre-morbid personality
Acute onset
Confusion
Precipitating cause
Depression/elation
Onset after age of 30
Married
Early treatment

require treatment and tend to relapse if it is discontinued. A third do poorly, responding only partially if at all to medication. The indicators of a good prognosis are shown in Table 6.4.

After a first illness that has responded well to treatment, medication should be stopped after recovery.

If the patient is recovering from the second or third episode of illness in a short period of time (two or three years), or where the illness has been very severe and caused major disruption to her life, maintenance medication should be continued for at least two years. Where the patient is co-operative oral medication should be used. Compliance may be improved by a once daily preparation (e.g. trifluoperazine spansules). If the patient cannot be relied on to take tablets regularly, she may agree to the routine of a fortnightly (flupenthixol decanoate) or monthly (haloperidol decanoate) depot injection. The use of antipsychotic medication and the incidence of side-effects should be monitored in all patients as part of clinical audit.

In all cases, regular review will be required to monitor change and to enable planning of other aspects of care. The emotional pattern of the family will indicate the advisability of a return home, the need for supported accommodation or a day placement. An educational package may be offered to high EE families. Other aspects of treatment planning have been considered in Chapter 7.

Serious side-effects and complications

The routine prescription of antiparkinsonian medication to cover the side-effects of antipsychotic drugs has been called into question by studies suggesting that this practice increased the risk of the patient developing tardive dyskinesia. This unpleasant, disfiguring and sometimes permanent condition produces involuntary writhing and grimacing movements. All patients receiving regular antipsychotic medication should be screened for the development of tardive dyskinesia. Small undulating movements of the tongue within the mouth may be the earliest sign. Later, jerky, writhing movements of the tongue and smacking lip movements are extended to involuntary movements of the jaw, face and limbs.

Dose reduction is the first step. About one-third of patients will improve following withdrawal of the antipsychotic, although the movements may at first get worse. For some patients whose psychosis becomes unacceptably worse on withdrawing the antipsychotic, the choice may have to be made between the possible permanent dyskinesia or the distress of the psychosis.

Neuroleptic malignant syndrome is a relatively rare complication of treatment using antipsychotics (neuroleptics). The patient becomes stiff, confused and develops a very high temperature. This may progress to coma and death unless appropriate measures are taken.

Other conditions

As schizophrenia is the condition most commonly encountered in rehabilitation work, the research findings on aetiology and treatment have been discussed in some detail. Substance abuse, learning disabilities and the problems of old age are covered in separate chapters. It is beyond the scope of this book to discuss the treatment of other conditions. A growing literature exists and the presentation of a review article to the team may help stimulate discussion about the most logical way of helping a chronically disabled person.

REFERENCES

American Psychiatric Association 1987 Diagnostic and statistical manual of mental disorders, 3rd edn revised. A.P.A., Washington

Barrelet L, Ferrero F, Szigethy L, Giddey C, Pellizer G 1990 Expressed emotion and first admission schizophrenia: nine month follow-up in a French cultural environment. British Journal of Psychiatry 156: 357–362

Barrowclough C, Tarrier N 1984 'Psychosocial' interventions with families and their effects on the course of schizophrenia: a review. Psychological Medicine 14: 629–642

Bateson G, Jackson D D, Haley J, Weakland J H 1956 Toward a theory of schizophrenia. Behavioural Science 1: 251–264

Bennum I, Lucas R 1990 Using the partner in the psychosocial treatment of schizophrenia: a multiple single case design. British Journal of Clinical Psychology 29: 185–192

Brown G W, Birley J L T 1968 Crises and life changes and the onset of schizophrenia. Journal of Health and Social Behaviour 9: 203–214

Brown G W, Bone U, Dalinson B M, Wing J K 1966 Schizophrenia and social care. Oxford University Press, London

Brown G W, Birley J L T, Wing J K 1972 Influence of family life on the course of schizophrenic disorders: a replication. British Journal of Psychiatry 121: 241–258

Caffey E M, Diamond L S, Frank T V, Grasberg J C, Herman L, Klell C J, Rothstein C 1964 Discontinuation or reduction of chemotherapy in chronic schizophrenics. Journal of Chronic Diseases 17: 347–358

Clare A 1980 Psychiatry in dissent, 2nd edn. Tavistock Publications, London

Crammer J, Heine B 1991 Use of drugs in psychiatry, 3rd edn. Gaskell, London

Crow T J 1983 Is schizophrenia an infectious disease? Lancet i: 173–175

Falloon I R H, Boyd J L, McGill C W, Razani J, Moss H B, Gilderman A M 1982 Family management in the presentation and exacerbation of schizophrenia: a controlled study. New England Journal of Medicine 306: 1437–1440

Hirsch S R, Leff J P 1975 Abnormalities in parents of schizophrenics. Maudsley Monograph No. 22, Oxford University Press, London

Karon B P, Vandenbos G R 1981 Psychotherapy of schizophrenia. The treatment of choice. Jason Aponson, New York

Kuipers L, Leff J, Lam D 1992 Family work for schizophrenia: a practical guide. Gaskell, London

Leff J P, Wing J K 1971 Trial of maintenance therapy in schizophrenia. British Medical Journal iii: 599–604

Leff J P, Kuipers L, Berkowitz R, Eberlein Vries R, Sturgeon D 1982 A controlled trial of social intervention in the families of schizophrenic patients. British Journal of Psychiatry 141: 121–134

Leff J P, Wig N N, Bedi H, Menon D K, Kuipers L, Korten A, Ernberg G, Day R, Satorius N, Jablensky A 1990 Relatives' expressed emotion and the course of schizophrenia in Chandigarh. British Journal of Psychiatry 156: 351–356

May P R A 1968 Treatment of schizophrenia: a comparative study of 5 treatment methods. Science House, New York

NIMH (National Institute of Mental Health) 1964 Phenothiazine treatment in schizophrenia. Archives of General Psychiatry 10: 246–261

Rycroft C 1972 A critical dictionary of psychoanalysis. Penguin, London

Singer M T, Wynne L C 1965 Thought disorder and family relations in schizophrenia. Archives of General Psychiatry 12: 187–212

Smith J, Birchwood M 1990 Relatives and patients as partners in the management of schizophrenia: the development of a service model. British Journal of Psychiatry 156: 654–660

Vaughn C, Leff J P 1976 The influence of family and social factors on the course of psychiatric illness. British Journal of Psychiatry 129: 125–137

WHO 1992 International classification of diseases: mental health disorders—tenth revision (ICD-10). World Health Organization, Geneva

7. Planning a care package

Clephane Hume

The way to a free and independent life is not to be well cared for. The right way is to train the disabled person to take care of himself.

Battgord

This chapter considers how treatment may be planned, including the use of various methods of documenting aims of treatment. The nature of the problem-solving process and its application to intervention in rehabilitation will be discussed. The design, planning and implementation of a care package, and who will be involved in this will be considered, together with some of the issues which face those setting up services and programmes.

It is important to note that various agencies may be involved in planning care packages, and the terminology used by different groups may vary, even when the meaning is the same.

HOSPITAL

The treatment planning process

Planning for therapeutic intervention, whatever the context, must be seen as a continuous process. The initial plan is only a starting point. Clear goals and identifiable steps towards achieving them are essential if confusion is to be avoided and interest maintained. The client will not remain motivated if he is not sure what he is aiming to achieve, and staff too will lose enthusiasm if there is no clear target.

Any rehabilitation programme must be based on an assessment of the individual's skills and limitations (strengths and weaknesses), so that realistic goals may be defined and the appropriate treatment regime devised (see Ch. 5). Reassessment and evaluation of results lead to modification of the programme and thus the treatment planning cycle continues. Achieving objectives through accomplishment of a goal allows termination of that particular aspect of the programme, or a change in emphasis.

Gradually, the person will develop skills and through practice and experience, reach his own level of competence, at which point intensive treatment may be terminated.

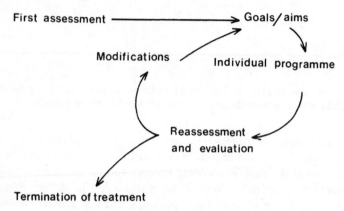

First assessment ⟶ Goals/aims

Modifications Individual programme

Reassessment and evaluation

Termination of treatment

Fig. 7.1 The treatment planning cycle.

Defining aims and goals/treatment objectives

The aim of treatment is the overall outcome which is desired.

For Jim, who has been in hospital for six months following treatment for his third episode of schizophrenia, the aim is to restore him to living in the community, independent of his family.

Goals are the smaller steps which require to be accomplished in order to achieve the overall aim. These may be of a long-term or short-term nature and it is important to note that the outcome of short-term goals may lead to modification of the long-term ones. It should be possible to measure the outcome of a goal in terms of its accomplishment.

It was decided that Jim's long-term goal would be to master the domestic skills required for living in a flat. First, he had to achieve various short-term goals such as menu planning and cooking simple meals, and keeping his own bedroom clean. It soon became obvious that budgeting was not one of Jim's strengths, and he did not feel confident about mastering this in relation to shopping for food. After much discussion, it was decided that the long-term aim should be modified to skills required for living in a more supportive environment, where meals were provided.

Identifying goals and establishing priorities

Identification of goals can only start after an assessment of the situation has been made (see Ch. 5). It is crucial that such an assessment should give attention to cultural needs (see Ch. 10). With a baseline which indicates the skills and deficits of the individual, there is a starting point for working out the long-term and short-term goals, and how these may be achieved.

The client may have his own clear goals in mind—getting a job, or staying in a hostel. Staff may consider that he may be able to cope with sheltered work or a group home. Joint discussion between the client, the care team and key others must precede the identification of aims, agreement on goals and the order in which these should be tackled, and strategies for accomplishing the goals.

Although the overall aim may be a significant change in the person's lifestyle, as in Jim's case, it is essential that the steps (goals) on the way to achieving this are of a size which the individual sees as being attainable. Start with tea and toast, not a three-course meal. Staged goals can then be set in the context of a general plan, which may require a range of services (see below).

The individual client's priorities may not coincide with those of his family or friends. Whether or not this is the case, family and significant other people in the person's life should be involved as early on in the planning of treatment as possible.

Goals may be reviewed at meetings with the individual, on a contractural basis, or reviewed in a group where targets are set and discussed by members. Staff will usually have preliminary discussions during regular progress reviews but it should be emphasised that the individual client should always be included in the decision-making process which determines priorities for treatment.

Recording treatment plans

It is possible to combine recording of information with the actual design of a treatment plan and different professions and units have their own ways of doing this. For example, the nursing care plan documents aims for the individual and who will carry these out.

Problem-oriented medical records (POMRs) may be used by the whole team and here there is clear division into problems identified, action to be taken, by whom and the eventual outcome (Fig. 7.2).

NAME	UNIT		
problem	action	by whom	outcome
Using public transport (Wants to visit brother)	1. Discuss what is involved	S. Maclean	Can identify bus number, stops and describe procedure
	2. Go into town for tea.	S. Maclean	
	3. Travel alone	Check "	
	4. Visit brother	Check "	
Dentures not fitting	Refer to dentist	K. Reid	Appointment made for 28th May, 10 am

Fig. 7.2   Example of problem-oriented records.

In determining priorities, it is sometimes helpful to list the strengths and weaknesses of the individual. This makes it easier to identify the assets on which to build, thus providing a positive focus for intervention. For example, strengths might include personal skills, stabilisation of symptoms and the availability of social support. Sometimes it may be necessary, for reasons beyond anyone's control, to prioritise areas which might not otherwise be ideal. If someone has to move to alternative accommodation more quickly than originally hoped or planned, survival skills for coping in the new environment will take precedence over longer term goals for leisure or occupation.

Designing a plan and implementing treatment

Once goals and priority areas for action have been identified, it is necessary to consider how treatment will proceed. Dyer (1988) stresses the dangers of 'going too far, too fast', and it is essential that the plan should reflect the level of demand with which the person can realistically cope. It is well known that providing too much stimulation/stress can lead to detrimental results. Achieving the correct balance for the person is not always easy, since no clear-cut guidelines can be consulted.

Depending upon the circumstances of work, it may be necessary to give attention to what treatment approach should be adopted in order to meet the person's needs most effectively. Brief consideration will be given to this here, in order to identify the approaches most commonly used in the rehabilitation process.

Humanistic

This is concerned with enhancing self-esteem by recognising the person as an individual and providing opportunities for achievement.

Behavioural

This recognises that behaviour is learned, and can therefore be modified by further learning. This approach may include the use of behaviour modification programmes which incorporate rewards or punishments, appropriate to the individual's values.

Cognitive

This focuses on the person's thinking in relation to emotion and behaviour. The aim is to reverse faulty thinking by the identification of negative thoughts and to encourage a positive outlook.

Often the cognitive and behavioural approaches are combined, using aspects of both, to focus on an application such as social skills training where both elements are applicable.

Rehabilitative

This approach uses education and compensatory techniques to modify or extend skills in order to achieve competence.

The benefit of using an identified approach is that it gives a guideline for planning and evaluating treatment and enables all those involved to work using a common focus. It is also possible to combine aspects of the different approaches into one, eclectic approach.

Once the approach to treatment has been identified, it is appropriate to consider what resources (staff, facilities and equipment) are required. (If resources do not match needs, this might of course lead to alteration of goals.) If time has to be specially allocated to take someone shopping, or a kitchen booked in order to practise cookery skills, it is important to check that everything has been organised in advance, so that treatment can proceed with minimum organisational interruptions. (A home visit without the key is a frustrating experience...) Knowledge of available resources is an important aspect of planning.

Modifying goals

Once treatment has been carried out and the person has had adequate opportunity to practise any necessary skills, the programme should be reviewed and evaluated. This is undertaken through further assessments (see Ch. 5), which will identify changes in the person's functional abilities. It may be relevant to continue the existing programme in order to establish learning more soundly, or to introduce new goals to replace those already accomplished. If there is a deterioration in function, this should be matched by modification of goals with the intention of maintaining skills for as long as possible.

The process of modification continues in a circular manner throughout the treatment process. Evaluation of the efficacy of treatment procedures should be routinely undertaken as a form of quality assurance—if they do not give favourable results, what is the reason for this?

Terminating treatment

It is almost always possible to identify goals which the client would like to achieve or which staff feel would assist the person to integrate into the community in the best possible way. There comes a time, however, when it is important to hand over the responsibility for identification of goals, and their pursuit, to the individual concerned. Rehabilitation may be a lifelong process but treatment does not always go on for ever. Equally, it helps no one to continue a treatment regime if no progress is being made. Staff must overcome their reluctance to terminate treatment. In some instances, this will be made easier by a contractural agreement to achieve particular goals or the arrangement of a fixed number of treatment sessions.

COMMUNITY

Community-based care management plans

In terms of recent UK legislation for care in the community, (National Health Service and Community Care Act 1990) the planning of care management plans bears many similarities to the processes described above, but the terminology is different. There is, however, a major focus on assessment of need (see Ch. 5) and client/carer participation in planning.

The care plan will identify the needs to be met and the services which will be required. These needs can then be linked to available resources so that a plan can be implemented and then monitored. In order to do this, the outcomes to be achieved must be specified, together with ways of measuring the results. Both the client and the management team should retain copies of the plan in order to clarify expectations.

It may be necessary to co-ordinate services provided by a range of agencies and wherever possible it is desirable to separate assessment of need from service provision. Clear, measurable objectives will clarify agreements and contracts between purchaser and provider and facilitate review and reassessment. Procedural manuals and referral schemes may be drawn up in order to facilitate communication between agencies. Such administrative structures will reflect the policies of individual authorities and standards or practice guidelines will be established in order to implement needs-based strategies.

Examples of needs

Needs are obviously many and various but some commonly expressed issues can be identified. These may be broadly divided into those which concern medical and psychological needs, skills and resource-based needs. There will inevitably be overlaps, and specialist areas to consider, so division here is purely arbitrary.

- Medical and psychological needs
  social contact
  increase in self-esteem and self-confidence
  supervision of medication
  support for carers
- Skills
  development of personal, life and domestic skills
  development of community living skills
  work skills/occupational opportunities
- Resource-based needs
  accommodation
  day care

Medical and psychological needs

Social contact

One of the greatest difficulties for many people with mental health problems is how to overcome the loneliness imposed by their illness. The causes of social isolation are obviously numerous, and may result from withdrawal linked to the illness process, a previous need to retreat from social contact in order to avoid the stress of interactions, lack of social skills and confidence in social situations, or loss of contact with friends. Whatever the reason, the person has an expressed need to build up social networks and establish non-threatening contacts with others.

Initially this may be accomplished through attendance at a day centre, or a social club where the person is welcomed in a supportive atmosphere. Such a centre will often include outings in its programme, so that the person becomes accustomed to moving about in the community at large. In this type of situation, it is necessary to ensure that 'special' events do not become the norm as a means of maintaining the programme. Equally, it is essential that there is a focus on social activities which are free, or at a minimal cost, since most people will not have a budget which permits expensive outings.

The realities of everyday life should also govern the choice of activities. Rare and expensive hobbies which might be very effective in promoting social contact are of little relevance. Discarding watching TV as being a sociable activity, the principal leisure pursuit of the majority of the UK population is going to the pub—which obviously has financial implications. The care package should therefore be realistic and flexible in meeting the needs of the individual.

Increase in self-esteem and self-confidence

This may be accomplished in many ways—through participation in activities which provide the chance to experience success, through social interaction and through the empowerment which client-centred care can promote.

Supervision of medication

This may be essential for ongoing symptom control and may be achieved through contact with primary health care staff or others with whom the person is in regular contact.

Support for carers

Family involvement in treatment is discussed in Chapter 9 —and recognition of the need for support for carers is now widely acknowledged. Responses might include self-help or support meetings or residential respite care to enable carers to take a holiday.

Skills

Personal/domestic skills

Most people living in the community will have a degree of independence in relation to personal life skills such as hygiene, grooming and clothes care. Use of medication may be more contentious but it may be essential to the person's ability to cope with everyday life.

Proficiency in domestic tasks—household management and cookery, may be more difficult and here the compilers of the care plan must consider whether it is more appropriate to aim to develop competency or to compensate for lack of skills by providing sheltered accommodation or attendance at a lunch club.

Community living skills

These may encompass everything from using public transport to literacy or arranging a visit to the health centre. The package might involve attendance at community education resources to improve writing and numeracy, or a social skills group at a day centre.

Work skills/occupational opportunities

Opportunities to gain remunerative employment may be severely restricted by the economic state of a country. If relevant, work skills can be developed and participation in voluntary work placements may provide fulfilment of some work-related needs.

Resource-based needs

Accommodation

Provision of a range of accommodation with different levels of support/supervision is an essential component of any mental health care service. The situation should exist where it is possible to select the preferred option for the individual, not the best of a limited range of choices.

Day care

As identified above, there is a need for social and occupational activities to enhance quality of life, as well as developing skills. Day care also provides a structure for the person's day — it is still the norm for people to leave their home each day, thereby having time away from their family. Evidence for the benefits of this in relation to preventing relapse in chronic mental illness, notably schizophrenia, is well documented by Leff and others (see Ch. 9).

Co-ordinating a care package

In the current context of care in the UK, there are incentives for supporting people at home, rather than in institutional care and it is therefore necessary to ensure that resources are available to those in greatest need. Case/care management systems have been proposed to provide co-ordination and evaluation of community care (Ovretveit 1992).

In the context of multi-agency co-operation, it may be necessary to design a package combining statutory, voluntary and private sources of provision.

The number of people who could potentially be involved in this is extensive and daunting. Usually there will be input from people representing different types of services and an identified co-ordinator or key worker is required, who will meet the consumer's need to identify one person who is knowledgeable about his care plan. Liaison between different agencies and several mental health workers from different professions may be necessary in identifying the most appropriate course of action to take.

In matching the needs of the individual to the resources available, it is obviously essential to give consideration to costing. Different providers of services may be approached in constructing the plan and it is necessary to work to a budget in drawing up a programme.

More detail of models of management may be found in government guidelines (SSI SWSG 1991).

Who is involved?

A list might include any or all of the following:

the client   local authority (social work, housing)
family   national health service (primary health
friends   care and hospital services)

religious organisations	local mental health associations
community education	voluntary organisations
private agencies	mental welfare commission
job centre	disablement advisory service

The necessity for care managers, key workers or liaison workers is therefore obvious!

Those concerned must have regular case conferences at which to discuss the options available and ensure that packages meet the needs of those concerned—client and relatives. When psychiatric services bridge the gap between hospital and community, consultation is essential in maintaining continuity.

Dilemmas in planning of services

In addition to the problems of co-ordination described above, there are other issues to be considered.

One of the difficulties which may confront mental health workers is how to plan programmes which meet the needs of the individual while being in harmony with the aims of an overall programme. For example, a member of staff in a unit may recognise that John requires support while developing skills for using public transport, but commitments in the unit may make it impossible to take time away in order to achieve this. The consequence of this is frustration for staff and continued lack of skills for John. Equally, staff may not be on duty at times which are appropriate for participation in particular activities. Achieving flexible hours of work is not always easy, but managers should aim to facilitate this. In a rapidly changing arena, some understanding of the dynamics of change will help.

A day centre may have to meet targets identified by the management committee, which demand a given number of attendances each week. Patmore (1987) suggests that monitoring of budgets and producing statistics which look cost-effective may detract from meeting the needs of individual clients.

Most readers will be able to identify situations in which a unit programme is in operation, with group activities designed to help clients develop particular skills. It then becomes necessary to ask whether or not such activities will really meet the needs of the individual, or is s/he 'slotted into' the least inappropriate groups? In such a programme, do staff have time to talk to individuals or are they too busy keeping the activities running?

Sometimes the activity can overtake the therapeutic aims—for example who is going to make the sandwiches for the office contract, rather than identifying that Tom needs to develop cooking skills and undertaking this task would be relevant for him. This is contrary to the concept of need and development of individual packages, where services should be adapted to needs, rather than people being fitted into existing services.

Likewise, stimulating and enjoyable programmes may be a more attractive alternative than that of facing the realities of making one's own way in the harsh outside world. Avoiding creation of dependency is important in enabling people to become competent and self-confident.

It will be evident from the above, that a care plan must reflect the needs of the individual and that the consequent care package should be flexible in addressing these needs. Assessment has already been discussed, including assessment of need in which the consumers, client and carer indicate their priorities for action. In considering the development of a care package, it is important to identify some of the broad areas of need which commonly require consideration. It is also important to acknowledge that beliefs about illness will influence the responses to problems and approaches to treatment. These too may obscure the real needs of the individual if the staff subscribe firmly to a particular philosophy which is not readily acceptable to the person, e.g. a behavioural approach which does not tackle the underlying problems associated with an obsessive–compulsive state.

Community-based rehabilitation

An additional approach which is attracting attention is that of community-based rehabilitation (CBR), also known as community-integrated rehabilitation, which by its name implies that the location of treatment is outwith the hospital. More than this, it uses the local infrastructure, local people—including those who may have experienced disability themselves, and will also involve those not directly concerned with health care but who have a leadership role in the community—such as councillors or religious leaders.

Behind this approach is the notion that disability is accepted, without stigma, and that care for disabled people is a communal responsibility, not a matter of putting people behind closed doors. Treatment resources should be small scale and geographically close to where clients live and therefore easily accessible. Treatment should be realistic and appropriate and by using a wide range of people (informal carers) it can be cost-effective.

Planning a community service

Several factors of community life should be taken into consideration when developing a community programme (Gross 1982). The following questions may be asked.

What is the community profile?
The demographic structure of the population—the age range and distribution, and social class.
What are the employment/unemployment patterns and the actual types of work available?
Do people commute each day, have the majority of young people left to seek work elsewhere?
How do people spend their leisure time?
Who holds the power? (They may be useful allies.)
What are the values of the community? That is, the directions in which the people want to go or matters which they see as being priority areas. This should reflect general concerns such as employment and town planning and more obvious health issues such as substance abuse problems or day care for the confused elderly.

Developing a plan and factors to be considered in establishing a service

What are the identified needs?
What are the resources which can be harnessed to meet them?
What are the gaps between needs and existing provision?
Are there projects elsewhere which could provide a useful model?
Needs may be all too obvious and therefore easy to identify but it may be necessary to conduct surveys or consult with local people. It is necessary to determine the extent of need (see above) as well as the actual needs. Do you have five or 50 people in need of anxiety management or a depot medication clinic?
Are there local political factors or legal aspects of practice to consider?
What social support networks are available to clients?
What finance is available and what resources in terms of buildings?

Who are the supportive leaders and services—who will be helpful to you in establishing your programme?

How will clients be selected? Will there be self-referrals? Who will be priority users?

Who else is providing a service which may overlap with yours?

There is no point in duplicating existing provision or creating territorial antagonism. Your service should augment and complement what is already there, not conflict.

Do any of your ideas clash with spiritual values or community beliefs, e.g. a needle exchange for drug users.

What approach/philosophy/policies will you have?

Do you plan short- or long-term intervention, or referral on to other agencies?

What will be the involvement of users in the day-to-day running of the service? How much can it be consumer driven?

Publicity and/or marketing of the service must be considered. How will you advise people of what you can offer? Meetings, letters, posters, local papers? Marketing strategies should be aimed at potential purchasers so a knowledge of budgetary constraints and the limitations of contracts is important. Measurable objectives should be clear so that both the purchaser and the provider can evaluate the service.

Getting started

It is usually wise to start small, perhaps with a pilot scheme, establish your credibility, grow by 'word of mouth' and work to maintain the service.

Initially it can be difficult or alternatively there may be a rush of enthusiasm followed later by the hard reality of maintaining the service at full effectiveness. Personnel need encouragement if morale is to be maintained and motivation can slip if results are not apparent.

Leaders need external networks for consultation and support.

Follow up

The service should be evaluated (see Ch. 5). What is the ongoing pattern of use? What modifications should be made? Are needs being met?

If the service is not meeting needs or can be seen to be surplus to requirements it should not be maintained. This may be difficult to acknowledge.

CONCLUSION

'Getting it right' in terms of planning a care package is one of the key features in providing successful rehabilitation in mental health. It may be necessary to explore various routes before reaching the optimal management strategy. Equally, modifications according to changes in health status may be required, so that continued rehabilitation may in practice be a long-term concern. The focus on community programmes may require attention to the principles of CBR, but essentially packages must reflect the needs of the individual.

REFERENCES AND FURTHER READING

Affleck J W, McGuire R S 1984 The measurement of psychiatric rehabilitation status—a review of the needs and a new scale. British Journal of Psychiatry 145: 517–525

Clifford P, Charman A, Webb Y, Best S 1991 Planning for community care. Long stay populations of hospitals scheduled for rundown or closure. British Journal of Psychiatry 158: 190–196

Dyer J A T 1988 Psychiatric rehabilitation. In: Kendell R, Zealley A (eds) Companion to psychiatric studies, 4th edn. Churchill Livingstone, Edinburgh, Chapter 41

Fidler G 1984 Design of rehabilitation services in psychiatric hospital settings. RAMSCO, New York

Gross D 1982 Community practice—a framework. Proceedings of World Federation of Occupational Therapists Congress 2: 928–935

Ovretveit J 1992 Concepts of case management. British Journal of Occupational Therapy 55: 6

Patmore C (ed) 1987 Living after mental illness. Croom Helm, London

Stockwell F 1985 The nursing process in psychiatric nursing. Croom Helm, London

SSI SWSG 1991 Care management and assessment. Summary of practice guidance. HMSO, London

8. Teamwork

Ben Thomas

We trained hard; but it seemed that every time we were beginning to form up into teams we would be re-organised. I was to learn later in life, that we tend to meet any new situation by re-organising; and a wonderful method it can be for creating the illusion of progress, while producing confusion, inefficiency and demoralisation!

Petronius Arbiter 210 BC

Teamwork is a key feature of contemporary psychiatric rehabilitation service. The number of professions involved in providing rehabilitative care requires a team approach and suitable methods of co-ordination. Psychiatric rehabilitation has a long tradition of teamwork. It has also recognised the many difficulties experienced in this way of working. Many of these problems remain unresolved. Government policy to encourage the development of community services for the mentally ill and the need for effective co-ordinated arrangements between health and social services, primary health care teams and voluntary agencies make the resolution of these problems imperative. The Government's proposed solution to many of these problems is the introduction of case management and the proper assessment of patients' needs. Taken together these will form the cornerstone of high-quality care and ensure that packages of care will be designed in line with individual needs and preferences.

This chapter examines the feasibility of this way of working. It describes the complexities of multidisciplinary teamwork, some of the problems and conflicts that have been identified and discusses some of the solutions proposed. The chapter examines teamwork in the newer forms of community-based rehabilitation. If community care is to be effective and is to live up to its expectations then co-ordinated teamwork must be a key element. Teamwork means more than just bringing a group of professionals together albeit that they share a common purpose, it is a complicated process that requires a great deal of effort and mutual understanding.

113

Successful teamwork seldom happens by chance. Though the importance of teamwork is widely recognised, there is a paucity of research literature in this area. Wherever possible throughout the chapter research findings are drawn upon to explain the present position of teams in rehabilitation care. The research cited is by no means exhaustive but rather provides examples in the way teamwork has been investigated.

INTRODUCTION

Teamwork means organised co-operation between a set of people working together. For the purpose of this chapter, teamwork relates to multidisciplinary teams, those teams which consist of different occupational groups involved in the care and rehabilitation of patients with mental health problems. Teamwork is an essential prerequisite for the successful implementation of the changes in health and social care proposed in the Government's series of White Papers. An ever increasing number of professionals and agencies will need to work collaboratively to ensure that people receive the service they require. Local authorities, health service professionals and the independent sector including voluntary organisations must work in an effective partnership. Multidisciplinary teamwork has a long tradition in the provision of psychiatric services and the Government's recent concentration in these reports on doctors at the expense of other professionals in providing care has been criticised as clearly undermining the progress made in interdisciplinary and inter-agency work since the 1970s. Peck (1989) draws attention to the statement made in Working Paper 7 (Department of Health 1989), which states that doctors are the leaders of clinical teams for the patients under their charge. He suggests that this completely overlooks the complexity of multidisciplinary working in mental health teams.

The complexities and problems of multidisciplinary teamwork have been well documented (Parry-Jones 1986). For the most part, this consists of prescriptive literature. Despite the need for research into multi-professional teamwork being recommended in a Ministry of Health report (1968) little research into this important area of service delivery exists (Temkin-Greener 1983). One of the most thorough investigations into multidisciplinary team functioning in psychiatric rehabilitation has been carried out by Ranger (1986). Ranger designed and used five methods to investigate team functioning amongst three multidisciplinary teams in a non-traditional psychiatric setting. These included self-report questionnaires, interviews, observations and a diary report of work carried out by team members. The results of Ranger's study clearly demonstrated the lack of understanding that continues to exist amongst team members about each other's roles and the traditional views held about professional hierarchies, the consultant psychiatrist being clearly identified as the team leader.

The effectiveness and efficiency of teamwork in providing rehabilitative care for psychiatric patients still needs to be demonstrated. Despite this lack of evidence, teamwork not only continues to be regarded as one of the central features of rehabilitative services but is central to the current philosophy of mental health care provision. The idea of a 'key worker' has been extended and is now embodied in the concept of 'case management' which ensures that each care recipient will have planned for them a personalised package of services delivered in a coherent and monitored fashion. The achievement of effectively integrated health and social care in a complex multi-agency field like rehabilitation in mental health care should not be underestimated. In this chapter, some of the complex aspects of multidisciplinary teamwork in rehabilitation psychiatry are examined.

DEFINITION

In 1956, Modlin & Faris described the ideal multidisciplinary team as 'action orientated', its organisation determined by its problem-solving function. The integrality of its inner structure gives it flexibility and adaptability in dealing with clinical exigencies. Its useful philosophy of mental illness affords its component members a truly holistic view of the patient.

Bowen et al (1965) describe a team in terms of process whereby various professionals who make individual decisions concerning patients and who share a common purpose meet together to communicate and share knowledge from which plans are made and thus further therapeutic decisions influenced.

The Royal Commission on the National Health Service (1979) used the abbreviation MDCT for multidisciplinary clinical team, which they defined as 'a group of colleagues acknowledging a common involvement in the care and treatment of a particular patient'.

Ekdawi (1990) found that amongst 18 European rehabilitation services the core membership of teams comprises medical and nursing staff, psychologist, occupational therapist and social worker. Some teams include physiotherapists, speech therapists and teachers. He found that the services revealed a good measure of agreement on the services' aims and seven main components were shared by all. These consisted of multifaceted assessments, combined medical and social treatments, multidisciplinary work, involvement of the recipients and their relatives in the programmes, residential and day-care provisions, long-term support and continued evaluation of the facilities and the programmes.

Most services are based on a combined clinical and social approach, and the maintenance of medical treatment remains an essential task. Ekdawi suggests that English rehabilitation services in particular, attach great importance to medication. The three overlapping models of social care most commonly used consist of the development of skills and vocational abilities (Anthony et al 1986), creating suitable environmental supports, including sheltered accommodation (Pepper 1987), and the strengthening of coping abilities (Strauss 1986).

THE NEED FOR TEAMWORK

A number of arguments are made for the need of teamwork in psychiatric rehabilitation. Menninger (1930) suggests that teamwork resulted from the necessity for maximum service with minimum staff. The necessity for teamwork has been echoed by a series of Government reports and by all the major professional groups. The diversity of people's needs, their long-term care, the close work involved with their families, and the different social and occupational settings require input from a number of professionals (Watts & Bennett 1991). They suggest that teamwork including joint decision making is the only way to provide such comprehensive care. Similar arguments are made by Shepherd (1981) and Sims (1981) who suggest that the multidisciplinary approach in the field of psychiatric rehabilitation is required so that all the patient's needs can be met.

The Younghusband Report (1959) on social work services suggested professional co-operation and teamwork because of the fast growing complexity and scope of modern knowledge. They argued that no one profession dealing with the range of people's needs can make exclusive claim in relation to others and that each group has an essential contribution to make as well as its necessary overlap with others.

Occupational therapists expressed their concern with the Tunbridge Report on rehabilitation (DHSS 1972), which they felt did not consider their contributions to the multiprofessional team. The Trethowan Report (DHSS 1977) on the role of psychologists in the health service recommended that interprofessional relationships should be based on multidisciplinary teamwork, which the report argued reconciles the two principles of clinical and medical responsibility by recognising that each member shares responsibility for patient care, while retaining professional independence. The Management Advisory Service report (MAS 1989) in a major review of the role of clinical psychology proposed a model of service delivery based on the principle of shared care. They recommended that psychologists become fully independent practitioners, accorded equal status with medical practitioners, and assume responsibility for the psychological well-being of individuals served by and providing healthcare.

PROBLEMS AND CONFLICTS

Throughout the health service dissatisfaction is often expressed about the way in which teams operate (Marshall et al 1979). The reasons for this dissatisfaction are usually expressed from two opposing viewpoints. The first viewpoint is based around interdisciplinary rivalry, power struggles, status, conflict about leadership and the division of labour. These are said to give rise to the secondary effects of poor communication, goal ambiguity and low morale. Fried and Leatt (1986) suggest that often different disciplinary groups downgrade and disparage each other's contribution. Any team with a doctor in it tends towards a leader-centred approach with the doctor as leader (Kane 1975). McIntosh & Dingwall (1978) suggest that the doctor's dominance is reinforced because of gender and class status since doctors are usually men and the other occupational groups around them are women. Keddy et al (1986) suggest that nurse–doctor relationships are strongly influenced by the fact that historically nurses were often educated and employed by doctors. Sims (1986) describes these problems in terms of multiple disciplines of team members with different interests, priorities, perspectives and language. Negative stereotypical views of the value of other professionals' contributions are held by many professionals due to their socialisation and training, which prevents co-operation between disciplines. There is a lack of respect for other disciplines and different rules about what counts as valid information. Payne (1982) suggests that different occupational groups use different theoretical and knowledge bases, which makes inter-agency teamwork very problematic. In discussing the problems in multidisciplinary teamwork, Braga (1972) identifies the problem of role strain. This is usually described in terms of two aspects: role ambiguity and role conflict. Working in a multidisciplinary team produces inevitable conflict between the role a person assigns himself, those which his profession assigns him and those which his colleagues assign him.

A number of strategies are now employed to deal with many of these problems. Multidisciplinary groups can improve teamwork by joint training in common aspects of their work. There are certain core areas which are of mutual concern irrespective of their professional affiliations, for example, assessment, standards of care, mental health legislation and liaison between disciplines. The benefit of professional training occurring in institutes of higher education enables academic input between professions to occur at an early stage. This practice is continued in postgraduate education and training and many specialist courses are now run on a multidisciplinary basis, e.g. substance abuse, family therapy and counselling. Teamwork can also be improved when joint training covers new topics in which none of the team members would be expected to have prior expertise or knowledge, e.g. the care of people with HIV, or where new procedures or administrative structures are introduced, such as resource management or clinical audit. Another alternative is for each team member to provide training in some aspects of their own professional group's work to the other disciplines, thereby enhancing understanding by others of their role, knowledge, skills and particular expertise.

Team building is often regarded as the most important intervention in improving the effectiveness of working teams (French & Bell 1984). The aim of team building is to enable team members to diagnose how they work together, identify weaknesses and to make the necessary improvements. This may involve self-awareness training and the development of facilitation, confrontational and assertive skills. Much of this work developed from early studies of organisational behaviour and management and leadership styles, which identified teamwork as the fundamental building blocks of organisations. Alston (1974) reports the use of a communication training programme for the staff of one rehabilitation team. The results demonstrated significant improvements in communication skills and in favourable perceptions of other staff.

The lack of clarity between the professions of leadership, authority, responsibility and accountability often stems from the assumption that all team members are equal. Doyle (1977) describes a community mental health centre which was established with an egalitarian multidisciplinary team approach and which employed the concepts of role blurring, generalist worker and joint decision making. The new structure permitted no authority figure, and decisions were made by the staff as a group. All staff including the unit chief, a psychiatrist, and the psychologist, social workers, nurses and attendants were expected to rotate shifts and interchange jobs. After several months, staff became so preoccupied with defining their philosophical and therapeutic position that patients' needs were not met. Lack of direction, leadership and responsibility eventually resulted in considerable stress and conflict in the individual professionals. This was only relieved when the approach was changed and clear role definition, positions of authority and leadership were established.

Some writers continue to support the egalitarian team concept, (Bonn & Huber 1977). They suggest that role blurring gives the impression of indistinctness, indefiniteness and lack of clarity. Instead of the term role blurring they prefer the use of role expansion. This they define as a clear, planned addition to the function of an individual staff member, based on training and personal qualities, and leading to maximum use of that staff member for the benefit of the patient. Such a system prevents needless fragmentation of a patient's treatment and care. Whereas some overlapping of roles inevitably occurs this is used to the patient's advantage by having multiple kinds of individuals available rather than rigidly selected members of one discipline alone.

Leadership

Difficulties and misunderstandings are said to arise when the consultant psychiatrist exercises authority and assumes sole responsibility for the patients in his or her care. Traditionally such authority and responsibility are bestowed upon them by other team members and the senior medical person has been regarded as the natural team leader. It is necessary for each team member's responsibility for patient care to be defined and agreed with the team. Ritter (1989) suggests that once this process has occurred then each person is deemed accountable for carrying out that part of the treatment programme. When an unsatisfactory treatment programme is decided upon jointly by the team, all members are liable to be called to account. In the case of a satisfactory treatment programme being decided jointly but carried out negligently by one person, then that person is liable, not the team.

To work effectively it is generally assumed that teams need leadership. The benefits and drawbacks of leadership in groups and teams are widely documented. The emergence of a leadership hierarchy seems to be a universal feature of human groups, though an autocratic style of leadership is thought to be unpopular and less effective in achieving cohesiveness and a feeling of commitment to the group's goals by individuals. Batchelor & McFarlane (1980) argue that if doctors are no longer to be seen as leaders of the multi-disciplinary team, then such a change should be determined by patients' needs and that nurses or psychologists who undertook to lead the team should be educated for the role. While the needs of the patient should be the determining factor in deciding who leads the care required, in reality the interaction between the social, psychological and medical aspects of needs is often difficult to differentiate.

Ward rounds

Pollock (1986) suggests that ward rounds exemplify how teams function and give insight into styles of leadership. An observational study in which the content of ward rounds was analysed for 10 neurotic and 10 psychotic patients demonstrated that most of the time was taken up by discussions on medical and diagnostic issues (Sanson-Fisher et al 1979). Medical staff spoke almost eight times as much as non-medical staff, including nurses, and occupational therapists spoke the least. An experimental study by Fewtrell & Toms (1985) compared a new ward round format with traditional ward round procedures. The new ward round procedure consisted of a 'key worker' system whereby each qualified member of staff was allocated responsibilities for one patient, including participation in an assessment interview with that patient in the review meeting. The new format, in which patients were encouraged to voice opinions and raise questions, both amongst themselves and with staff, consisted of a balanced ratio of staff and patients attending simultaneously in an informal atmosphere. The new type of ward round produced a swing away from medical and diagnostic issues to more discussion on domestic and social matters. However, it was not demonstrated whether this resulted from reducing the status of the medical staff within the group.

Blurring of roles

The opposing viewpoint put forward as the possible reason for the inability of teams to function effectively stems from the difficulty to differentiate clearly between the appropriate professional contributions of staff. Fischer & Weinstein (1971) suggest that the blurring of professional distinctions in the team approach leads to the abandoning of individual professional responsibilities with the result that the needs of patients are not met. The blurring of professional roles and skill sharing are characteristic features of contemporary work in the mental health field. Most people in the caring professions have some elementary training in counselling techniques, establishing, maintaining and supporting relationships with patients, group therapy and stress management. Further, some professionals undertake advanced training in various therapies, such as behaviour modification, behaviour psychotherapy, psychoanalysis, cognitive therapy, family therapy and psychodrama.

Professional distinctions have been examined through research and a number of reports from the viewpoint of particular disciplines. The role of psychiatric nursing has come under continual scrutiny (Towell 1975, Cormack 1976). The results of Cormack's study demonstrated that there was a marked discrepancy between the prescribed role of the psychiatric nurse and the reality of the work carried out by psychiatric nurses. Rather than assuming a therapeutic role in their own right nurses spent most of their time gathering clinical data relating to signs and symptoms of psychiatric illness and monitoring the success or failure of physical treatments. Cormack & Fraser (1975) suggest that nurses work according to the prevailing medical ideology and that they are dependent on the psychiatrist to allocate an active part in the treatment programme. The development of nursing knowledge and the introduction of nursing models and theoretical frameworks are seen as a means to delineate the unique contribution of nurses and to loosen their ties from medical hegemony (Peplau 1982).

Jorsh (1991) agrees with the principle of the nurse becoming an independent practitioner and not being subservient to medicine, but warns that this should not be at the expense of the multidisciplinary team. He suggests that psychiatry and psychiatric nursing have a commensal relationship and that each must be aware of their abilities and limitations to co-operate within the multidisciplinary team. All mental health practitioners must be familiar with descriptive psychopathology, being the basis of psychiatric diagnosis and psychiatric syndromes. To assist in sharing knowledge and understanding across disciplines Jorsh recommends each discipline having teaching input with different professional groups.

The MAS report (1989) observed that the role of the clinical psychologist is ambiguous, confused with other disciplines and by the variety of ways in which psychology services are delivered and practised. The report suggests that whilst a multidisciplinary team approach is desirable in terms of quality and scope of care it is able to provide, there are often problems resulting from an absence of mechanisms to co-ordinate, direct and control the activities of the team as a corporate entity. The report proposes that the process for delivering psychological services through other disciplines becomes formalised, with a defined responsibility for the psychologist in teaching and supervising other staff who are using psychological interventions in their work. The use of psychological skills is not confined to clinical psychologists. They are used extensively by a wide range of healthcare staff. The report outlines the range of psychological skills possessed across the various disciplines within a skills framework related to three levels of activities (see Fig. 8.1).

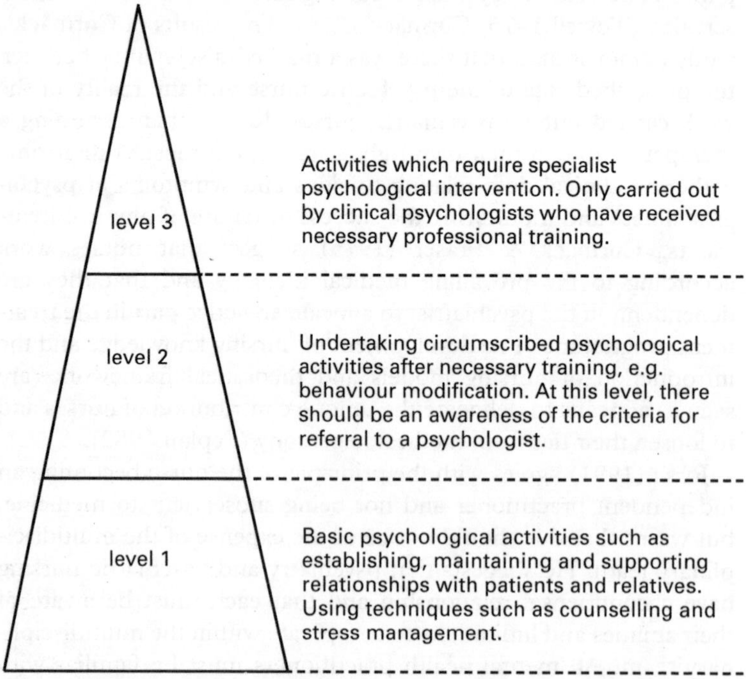
level 3
Activities which require specialist psychological intervention. Only carried out by clinical psychologists who have received necessary professional training.
level 2
Undertaking circumscribed psychological activities after necessary training, e.g. behaviour modification. At this level, there should be an awareness of the criteria for referral to a psychologist.
level 1
Basic psychological activities such as establishing, maintaining and supporting relationships with patients and relatives. Using techniques such as counselling and stress management.

Fig. 8.1 Framework of multidisciplinary psychological skills.

The framework provides a useful starting point to examine each discipline's contribution through the multidisciplinary team in providing comprehensive care to patients. The use of skills as opposed to roles may be one way of overcoming previous conflicts. Between all disciplines there will be some skill sharing while each discipline will possess their own particular skills for which they had specialist training. The skills required should be determined by the needs of the patient.

Payne (1982) attempts to find the middle ground between these two perspectives. He suggests that most writers propose that both these perspectives are undesirable and inappropriate in a multidisciplinary team. He argues that the appropriate way of co-operating is to keep the ideals of the occupational groups as a reference point and negotiate on tasks and boundaries. Involvement in a multidisciplinary team requires of members that they have a strong idea of their own occupational role and skills, can explain it and demonstrate their practice. Effective co-operation between members requires mutual respect and a clear understanding of the roles and skills of the other professionals involved.

KEY WORKER AND CASE MANAGER

If difficulties of definition, responsibility and communication exist between members of the multidisciplinary team, it is not surprising that patients are confused when having to relate to a variety of professionals to have their needs met. One way of dealing with this is the appointment of a contact person for the patient with the specialist skills of the team members channelled through this person. Additionally, the recognition that team members may have similar and overlapping skills and to overcome the difficulties of co-ordination and communication led to the adoption of the concept of 'key workers'. During the 1970s, the idea of the key worker became increasingly popular. A key worker is allocated to a specific client and serves as a contact point mobilising services and resources, co-ordinating and organising the health and social care for that individual. However, Ekdawi (1990) reports that many English services, while supporting the key worker principle, backed by the team, work on the assumption that the consultant remains the point of reference, the co-ordinator and the provider of continuity.

Central to the reorganisation of services outlined in 'Caring for People: Community Care in the Next Decade and Beyond'

(HMSO 1989) is the system of case management. Case management is a popular element in service delivery in America. Intagliata (1982) suggests that the increased popularity of case management arose in response to the need to plan and co-ordinate highly complex and fragmented services and to ensure that deinstitutionalised patients received adequate and appropriate community care services. There are numerous definitions of case management. It is generally accepted that case management is a process or method for ensuring that clients are provided with whatever services they need in a co-ordinated, effective and efficient manner. Intagliata lists the six main components of case management.

1. A comprehensive assessment of individual needs.
2. The development of an individual 'package' of care to meet those needs.
3. Ensuring that the individual gains access to these services—this may entail considerable outreach work, i.e. going along with the client to the housing, or social security office or day centre to ensure that they are able to actually obtain whatever service they need and that it conforms, as far as possible, to their expressed wishes and desires.
4. Monitoring the quality of services provided and liaising with service providers if the quality or content of service does not meet what is required and, if necessary, attempting to change them, i.e. case managers may be proactive in actually changing and shaping services.
5. Adjusting levels of support according to fluctuating levels of functioning.
6. Providing long-term commitment.

There is only a small amount of contradictory evidence which has examined the effectiveness of case management. When compared to traditional aftercare services patients in the case management programme receive more services, cost more to maintain, had higher relapse rates and had no increases in assessed quality of life (Franklin et al 1987). Other exploratory studies which have examined the effectiveness of case management have produced more promising results, including reduced rates of hospitalisation and high rates of individual goal attainment (Rapp & Wintersteen 1989). Shepherd (1991) suggests that the variability in outcome reported in different studies may be accounted for by the kind of case management procedure which is adopted and how implementation is affected by local organisational constraints.

Introducing a case management approach into the care of the mentally ill without testing its applicability has been criticised by Holloway (1990). He argues that the bureaucratic concept of case management stems from experience in pilot projects involving the elderly and mentally handicapped. He believes that precious resources will be syphoned off to pay case managers who will have little direct client contact, so diminishing front-line services and further demoralising direct care staff. Harris & Bergman (1987) argue that rather than just providing an administrative role case managers should cultivate the therapeutic aspects of their relationships with clients to help them deal more effectively with their problems. O'Donnell (1989) warns that though the principles of case management are sensible and straightforward, because of the complex multi-agency nature of community mental health care the practicalities of its introduction should not be underestimated. The role of case manager combines elements of many different mental health professions. Shepherd (1991) suggests that the core skills necessary for case managers to operate effectively still need to be identified. Unless such problems are sorted out then they may contribute further to the familiar difficulties of interprofessional rivalries, role ambiguity and role conflict.

Whatever the fate of implementing case management good teamwork is an essential prerequisite. Case managers will need to identify the appropriate contributions required from each professional and their accountability. Test (1979) suggests that case management is best seen as a team responsibility both in terms of decision making and providing continuity of care. There are presently many expectations of case management; however, to regard it as the solution to all the problems of multidisciplinary teamwork and the co-ordinating and maintaining of continuity of care seems more than a little naive.

PATIENT INVOLVEMENT

Holland (1983) suggests that the acceptability of a service to its users is crucial, since intolerable or unsatisfactory provisions will be underused, even if they are effective and efficient in other respects. This argument is even more pertinent for people with a mental illness where long-term care and rehabilitation may be necessary. Ekdawi (1990) suggests that rehabilitation programmes may well founder if the rehabilitee's co-operation is not enlisted. Government direction in health care emphasises the need for patient satisfaction with services, which is closely associated with patient involvement in the decision-making process and their ability to make informed choices. Several studies have begun to investigate patients' satisfaction with the services they receive and their views regarding the care and treatment provided by individual disciplines.

Some studies have examined patients' understanding of the various roles of members of multidisciplinary teams. Ranger (1986) reports that patients have a very traditional view of multi-disciplinary team functioning. The patients regarded nurses and doctors as being the disciplines most involved in assessment and treatment, with doctors being in charge. Patients' views on psychologists were consistently low, which reflected an uncertainty about the role of the psychologist. Ranger suggests that this is hardly surprising since the study also demonstrated that other disciplines in the teams were unsure about the psychologist's role. Social workers were also ranked low on involvement with patients, except in the area of liaison outside the hospital which is seen as their traditional role. This finding was again reflected by the ratings of other disciplines on the involvement of social workers in the team's work. Patients saw themselves as being less involved than any of the staff disciplines in all areas except occupational therapy, where they rated themselves as more involved than social workers but less so than any other discipline.

COLLABORATION

Collaboration between team members is an essential prerequisite for effective team functioning. Collaborative practice has been described as a planned system through which health care professionals work to ensure consistent, quality patient/family care (Koerner et al 1986). Presently little research exists which demonstrates how much collaboration occurs between team members. Weiss and Davis (1985) tested collaborative practice scales in an attempt to determine the elements of collaborative practice between nurses and doctors; however, their results were inconclusive.

The introduction of formalised audit in health care provides another perspective from which to consider collaboration in teamwork. Government direction is towards the separation of medical audit from the auditing of nursing and other disciplines allied to medicine. This is clearly evident by the large amount of funding allocated to medical audit compared to the small amount of funding made available to all the other disciplines. In psychiatry, the adoption of the term clinical audit to encompass all those disciplines involved in the care of patients demonstrates the collaborative nature of the work and the necessity to analyse critically this work from a team perspective. Fenton et al (1990) describe multidisciplinary case conferences which are held on a regular basis and which involve all members of the health care professions. Howden-Chapman (1990) suggests that audit which is exclusively medical offers a limited scope in specialties where decision making and care are a matter of teamwork and it is methodologically impossible and undesirable to audit the contribution of one team member. In a mental health service, decisions about admission, treatment, discharge and rehabilitation are not taken solely by doctors and the concept of audit should therefore be expanded to mean clinical audit and should encompass the whole team.

TOWARDS A SOLUTION OF OLD PROBLEMS

The continuing movement towards community care for the rehabilitation of people with a mental illness means that many of the issues around multidisciplinary teamwork will need to be resolved — notably whether multidisciplinary teamwork can be adapted and developed for community-orientated services and whether the traditional problems and discrepancies related to professional rivalry, status and power struggles and role confusion can be ironed out and service provision improved. Simply moving out of the hospital with its organisational structure is not enough to rid the team of these problems. Research into primary health care has demonstrated that these problems are as much in existence amongst community health workers as professionals who are hospital based (Sheppard 1986). It seems likely that improvements will only occur if time and energy are given to training and team building needs. Rubin et al (1978) describe team development programmes in American community health care organisations. They suggest that health care workers seemed to prefer an expert prescriptive medical model rather than a collaborative participative, non-directive model. The authors found that one of the major problems of team functioning was that conflict is not brought out into the open and confronted but usually avoided or covered over. When it does emerge decision making is authoritarian, rather than collaborative with the medical profession having the last word.

In moving towards community care, the Government has encouraged the replacement of large psychiatric hospitals by a more appropriate range of flexible services. Stuart & Sundeen (1983) suggest that in the community professionals increasingly seem to perform tasks using strikingly similar skills. A number of people have argued that a new breed of professional may be required in the form of generic community mental health workers. The advantages are that generic staff would be better placed for new services, with new types of training and possibly the creation of a new employer incorporating the relevant portions of personal social services, the health service and the independent sectors. Some countries such as Norway have already adopted this approach. In Canada, the Mental Deficiency (institutional) Nursing Programme was discontinued in 1972. This was replaced by Rehabilitation Counsellor Programmes. However, this was subsequently found to be premature and considerable modifications have had to be made to this programme in response to a growing number of concerns over the needs of clients.

The solution is probably to be found somewhere between these two perspectives where professionals retain their own identity and key areas of responsibility and where different members recognise the skills and expertise of others and are content to put them to good use; where instead of energy being used to protect and enhance professional domains, areas of overlap, role blurring and skill sharing are acknowledged and made the best use of both with regard to resources and time for the benefit of the patient. These problems have recently been addressed by a number of studies using an organisation development approach. Such an approach identifies the key issues faced by any team as, in order of priority, goals, roles, procedures and interpersonal relationships. Iles and Auluck (1990) describe one such approach with a community team with representatives from five different professions and drawn from three different employers. The clarification of specific and overlapping professional skills and competencies, attention to role conflicts, and the clarification of accountabilities of team members to the team as a whole, to the team leader and to professional superiors outside the team all emerged as important issues requiring resolution.

CONCLUSION

It seems that if the objective of multidisciplinary teamwork in providing psychiatric rehabilitation is to optimise the capacity of individuals to reach their potential and to live as independently as possible then individual disciplines have to reject the notion of their monopoly in achieving this. This requires an acknowledge-ment of the need for collaborative working and the appreciation of every team member's contribution. Role blurring and skill sharing greatly increase the extent of need which can be addressed. This, however, is not to say that there are not skills or a role which is uniquely the domain of each member of the multidisciplinary team. The careful assessment of individual patient needs is a good starting point. However, work in this area has only just begun and there is yet no agreement on how this should be carried out or of any standardisation (Brugha et al 1988).

It seems that multidisciplinary teamwork is here to stay. Nevertheless, the performance of rehabilitation multidisciplinary teamwork needs to be regularly evaluated so as to justify its existence and to enable future planning and consequent expendi-ture of resources and valuable professional time. The monitoring of the effectiveness of multidisciplinary teamwork will greatly enhance the present state of knowledge and lead to improved functioning. Further research is needed to develop maximally efficient methods of delivering rehabilitation services through effective teamwork. In future it seems that social services are to become responsible for ensuring that there is assessment of individual need, the design of care arrangements and for ensuring that these are delivered within the constraints of available resources. Nevertheless, while it may be appropriate for the lead of services provision to be taken by social services, it is important to realise that this does not mean ownership of the service. They will have to work closely with health services and other agencies and only through pursuing effective teamwork will success be achieved in meeting patients' needs.

REFERENCES

Alston P P 1974 Multidiscipline group facilitation training: an aid to the team approach. Rehabilitative Counselling Bulletin 18: 21–25

Anthony W A, Kennard W A, O'Brien W F, Forbes R 1986 Psychiatric rehabilitation. Community Mental Health Journal 22: 249–264

Batchelor I, McFarlane J 1980 Multidisciplinary clinical teams. Kings Fund Centre, London

Bonn E M, Huber H M 1977 Egalitarianism in a mental health centre: a commentary. Hospital and Community Psychiatry 28: 526–527

Bowen W T, Marler D C, Androes C 1965 The psychiatric team: myth and mystique. American Journal of Psychiatry 122: 687–690

Braga J L 1972 Role theory, cognitive dissonance theory and the interdisciplinary team. Interchange Vol. 3: 69–78

Brugha T S, Wing J K, Brewin C R, MacCarthy B, Mangen S P, Lesage A, Mumford J 1988 The problems of people in long-term psychiatric day care. Psychological Medicine 18: 443–456

Cormack D 1976 Psychiatric nursing observed. Royal College of Nursing, London

Cormack D, Fraser D 1975 The nurse's role in psychiatric institutions Paper 2. Nursing Times 71 (52): 129–132

Department of Health 1989 Working Paper 7. HMSO, London

DHSS 1972 Rehabilitation (The Tunbridge Report). HMSO, London

DHSS 1977 Role of psychologists in the health service (Trethowan Report). HMSO, London

Doyle M C 1977 Egalitarianism in a mental health centre: an experiment that failed. Hospital and Community Psychiatry 28: 521–525

Ekdawi M Y 1990 The components of psychiatric rehabilitation services. In: Weller M (ed) International perspectives in schizophrenia: biological, social and epidemiological findings. John Libby, London

Fenton G W, Ballinger B R, Ballinger C B, Naylort G J 1990 Medical audit in a Scottish psychiatric service. Psychiatric Bulletin 14: 136–139

Fewtrell W D, Toms D A 1985 Patterns of discussion in traditional and novel ward-round procedures. British Journal of Medical Psychology 58: 57–62

Fischer A, Weinstein M R 1971. Mental hospitals' prestige, and the image of enlightenment. Archives of General Psychiatry 25: 41–45

Franklin J L, Solovitz B, Mason M, Clemons J R, Miller G E 1987 An evaluation of case management. American Journal of Public Health 77: 74–78

French W L, Bell C H 1984 Organization development. Prentice Hall, Englewood Cliffs, New Jersey

Fried R J, Leatt P 1986 Role perceptions among occupational groups in an ambulatory care setting. Human Relations 39: 1155–1174

Harris M, Bergman H C 1987 Case management with the chronically mentally ill: a clinical perspective. American Journal of Orthopsychiatry 57: 51–56

HMSO 1989 Caring for people: community care in the next decade and beyond. Command Paper 849. HMSO, London

Holland W W 1983 Evaluation of health care. Oxford University Press, Oxford

Holloway F 1990 Caring for people: a critical review of British Government policy for the community care of the mentally ill. Psychiatric Bulletin 14: 641–645

Howden-Chapman P 1990 A climate of trust. The Health Service Journal Vol. 100 (No. 5192): 402–403

Iles P A, Auluck R 1990 From organizational to interorganizational development in nursing practice: improving the effectiveness of interdisciplinary teamwork and interagency collaboration. Journal of Advanced Nursing 15: 50–58

Intagliata J 1982 Improving the quality of community care for the chronically mentally disabled: the role of case management. Schizophrenia Bulletin 8: 655–674

Jorsh M S 1991 The changes in the education of psychiatric nurses: do psychiatrists have a role? Psychiatric Bulletin 15: 339–340

Kane R A 1975 Interprofessional teamwork. Syracuse University, New York

Keddy B et al 1986 The doctor–nurse relationship and historical perspective. Journal of Advanced Nursing 11: 745–753

Koerner B L, Cohen J R, Armstrong D M 1986 Professional behaviour in collaborative practice. Journal of Nursing Administration 16: 38–43

McIntosh J, Dingwall R 1978 Teamwork in theory and practice. In: Dingwall R, McIntosh J (eds) Readings in the sociology of nursing. Churchill Livingstone, Edinburgh

Management Advisory Service 1989 Review of clinical psychology services. MAS, London

Marshall M, Preston-Shoot M, Wincott E 1979 Teamwork: for and against. BASW Publications, Birmingham

Menninger K A 1930 The human mind. A A Knopf, New York

Ministry of Health 1968 Psychiatric nursing: today and tomorrow. HMSO, London

Modlin H, Faris M 1956 Group adaption and integration in psychiatric team practice. Psychiatry 19: 97–103

O'Donnell O 1989 Mental health care policy in England: objectives, failures and reforms. Centre for Health Economics, York

Parry-Jones W L L 1986 Multidisciplinary teamwork: help or hindrance? In: Steinberg D (ed) The adolescent unit: work and teamwork in adolescent psychiatry. John Wiley, Chichester

Payne M 1982 Working in teams. Macmillan Press, London

Peck E 1989 Working for psychiatric patients? Mental health services and the White Paper. Psychiatric Bulletin 13: 407–408

Peplau H E 1988 interpersonal relations in nursing: a conceptual frame of reference for psychodynamic nursing. Macmillan, Basingstoke

Pepper B 1987 A public policy for the long-term mentally ill. American Journal of Orthopsychiatry 57: 452–457

Pollock L 1986 The multidisciplinary team. In: Hume C, Pullen I (eds) Rehabilitation in psychiatry. Churchill Livingstone, Edinburgh

Ranger S 1986 Functioning of the multidisciplinary team: a study of 3 teams in a psychiatric rehabilitation setting. Institute of Psychiatry. Unpublished M Phil, London

Rapp C A, Wintersteen R 1989 The strengths model of case management: results from twelve demonstrations. Psychosocial Rehabilitation Journal 13: 23–32

Ritter S 1989 The multidisciplinary clinical team. In: The Bethlem Royal and Maudsley Hospital manual of clinical psychiatric nursing principles and procedures. Harper Row, London

Royal Commission 1979 Royal Commission on the National Health Service. HMSO, London

Rubin I M, Plovnick M S, Fry R E 1978 Task oriented team development. McGraw-Hill, New York

Sanson-Fisher R W, Poole A D, Harker J 1979 Behavioural analysis of ward rounds within a general hospital psychiatric unit. Behaviour Research and Therapy 17: 333–348

Shepherd G 1981 The nature of psychiatric disability. Paper presented for MINDOUT (National Association for Mental Health) January 1981

Shepherd G 1986 Social skills training and schizophrenia. In: Hollin C R, Trower P (eds) Handbook of social skills training: volume 2. Pergamon Press, Oxford

Shepherd G 1991 Psychiatric rehabilitation for the 1990s. In: Watts F N, Bennett D H, Theory and practice of psychiatric rehabilitation, 3rd edn. Wiley, Chichester

Sims A 1981 The staff and their training. In: Wing J K, Morris B (eds) Handbook of psychiatric rehabilitation practice. Oxford University Press

Sims D 1986 Interorganization: some problems of multiorganizational teams. Personnel Review 15: 27–31

Strauss J S 1986 What does rehabilitation accomplish. Schizophrenia Bulletin 12: 720–723

Stuart G W, Sundeen S J 1983 Principles and practice of psychiatric nursing. C V Mosby, St Louis

Temkin-Greener H 1983 Interprofessional perspectives on teamwork in health care: a case study. Milbank Memorial Fund Quarterly 61: 641–658

Test M 1979 Continuity of care in community treatment. In: Stein L (ed)

Community support systems for the long-term patient. C A Josey-Bass, San Francisco

Towell D 1975 Understanding psychiatric nursing. Royal College of Nursing, London

Watts F N, Bennett D H 1991 Management of the staff team. In: Watts F N, Bennett D H Theory and practice of psychiatric rehabilitation, 3rd edn, Wiley, Chichester

Weiss S J, Davis H P 1985 Validity and reliability of the collaborative scales. Nursing Research 34: 299–305

Younghusband Report 1959 Report of the working party on social work in social authority health and welfare services. HMSO, London

9. The family and rehabilitation

Colin Elliot

I am the family face;
Flesh perishes, I live on.

Thomas Hardy, **Heredity**

INTRODUCTION

Psychiatry is still very much in its infancy. Only recently has there been some convergence between the different schools of thought. Over the past three decades, views on the genesis of psychiatric illness have been opposed. At one end of the spectrum was the view that mental disorder was an illness, biological, chemical or genetic in its origins; at the other, that psychiatric illness was nothing more than a social construct (Szasz 1960) or the product of dysfunctional families, more often pathological parents (Laing 1967).

Recent developments in the use of drug treatments, particularly when targeted at specific disorders, confirm the importance of the physiological/chemical aspects of mental ill-health. The lack of empirical evidence and validating research of social and dynamic views of the origins of mental illness means they have largely been abandoned. That said, it is clear that the stereotype images created in the late 60s and early 70s of 'passive fathers' and 'schizo-phrenogenic mothers' still exist. They are still used, but much more covertly, often as a shorthand communication between professionals to convey negative images of parents.

The advances in chemical research and treatment mean families are at risk of being marginalised. They can be seen as having little to contribute except to confirm aspects of medical history at the point of admission and at discharge, to provide practical support—particularly over accommodation.

It is the author's view that families involved in the rehabilitation process receive messages which often reflect these perceptions. Often they are excluded as irrelevant or kept at a distance, viewed as potentially or actually destructive to the rehabilitation process. These perceptions are inaccurate and do not reflect the valuable contribution families make. They also ignore the family's need for support in its own right. This chapter outlines a variety of approaches reflecting these convictions.

Firstly it is important to clarify our terms of reference. The 'family' is used within its widest meaning to include relationships that are formulated within the law—husband, wife, son, daughter, mother and father. It also includes those relationships which can be described as 'significant' and long-standing but not consolidated in a legal manner. This broadening of views on the family is reflected in some mental health legislation such as The Mental Health Acts of England and Wales and Scotland (1983 and 1984). These recognise that the reality for some people may be that their immediate family may have a less significant relationship than an unrelated companion or partner. In other words, traditional constructs of the family have changed as patterns of living have evolved. Kinship relationships are now much looser and this has an effect on the rehabilitation process. Families can be physically quite separate from each other and the nature and structure of family relationship may be at odds with the traditional view of the family, 'mum, dad and 2.3 children'. For example figures suggest the number of families living in single-parent households in the Western world has risen very significantly over the past 20 years.

The meaning of the word 'rehabilitation' in psychiatry has also changed and become quite ambiguous. Some view it as a process which involves all psychiatric treatment. Within this framework rehabilitation starts with the initial contact and works towards an optimum return to normality. Traditional views of rehabilitation in psychiatry are that specialist programmes need to be organised for certain individuals with particular difficulties. This means people who have very severe recurring illnesses and those who are significantly handicapped by the effects of their particular disorder. The aim is to help these individuals re-integrate into society and function at their optimum level within the limitations imposed by their disabilities. Failure to do this means they would most likely remain in institutional care or exist within communities, functioning at less than optimum or desirable levels and often highly dependent on their individual families.

Rehabilitation programmes can therefore be highly successful, of short duration and applicable to all individuals with a mental health problem or intensive, long-term, extremely problematic and focused on a particular but small sub-set of the general psychiatric population. The author favours the latter description as it offers a specific focus to a particular set of difficulties that are not universal to all those with mental health problems. To embrace the former view, is to some extent, a failure to recognise these highly specific needs. This does not deny the need and sense of planning ahead and the development of contingency plans in general psychiatric care. What is being stressed is that this particular group of patients has very specific problems and these need to be addressed as soon as possible in the treatment process as a vision of the future needs to be developed and myopia avoided. This point is explored in more detail later in the chapter.

WHO ARE WE TALKING ABOUT?

The improved sophistication of chemical treatments means the vast majority of individuals who experience mental ill health are treated in the community by primary carers (Goldberg & Huxley 1980). Those admitted to hospital are usually treated and discharged within a few weeks. The days of psychiatric hospitals filled with 'young chronic patients' languishing in refractory wards are, thankfully, long gone. That said, this dreadful state of affairs and the moral outrage it provoked, galvanised many forward-looking institutions into developing rehabilitation programmes. This eventually led to many individuals being discharged into the community where they blossomed. These successes encouraged institutions to take risks in discharging long-stay patients and they invested considerable resources in this area (Wing 1977).

The success of this approach meant that over time those patients being considered for discharge were more extensively debilitated and used to life within an institutional regime. That is, it was questionable whether or not they would want to leave hospital and if they did, would this offer them a better quality of life, and at what cost, to them, their families and society in general? The advancing costs of institutional care and the decay of many hospitals in the West have resolved this question. Many people who would not normally be considered as 'rehabilitation material' are being relocated in the community. Ironically, many of the very large and unprogressive institutions who had resisted rehabilitation programmes have been at the forefront of this process. The quality and extent of support on offer have been extremely variable and have provoked concern from many bodies. In those situations where individuals are well cared for, often in small-scale supported housing schemes, the quality of life of former long-stay patients has improved a little and costs have been contained. The indirect effect of these actions has been to raise the profile of rehabilitation again when it had fallen into the doldrums after the high-profile successes of the 60s and 70s.

Rehabilitation is now focused on two quite distinct groups. One group, as detailed above, have had long-term residence in hospital and are quite debilitated by their individual psychiatric problems. The motivation to relocate this group has been forced on hospital authorities by the unacceptable financial realities of high-cost hospital care and the deteriorating fabric of many institutions. The other, is a younger population who live in the community in a variety of situations and who have recurrent admissions to hospital. These admissions can be brief but frequent, of a crisis nature or protracted and irregular in occurrence. Many individuals in this group have chronic housing problems and are highly visible 'on the streets'. In some countries, their plight has been the focus of considerable media attention and the stimulus to new mental health legislation in both the United Kingdom and the United States.

What is common to both groups is that their respective difficulties do not respond particularly well to current modes of intervention. Many of their symptoms are unresponsive to medication. Individual behaviours can be extremely odd, complex and problematic. It is likely that these individuals will present complex clinical pictures where it is difficult to disentangle illness from personality factors, life experience and social circumstances. As such, they present considerable challenges, not least because they are unattractive within the current priorities in psychiatry which has tried to emulate the rapid turnover in beds in acute medicine. There is a considerable pressure to move the older group out of hospital and a desire to maintain the younger population in the community lest they become the new generation of chronic long-stay patients. In reality, many institutions no longer have a provision for this population, being geared to either acute admissions and high bed turnover or the long-term care of psychogeriatric patients with only a very small quota of beds being retained for individuals with longer term needs. A common theme to both groups is the desire to conduct rehabilitation in the community.

The family groups and contacts of these two groups also differ. Many of the long-stay patients in the rehabilitation process have lost contact with their families over the period of hospitalisation. Other families and relatives who are still in contact may have become used to the person's circumstances and 'odd' behaviour. The prospect of discharge can raise considerable anxiety for them. The families of the younger, community-based population are more likely to be in closer proximity and as such more exposed to the individual's problems. Many will also be in the position of still coming to terms with the person's illness and its likely outcome.

As stated the vast majority of people with mental health problems recover with the minimum of intervention over a relatively short period of time. Rehabilitation for these individuals and their families is not an issue. The difficulties the individual and family experienced will have limited impact on the rest of their lives. This does not mean that these difficulties are not significant or traumatic to the individuals concerned, far from it. The difference is in the **length** and **depth** of the illness and the **degree** of impairment it signifies for the person's normal functioning and integration in society. Whilst this group is a sub-set of the general psychiatric population its size should not be underestimated. Hughes (1991) estimates in excess of 100 000 people in the United Kingdom are severely disabled by schizophrenia alone. So, whilst it is important to recognise that the rehabilitation process is not relevant to all, it has particular relevance for a significant number of people, many who are extremely disabled and difficult to help.

WHAT SUPPORT DO FAMILIES NEED?

Families frequently complain that they are excluded from care planning discussions. This may be a reflection that the family involvement is seen to be unwelcome or unnecessary. In many cases the specific complaint is that they are not told what is wrong, in some instances for many years (Hatfield 1983). Clare (1985) makes the point that if nothing else, diagnosis allows us to predict the likely outcome and course of an illness. We can have some sympathy with psychiatrists who feel pressurised into making a premature diagnosis when the clinical picture is still emerging. Yet this has to be balanced against the needs of the individual and the family who are often desperately trying to make sense of the situation in which they find themselves—particularly so when the mental health problems are emerging for the first time. The needs of psychiatry to hide its embarrassment at not knowing the answers to relatives' questions should pale into insignificance when compared to the families' needs for information, comfort and reassurance.

Individuals and families have to take stock of the situation and look ahead in the same way as the professionals. For many, this is a period of considerable emotion often likened to a protracted grief reaction. Considerable adjustments need to be made in the way that the family member is perceived and this often involves behavioural and relationship changes. A balance must be found in what can be realistically expected of the person and this usually requires a considerable shift in expectations for everyone concerned. This process takes time and often requires a great deal of support. The analogy with grief is helpful as it suggests a process which must be gone through which often involves disbelief, self-blame, anger, sadness, a sense of loss and eventually re-adjustment. Families, like individuals, can and frequently do get 'stuck' at various points in this process. For example, there is a tendency to minimise the severity of the illness. (This is often colluded with by professionals not wishing to be seen as the harbingers of bad news.) Consequently, expectations are artificially maintained, often placing considerable strain on the patient who in turn goes on to 'fail' when his/her mental health does not improve, relapses occur or the individual fails to attain unrealistic goals (Wing 1977). The messages given at this stage often undermine and minimise the need for compliance with medication (Smith & Birchwood 1987). Equally, the extent of the illness can be exaggerated by the family and this in turn can lead to overprotection. This can undermine the individual's confidence in his/her abilities and create dependency which will work against the rehabilitation process. The idea of adjustment, which can be viewed as the beginning of the rehabilitation process, needs to be facilitated by clear communication at the outset, that the person has severe difficulties. This information needs to be given and heard. Avoiding this responsibility serves no purpose except to leave families without crucial facts. It also blurs the planning process and does not address the longer term needs of the individual. While difficult, painful information may have to be communicated, the positive effect can be that the diagnosis and prognosis are well considered and energies become focused on future care.

Irrespective of whether someone is being rehabilitated after a prolonged admission or being maintained in the community, consideration should be given to how the family is best involved. Families often need guidance on how to react and behave as they may be dealing with behaviour and emotions that are new and frightening. Where possible and appropriate, an alliance should be constructed between the professionals involved, the individual and his/her family, particularly if the family are to play a significant part in the support system. The proximity and character of the relationships, taken in conjunction with the individual's wishes will determine the nature of the involvement with the family. It is important that these decisions are taken for the right reasons. That is, it is easy to fall into the trap of minimising the needs of the family or rationalising away its involvement as unnecessary. This point has been made in numerous studies which found the needs of families were frequently neglected and services were unresponsive (Bells 1978, Creer & Wing 1974, Hatfield 1979, Holden & Lewine 1982). Facing up to the true extent of family need in the rehabilitation process has considerable resource and skill implications. Many families need intense support, often for very long periods. As noted, the need for high turnover militates against this. Professions historically linked to the long-term support of families, most notably social work, have been directed into other areas of practice, in particular statutory child care work (Loxley 1988). This trend appears to be continuing and this raises the worry that the important area of rehabilitation and the needs of families may be neglected. It has also been observed (Rushton 1987) that working with human pain and distress is extremely stressful for professionals working in this field and as such it is common to adopt defensive postures that put distance between us and the source of stress, in this case families and relatives. Providing support is costly in many ways.

Evidence from studies (Gibbon et al 1984) show that the vast majority of families living with someone with a long-standing psychiatric complaint experience considerable emotional and physical hardship. For example, many close relatives become enmeshed in the patient's delusional systems and are treated in an abusive manner and often live in fear of violent eruptions. Considerable pressure is often present in marital situations as the couple try to readjust to illness in the family. This often means a period of self-reproach, mutual blaming and extreme tension which in some cases can lead to complete marital breakdown. It has long been recognised that long-term psychiatric illness can precipitate a downward financial and social spiral, often because less income is coming into the household. Support therefore needs to be delivered on a number of levels. This variety often means that these needs have fallen between the boundaries of the different professions in the rehabilitation system. At a wider level, this frequently leads to a dispute between health care agencies and local authorities. Some of this reluctance to get involved can be simply because the process of supporting the individual with a long-standing illness and their family is labour intensive and as such costly. Living with someone who has a long-standing psychiatric illness which is not particularly responsive to treatment is extremely taxing. Families need to have the opportunity of a break. This need has to be accepted by the family so that they do not experience guilt when in touch with their feelings of having 'had enough' and wanting time away from their relative. This should be seen as a natural process.

In periods of crisis, families need to feel that they have reasonable access to services. That is, they should not be made to feel that they are a nuisance or experience guilt for making demands and requesting support. In the past, this has often been the case because of the unfortunate stereotype images projected onto relatives. This point underlines the need for alliances to be formed between relatives and professionals. Rivalries and mutual criticisms can arise quite easily as the locus of care moves between the family and the surrogate professional carers. It is the author's view, that one of the primary roles in working with families is to confront this rivalry as soon as possible and work through it so that relationships do not become 'split' and unhelpful.

WHAT CAN BE DONE TO HELP?

It has been recognised for a long time that certain types of interactions between patients and their families can impede the rehabilitation process and result in re-admission (Vaughn & Leff 1976). Considerable research in this area has produced evidence that social intervention, combined with medication reduces relapse. Behaviour that is overly critical is seen to be of particular importance as is the face-to-face expression of emotion. Falloon & Shanahan (1990) and Birchwood et al (1988) have proposed models of psychosocial intervention that aim to lessen family tensions through improved communication — in particular, how requests for behavioural change are made, how individuals listen to each other and make reciprocal conversation. Families are also encouraged to develop their problem-solving skills so as to avoid stressful situations. This highly pragmatic approach has gone a long way to counter the view of families that the notion of high expressed emotion (HEE) was pejorative and a denial of their legitimate concern for the family member (Mueser 1992). Unfortunately, there is little evidence to suggest that the potential of this style of intervention has been fully exploited.

Many individuals who require rehabilitation choose to live away from home. This can be a recognition of the negative effect that their family has or more probably, a reflection of the normal maturational process. That is, in many cultures it is normal for young people to move away from the parental home and establish independent life-styles. This process should not be restricted by mental health problems or the rehabilitation process. That said, it is difficult for some families to 'let go' when there are valid concerns over the individual's future mental health. In these situations, which predominantly pertain to young people and their parents but not exclusively, considerable intervention may be required to manage family feelings of separation. Parental anxiety can be particularly high and considerable reassurance and explanation may be needed. If the family is still coming to terms with the illness, the situation can be even more complex. In practice, families often look for guarantees where none can be given. If the individual relapses or his/her domestic situation breaks down, blame can be attributed to the professionals involved on the basis that it would not have happened if the individual was living at home. Consequently, it is important to anticipate this and discuss its possibility with the family.

The significance of having open, clear and frequent communications with the family cannot be overstated. This is particularly so when important changes are being proposed, for example, when a move to supportive accommodation is being advised. Many families are in a position where considerable trust has to be invested in the professional groups managing the rehabilitation process. This trust has to be developed and not automatically assumed. A successful method of developing this rapport is to establish support groups between relatives and carers while the individual is in hospital. This allows information and experience to be shared but does require considerable skill from those leading the group. These groups, no matter how valuable, should not be seen as an alternative to individual meetings between carers and families but rather as supplementary to them. Good experiences in these groups can lead to families developing contacts with self-help and support groups once the individual has moved away from hospital; for example, the National Schizophrenia Fellowship (NSF) in the United Kingdom and the National Alliance for the Mentally Ill (NAMI) in the United States.

As indicated earlier, families need to feel that they can have access to supports in periods of crisis. (This can be extended to include voluntary organisations who offer residential accommodation.) Individuals who have long-standing psychiatric problems and their families can experience difficulty in gaining readmission to hospital. This is often based on the view that little can be done to change the individual's behaviour and that the cause of the crisis is domestic factors. What is often required is 'time out'. While access to respite facilities can play a part, what is required is a crisis intervention service. These services have particular relevance to families and can be the difference between the families breaking down or resolving and learning from their difficulties.

It has been recognised for some years that respite care is important for families. However, while there has been considerable growth in respite facilities for the elderly and individuals with learning difficulties over the last decade, there has not been a corresponding expansion in the area of mental health. Families have often been confronted with the reality of no option or the unattractive alternative of a readmission to hospital. This has often been taken up but at the expense of sending the wrong message to the family member and leaving a residue of guilt. Within the author's particular geographical location, a variety of initiatives are being encouraged. These range from 'share the care' schemes facilitated by the local authority, where other families provide respite, to a national residential resource run by a voluntary organisation. In this unit which specialises in respite, having time away from the usual living situation is seen to be normal and highly desirable for everyone concerned, not least the individual with mental health problems.

The level of stigma related to mental ill health remains consistently high. This fact does not appear to be altered by public education programmes or indeed the prevalence of mental ill health. The adjustment process that individuals and their families need to make is not made any easier by these negative attitudes. Where someone has a serious medical problem, it is likely that they and their family will receive considerable sympathy and understanding. In contrast, those who have serious mental health problems tend to conceal this fact for as long as possible. Some individuals and their families live in fear of being discovered. This can mean that families can become quite isolated from their normal social contacts. These processes and reactions can in themselves exacerbate the primary problem. In response to this, many families derive considerable support from self-help groups. There is a desire to be involved and a wish for more information on the illness. This is thought to be universal, irrespective of the particular diagnoses (Muesar 1992). These groups can provide very tangible support in the form of education, information and access to people in a similar situation. Within these supportive structures, many families develop the strength to 'come out' and be open about their situation. It is often the case that once a contact is made, a relationship will develop that is sustained for many years. Professionals can play a significant role in the formation of these groups where none exist and where they do, in encouraging families to make maximum use of them.

THE FUTURE

The nature of psychiatric rehabilitation services has changed considerably over a relatively short period of time. This is closely linked to developments in psychiatric treatments. These developments have allowed psychiatry to move away from institutional care. While a steady trickle of individuals with particular needs are rehabilitated from a hospital base, the vast majority are cared for in the community having had a brief period of admission. Rehabilitation has become, and will continue to be, a community-based activity. As such, the focus of energy is on the development and maintenance of individuals within their chosen social systems. These vary from person to person but often involve family members. Consequently, there is a growing recognition of the important role that families play in community care. Similar comparisons can be made with voluntary organisations which have expanded while the large psychiatric institutions have retracted. These changes require a considerable shift in power and perception. That is, professional groups need to enter into power sharing relationships with these new partners. Some will find this transition easier than others.

REFERENCES AND FURTHER READING

Bells C 1978 Social networks, the family and the schizophrenic patient. Schizophrenia Bulletin 4: 512–520

Birchwood M et al 1988 Schizophrenia — an integrated approach to research and treatment, part 4. Longman Publications, London

Brandon D 1988 The crumbling institutions of mental health. Social Work Today 19: (39)

Clare A 1985 Psychiatry in dissent: controversial issues in thought and practice, 2nd edn. Tavistock Publications, London

Creer C, Wing J K 1974 Schizophrenia at home. Institute of Psychiatry, London

Falloon I R H, Shanahan W J 1990 Community management of schizophrenia. British Journal of Hospital Medicine 43 (January)

Gibbon J S, Horn J H, Powell J M , Gibbons J L 1984 Schizophrenic patients and their families. A survey in a psychiatric service based in a DGH unit. British Journal of Psychiatry 144: 70–77

Goldberg D, Huxley P 1980 Mental illness in the community. The pathway to psychiatric care. Tavistock Publications, London

Hatfield A B 1979 Help-seeking behaviour in the families of schizophrenics. American Journal of Community Psychology 7: 563–569

Hatfield A B 1983 Coping with mental illness in the family: the family guide and the leader's guide. University of Maryland

Hatfield A B, Lefley H P (eds) 1987 Families of the mentally ill: coping and adaptation. Cassell Education Limited, London

Holden D F, Lewine R R J 1982 How families evaluate mental health professionals, resources and effects of illness. Schizophrenia Bulletin 8: 626–633

Hughes J 1991 An outline of modern psychiatry, 3rd edn. John Wiley, England

Laing R D 1967 The politics of experience. Penguin, Harmondsworth

Loxley A 1988 The marginalisation of hospital social work: a threat to resist. Social Work Today 19: (20)

Mueser K T 1992 An assessment of the educational needs of chronic psychiatric patients and their relatives. British Journal of Psychiatry 160: 674–680

Rushton A 1987 Stress amongst social workers. In: Payne R, Firth-Crozens J (eds) Stress in health professionals. John Wiley, Chichester

Smith J V, Birchwood M J 1987 Specific and non-specific effects of educational intervention with families living with a schizophrenic relative. British Journal of Psychiatry 150: 645–652

Szasz T S 1960 The myth of mental illness. American Psychologist 15: 113–118

Vaughn C E, Leff J P 1976 The influence of family life on the course of psychiatric illness. British Journal of Psychiatry 129: 125–137

Wing J K 1977 Schizophrenia and its management in the community. National Schizophrenia Fellowship, London

10. Transcultural aspects of rehabilitation

David Mumford

All human beings are born free and equal in dignity and rights.
Universal Declaration of Human Rights 1948

INTRODUCTION

Rehabilitation and culture

Many people have attempted to define 'culture'. I favour Tyler's (1874) definition:

'that complex whole which includes knowledge, belief, art, morals, law, custom, and any other capabilities and habits acquired by man as a member of society'.

Rehabilitation exists in a cultural milieu. It cannot be achieved in isolation from family and friends, from the particular community to which the person belongs. What is more, the rehabilitation process is itself a cultural task. It aims to restore those 'capabilities and habits acquired by man as a member of society' which have been lost or impaired.

When the person comes from the same cultural group as ourselves, it is easy to overlook the cultural character of rehabilitation. But when he or she comes from a *different* culture, then a whole lot of issues arise. This chapter looks at some of these issues.

Recent migration into Britain

Throughout human history, people have migrated from place to place, whether in search of work, for a new and better life, or to escape from persecution. Rack (1982) calls these three kinds of migrant Gastarbeiters ('guest-workers'), settlers and exiles, and describes the different psychological stresses on each group.

The last 100 years has seen some of the greatest-ever movements of population, particularly from Europe to the New World, and from Asia into Europe. Britain has received several waves of immigrants during this century. The Irish continued to migrate to find work, as they did throughout the 19th century. In the 1930s, Jews were fleeing Nazi persecution. East Europeans came during and after the 1939–1945 war. British post-war economic recovery drew in workers from the Commonwealth: West Indians in the 1950s and Indians, Pakistanis and Bangladeshis in the 1960s. Most cities in Britain now contain significant ethnic minorities.

WORKING ACROSS CULTURES

For several years, the Transcultural Psychiatry Unit at Bradford has organised study days for nurses, doctors, social workers and other mental health professionals, covering the principles of transcultural work. The programme focuses on three basic issues: language, culture and adaptation.

Language

Effective communication is essential to any psychiatric assessment or treatment. Patients without fluent English are severely disadvantaged when using the existing psychiatric services. In a few places, the NHS employs interpreters who can be called upon at short notice; sometimes a nurse or doctor can be found who speaks the patient's language; but for the most part, mental health professionals have to make their own *ad hoc* arrangements.

Patients from the Indian subcontinent who speak little English will often attend hospital with a young son or daughter to interpret for them. It is surely unprofessional and inappropriate to rely on a family member, particularly a child, to interpret during a psychiatric interview.

Even where a trained interpreter is available, effective use of an interpreter is a skill that has to be learned. It is a great advantage to work closely with one particular interpreter, who then becomes a valuable member of the multidisciplinary team. This has certainly been the experience in Bradford, following the appointment of a 'communications assistant' to the Transcultural Psychiatry Unit.

Culture

Building a therapeutic relationship lies at the heart of all mental health work. When patient and helper come from different cultures, difficulties are bound to arise. Each person brings to the encounter a different set of beliefs and expectations and assumptions. Prejudice and misunderstandings need to be recognised and overcome on both sides.

Culture also determines the ways in which people signal emotional distress. The mode of presentation of mental disorders and expression of psychiatric symptoms differ between ethnic groups. For example, people from non-Western cultures suffering from anxiety or depression tend to give more prominence to somatic symptoms rather than psychological symptoms. (For a fuller discussion of these somatic symptoms, see Mumford et al 1991.)

Sometimes it may be difficult to decide whether a particular complaint or piece of behaviour is a sign of mental illness or not. It is a common pitfall to diagnose as psychotic an African or an Afro-Caribbean whose acute stress reaction consists of excited behaviour and prominent religious ideas (Rack 1982).

It is also difficult for a helper to understand and appreciate the social and domestic stresses, crises and problems which may lie behind the psychiatric disorder. He or she needs to find out whether the response to the stresses is excessive and out of keeping with cultural coping strategies. It is important to check this out with someone else from the same cultural background as the patient.

Concepts of health and disease vary greatly between cultures, as do patterns of behaviour appropriate to the 'sick role'. For example, many South Asian patients believe they must rest while they are ill. They may regard activities such as occupational and industrial therapy as harmful. Such cultural attitudes run counter to the model of rehabilitation that emphasises restoration of function through activity.

Adaptation

Migrants find themselves living in a strange and unfamiliar culture, and react in a variety of ways. Some wish to assimilate and adopt the customs, habits and dress of their adopted home. Others re-assert their culture of origin and even become a walking caricature of it.

Members of ethnic minorities often experience multiple stresses:

unemployment, social and economic deprivation, poor housing in inner-city areas and racism. Some are grateful for their new opportunities in life and accept the many difficulties they encounter. Others become embittered and resentful, particularly in the face of racial prejudice and hostility. (For a full account of the variety of psychological reactions to unfamiliar environments, see Furnham & Bochner 1986.)

The children of immigrants have a wholly different experience from their parents. The 'second generation' grows up in Britain without any direct experience of their parents' country of origin. They imbibe British culture at school and develop social habits and career aspirations from their British schoolfriends. They may find themselves in conflict with their parents who wish to preserve the distinctive cultural values of the family.

Most of this chapter is concerned with the first generation of the ethnic minorities: people who have come to Britain as adults with their cultural identity and cultural values already formed in their country of origin. The issues in rehabilitation for the second generation are different and will be discussed only briefly in this chapter.

THE REHABILITATION PROCESS

Referrals

There is accumulating evidence that members of ethnic minorities are referred to psychiatrists less often than indigenous British people (Ineichen 1990, Lipsedge 1991). It is unlikely that they experience significantly less mental illness. The lower referral rate may be because their GPs are less efficient at recognising psychiatric disorders, or because they themselves are less willing to accept a psychiatric referral, or because of deficiencies in the psychiatric services.

The process of referral to the psychiatric rehabilitation team is likely to be affected by similar factors. Rehabilitation may be perceived by referring agencies as less relevant to the needs of ethnic minority patients. Cultural stereotyping may cause referrers to anticipate poor compliance (Afro-Caribbeans) or existing strong family support (South Asians).

Admission to a rehabilitation unit

Following referral, the patient may be admitted or transferred to a rehabilitation unit in a psychiatric hospital. Admission to a psychiatric hospital can carry important consequences for the ethnic minority patient and his/her family. The stigma of mental illness is generally greater among ethnic minorities and can have far-reaching effects. For example, in tightly knit South Asian communities, it may make it difficult to arrange the marriage of a younger daughter.

As a result the patient's family may resist and try to obstruct a hospital admission, especially if this is to be for several months. It may be useful to arrange a home visit to explain its purpose and to allay their fears. If possible, the visit should involve a member of the rehabilitation team who comes from a similar ethnic background.

When admitted to a psychiatric hospital, the patient from an ethnic minority will probably feel lost in an alien environment. This has a double aspect. The 'hospital culture' will seem strange and threatening; and many everyday things which we take for granted may be unfamiliar. To appreciate what they are experiencing, try to imagine what it would be like to be admitted to a psychiatric hospital in India or China.

Assessment

The assessment of patients from an ethnic minority background is likely to present a variety of new problems. Most assessments in rehabilitation units would aim to identify difficulties and needs in a wide range of activities of daily living: domestic tasks, social skills, leisure activities and taking responsibility for medication.

All these are culturally based activities, and reflect the roles and expectations and values of people living in Britain at the end of the 20th century. The list might look very different if you were doing psychiatric rehabilitation in Nepal or New Guinea. For example, performance of religious activities might take a higher priority than 'leisure' among many traditional cultures.

Sex roles are often more sharply demarcated in non-Western cultures than in the contemporary Western world. For example, a man may be unwilling to be assessed on cooking or other domestic tasks if his cultural code decrees that this is 'women's work'. A woman may have little interest in pottery or gardening.

Assessments in rehabilitation are undertaken in four ways: by interview, by observation of task performance, from relatives and other informants, and by self-rating questionnaire. The balance between these four methods may differ when assessing someone from an ethnic minority background. For example, if there are communication difficulties with the patient, greater reliance is placed on interviews with relatives who speak more fluent English. The use of questionnaires may be restricted, both because of poor literacy and also through lack of familiarity with the questionnaire format.

The interpretation of information gleaned may also cause difficulty: the same social behaviour can carry quite a different significance in another cultural setting. At interview or during observation, a lack of awareness of the cultural meanings of gestures or actions by professional staff may therefore lead to misinterpretation and misunderstanding.

Assessments must be made relative to the culture and social class of the patient. If you are not sure about the cultural norms, make enquiries. A good motto is, 'If in doubt, check it out'. Family and friends are usually only too willing to act as cultural interpreters, if the approach shows genuine interest and is non-judgmental. However, a word of warning is needed, not to rely on the family alone: in some cultural groups, the family may accept mild degrees of chronic illness as invalidism, and exaggerate the level of disability.

The rehabilitation plan

The next stage is for the multidisciplinary team to draw up a rehabilitation plan. Cultural issues loom large. Are the priorities to be set according to the patient's cultural norms and personal aspirations or those of the rehabilitation team?

There are two extremes to be avoided. One is to ignore the cultural dimension and devise the plan without taking account of the patient's cultural distinctiveness. Rehabilitation should be concerned with *relevant* social, domestic and work skills. The other extreme is to operate only with stereotypes of how people from that particular ethnic group live and what they would like to achieve. Prepare to be surprised!

Take the example of cooking. It is generally 'out of culture' for men to do the cooking in many ethnic minority households. Such men with psychiatric disabilities are less likely than indigenous Britons to live alone. On the other hand, many older Asian men came to Britain to work before sending for their wives and children: they may be able to cook and be proud to show off their skills. Including cooking skills in a rehabilitation plan might (or might not) be seen as irrelevant and encounter consumer resistance.

The experience of colleagues in Bradford is that people often enjoy doing something 'out of culture'. Some Asian men like learning to cook, others enjoy gardening, which is usually regarded as low-status work. As patients they may learn useful skills which they would never have had a chance to acquire had they not been on a rehabilitation programme.

In this respect, rehabilitation is like psychotherapy, which often finds itself running 'counter-culture', working against prevailing cultural norms (Bavington 1992). For example, an Asian woman may seek appropriate ways to become more assertive in her marriage, or to find new practical outlets for her abilities. Existing cultural norms are not the last word in the development of a person's potential.

Besides, cultures are always changing and developing: cultural values and ideals never stand still. The experience of living in Britain is changing the behaviour and values of members of non-Western cultural groups in profound ways. A knowledge of what happens in Pakistan, for example, is becoming less and less useful as a guide to understanding Pakistanis settled in Britain.

At times, a feeling of helplessness may overwhelm mental health professionals when faced with these cultural complexities. They may become acutely aware of their lack of understanding of the language and culture of the patient they are trying to help. They feel they are stepping on toes, doing or saying the wrong things, imposing Western values, creating obstacles and barriers to therapeutic progress. Such feelings tend to make us want to shy away from this area of work. I think that this response should be resisted. Yes, a professional from a different cultural background may make mistakes. But patients are usually forgiving: they recognise good motives and genuine concern on the part of those who are trying to help them.

Implementation

The implementing of a rehabilitation plan requires effective co-operation among the members of the multidisciplinary team. With some patients, the team may face difficulties with language and cultural understanding. The choice of an appropriate key worker may be important. Where the local area has a significant ethnic minority population, it is highly desirable that the team should include at least one representative of that ethnic group.

Engaging ethnic minority patients in the rehabilitation process may present its own problems. Their more relaxed attitude to time-keeping may cause some frustration among staff. Attendance at a day hospital may run into difficulty if there is a reluctance to use public transport. Requests for special arrangements need to be handled sensitively. For example some traditionally minded Muslims may ask for *halal* food and women-only areas (*purdah*).

Difficulties may arise in persuading medically orientated patients that rehabilitation *is* treatment: some may feel that only tablets or injections are effective. Certain types of activity may be more acceptable than others. In Bradford, colleagues have found that many South Asian patients prefer work-based occupational activities (woodwork, sewing, typing) to games and leisure activities. Work gives a sense of fulfilment and improves self-esteem. Art therapy and other expressive activities may be seen by some as pointless and affect their motivation to participate. However, other patients have participated in such groups and found them enjoyable and beneficial.

Afro-Caribbean patients are often more comparable with Caucasian patients in their attitudes to rehabilitation programmes. Outings are popular with all ethnic groups. Keep-fit and beauty/self-care groups seem to be appreciated by most women.

Many rehabilitation units encourage involvement in various 'satellite' activities that may be available in the hospital or the community. For example, in Bradford many Asian patients have benefited from attending a long-running Urdu-medium supportive psychotherapy group. If there are several patients from the same linguistic group in the rehabilitation unit, a special support group may be desirable.

Within the rehabilitation unit, there are many opportunities to break down ethnic suspicions. An Asian cookery group may be very popular among indigenous British patients. Asian women will often be delighted to pass on cooking skills and knowledge to others who want to learn, with significant effects on their confidence and self-esteem. Such collaboration and co-operation can carry far-reaching benefits for relationships within the rehabilitation unit.

Evaluation

A vital part of any rehabilitation process is the evaluation of how far its goals have been achieved. In Chapter 1, the overall aim of rehabilitation is stated as 'to restore the individual to his maximum level of independence, psychologically, socially, physically and economically'. The importance given to *independence* may be seen, to some extent, as a Western cultural emphasis. Traditional Asian families value *inter*dependence; they expect to support their family members if they have an illness. Perhaps a broader term like 'competence' would be more appropriate, encompassing cultural, social and individual goals of rehabilitation.

If the goals of rehabilitation are not achieved, it will be important to consider whether there are cultural or attitudinal reasons for this failure. The rehabilitation plan may not have been sufficiently culturally sensitive and may have set unrealistic goals; or there may have been unforeseen cultural obstacles in the implementing of realistic goals.

Sometimes poor compliance and absenteeism may limit what can be achieved. The possible reasons for non-attendance need to be analysed. There may be a lack of understanding of the purpose and benefits of rehabilitation; the activities may be culturally irrelevant; mixed gender groups may be unacceptable; the patient may feel excluded because of limited comprehension of the English language; in the patient's cultural group, the sick role may demand rest rather than activity.

A failure to achieve the stated goals of rehabilitation is likely to result from a combination of 'patient factors' and 'service factors'. The challenge to the rehabilitation service is to keep cultural obstacles to a minimum, to strive for greater cultural sensitivity, so as to increase the likelihood of a satisfactory outcome.

Discharge/placement

Decisions about discharge of patients hinge on the type of family and social support available. Patterns of family life and family structure vary greatly among ethnic minorities. Many South Asians belong to a traditional extended family which offers both support and control over family members (Lau 1986).

In the extended family system, *authority* is largely conferred by age and rank; all important decisions are taken by the head of the household. Highly structured *kinship ties* define the individual's role, duties and obligations within the larger family. *Parenting functions* are not restricted to the biological parents; shared or multiple parenting is common. *Adolescence* has different developmental tasks from the West, with less emphasis on separation and individuation. *Marriage* carries wholly different expectations, and the choice of marital partner is usually made by the parents. Aspects of decision making and financial interdependence may be retained even though the family members are dispersed geographically.

Many Afro-Caribbeans, on the other hand, have a more informal family structure. The experience of slavery has had a profound effect on marriage and child-rearing (Burke 1986). The responsibility for bringing up children often falls largely on the mother, who may not have the support of the children's father or wider family unit.

These differences in family structure affect the task of involving the family in the rehabilitation process. Asian families may wish to look after their own members, rejecting offers of professional help. Afro-Caribbeans may welcome help, but may have limited coping resources within the family.

As a consequence, Asians are probably less likely than Afro-Caribbeans or Caucasians to be placed in hostel accommodation. Attendance at out-patient appointments may be more irregular with certain ethnic minority groups and requires more vigorous domiciliary follow-up.

SOME CURRENT ISSUES AND PROSPECTS

Service provision

A major dilemma facing those who plan psychiatric services for ethnic minorities is between a separate unit or facility and an integrated psychiatric service. Are the mental health needs of ethnic minority patients best served by a distinct and identifiable service, with all the risks of marginalising them further? Or does the ethical and political consideration of avoiding any suggestion of apartheid demand a fully integrated service?

At times, a rehabilitation programme for ethnic minority patients may require separate activities. This can pose tricky ethical dilemmas. Few would argue in favour of a wholly separate department for ethnic minority patients. Yet a good rehabilitation service needs to be individually tailored and culturally sensitive.

If no specialist facilities in transcultural psychiatry are developed, will the necessary professional skills ever be acquired, or new clinical approaches to assessment and treatment be pioneered? What is required is not a different standard of psychiatry, but the opportunity to offer the same standard of service to people who may be disadvantaged at present by reason of language, culture or ethnicity.

There are also dilemmas around the recruitment of mental health professionals from the ethnic minorities, especially from the Afro-Caribbean community where few reach professional status. There are substantial numbers of South Asian psychiatrists employed in the NHS, but they may encounter difficulties if they come from a different religious, linguistic or social class background from their South Asian patients. Attempts at selective recruitment and training from among British-born Asian or Afro-Caribbeans may not succeed in improving services for these ethnic minorities, since they may not return to work in the same community but prefer to seek employment in other areas of the country, unless suitably encouraged.

Ethical and political issues

The current climate of racial politics in Britain gives rise to many dilemmas for mental health professionals. There are those who have argued that only a black person may treat a black person: that the imbalance of power and social status is so great between black and white people that any therapeutic alliance between a black patient and a white professional is intrinsically harmful. From a cultural viewpoint, some might insist that only a person who has grown up in a village in the Punjab can really understand a Punjabi woman who presents in emotional distress.

On the other hand, it may sometimes be advantageous that the therapist and patient have different cultural backgrounds. A therapist who does not share all the hidden cultural assumptions with the patient may have a clearer view of the patient's difficulties. In Bradford, many girls of Asian parentage who were born in Britain prefer a therapist from the majority community, who they believe will endorse aspirations that may run counter to their family and their community.

However, a particular problem arises where the patient has been subject to racial harassment or has been the victim of a racist attack. This requires skilled psychotherapy; it may be difficult for white therapists to undertake this work, unless they feel confident in handling the powerful negative transference that may arise towards a representative of white society.

A way forward?

What can be done to keep transcultural psychiatry within

mainstream British psychiatry, rather than becoming a marginalised minority interest? In my view, any mental health team offering a psychiatric service to ethnic minority groups should contain a wide ethnic mix among its members. The hope is that friendships will grow up between members of the multi-ethnic team which will dissolve racial and cultural stereotyping. Every mental health professional must examine his or her attitude and assumptions towards members of other ethnic groups. Few, if any, human beings are free of negative attitudes to people who are different.

In building a multi-racial mental health team, any negative or discriminatory behaviour among team members needs to be identified and brought into the open. Each person should 'own' their bit of racial prejudice, but must not be brow-beaten into taking on the responsibility and guilt for racism in other members of their ethnic group. It is only by such honesty and the building-up of trust and goodwill that team members can offer each other the professional support and encouragement needed when faced with the inevitable tensions and difficulties encountered in this kind of work. Mental health professionals cannot change British society, but they can set an example of multi-racial teamwork in the task of bringing good psychiatric care to their ethnic minority patients.

There are many difficulties in offering relevant psychiatric services to ethnic minorities in Britain. What is urgently needed is for all mental health professionals to receive more training in the appreciation of cultural factors in mental illness, and to develop a greater sensitivity to the effects of racial and social disadvantage.

Acknowledgements

While writing this chapter, I have benefited greatly from discussions with several colleagues at Lynfield Mount Hospital, Bradford; especially John Bavington, Kath Mashinter and Jill Vogler.

REFERENCES

Bavington J T 1992 The Bradford experience. In Kareen J, Littlewood R (eds) Intercultural therapy: themes, interpretations and practice. Blackwell Scientific Publications, Oxford

Burke A W 1986 Racism, prejudice and mental illness. In: Cox J L (ed) Transcultural Psychiatry, Ch. 9. Croom Helm, London

Furnham A, Bochner S 1986 Culture shock: psychological reactions to unfamiliar environments. Methuen, London

Ineichen B 1990 The mental health of Asians in Britain. British Medical Journal 300: 1669–1670

Lau A 1986 Family therapy. In: Cox J L (ed) Transcultural psychiatry. Croom Helm, London

Lipsedge M 1991 Culture influences on psychiatry. Current Opinion in Psychiatry 4: 324–330

Mumford D B, Bavington J T, Bhatnagar K S, Hussain Y, Mirza S, Naraghi M M 1991 The Bradford Somatic Inventory: a multi-ethnic inventory of somatic symptoms reported by anxious and depressed patients in Britain and the Indo-Pakistan Subcontinent. Br J Psychiatry 158: 379–386

Rack P R 1982 Race, culture and mental disorder. Tavistock, London

Tyler E B 1874 The origins of culture. Reprinted 1958; Harper & Row, New York

FURTHER READING

Cox J L (ed) 1986 Transcultural psychiatry. Croom Helm, London

Furnham A, Bochner S 1986 Culture shock: psychological reactions to unfamiliar environments. Methuen, London

Kleinman A, Good B J (eds) 1985 Culture and depression. University of California Press, Berkeley

Leff J P 1988 Psychiatry around the globe: a transcultural view, 2nd edn. Gaskell, London

Rack P R 1982 Race, culture and mental disorder. Tavistock, London

Watson J L (ed) 1977 Between two cultures: migrants and minorities in Britain. Blackwell, Oxford

11. Substance abuse

Ben Thomas

If you'll believe in me, I'll believe in you.
Lewis Carroll **Through the Looking-Glass**

This chapter is concerned with the rehabilitation of people who abuse drugs and alcohol. Contemporary substance abuse services attempt to view treatment and rehabilitation as part of the same process; the previous dichotomy between the two has been identified as counter-productive. Short-term treatment responses to substance abuse have produced limited results. For many people, a long-term response is required involving effective co-ordinated arrangements between health and social services' authorities, primary health care teams and voluntary agencies. Services have undergone many changes during the past few years, most notably the move from remote, specialist in-patient facilities to those which are more easily accessible and locally based. Much of the chapter describes the different types of facilities available and the services they offer. Traditionally services for people who abuse alcohol have developed separately from those for people who abuse drugs, and this is reflected in the literature. In reality this division is artificial. Many of the principles underlying rehabilitation programmes are similar if not the same and where an attempt is made to reflect this mutuality, alcohol may be substituted for drugs and vice versa. However, for the sake of clarity some services are described separately. Recent recommendations particularly in the area of training suggest a more integrated approach to substance problems. This is reflected by the sharing of many popular treatment approaches and preventative programmes. Most importantly rehabilitation is not just about underlying principles, interventions or facilities; it is about the people who provide the services and how they interact with the people who require help. For too long people who abuse substances have been stereotyped and stigmatised. Perhaps the biggest change is in the area of professional attitudes towards a more thoughtful and responsive approach.

INTRODUCTION

The increase in the prevalence of HIV infection amongst intravenous drug users has once more brought substance abuse to the forefront of social debate. The controversial nature of substance abuse is highlighted by the polarisation of opinion regarding the provision of sterile injecting equipment to drug users and the wider debate of drug legislation. The harmful consequences of drug abuse have largely been ignored by the general public. The increase in the incidence of AIDS among injecting drug users has been influential in raising awareness amongst the general population about drug abuse probably for more selfish reasons rather than genuine concern or understanding of drug users. Professionals continue to grapple with the problem. Many now support the philosophy of risk reduction and harm minimisation, while others feel that such a policy is condoning, if not positively encouraging drug misuse and dependency. There also remain those whose impulse is to blame, reproach and moralise. Just like people with HIV infection, those who use mind-altering substances are accused of only having themselves to blame and thought to be undeserving of professional help and public expenditure. Recent Government proposals begin to address this debate. In the Government report 'The Health of the Nation' (1991) a balance between individual responsibility and Government action is strongly recommended. The area of substance abuse straddles this precarious balance. There is considerable emphasis in the report on the need for people to change their behaviour, particularly in the areas of smoking, alcohol consumption, safer sex and intravenous drug use. The Government also recognises its need to intervene in these areas not only in terms of prevention and health promotion but also in the form of law and regulation.

The nature of substance abuse is complex and compounded by the different substances which are currently used, the variety of effects produced and its political, social, legal and medical consequences. In the space of one chapter it is not possible to summarise the major conceptual changes and all the developments which have taken place in the area of addiction. For the most part the focus is on rehabilitation of people who abuse drugs and alcohol and current service provision. The apparent failure of treatment in terms of outcome frequently highlighted in the substance abuse literature (Thorley 1983, Allsop & Saunders 1988) means that rehabilitation support and maintenance are essential components in the effective management of those affected.

The diffuse nature of substance abuse has produced an evolving multidisciplinary approach to the variety of problems caused. Innovative services with easy access have developed including telephone help lines, needle exchange clinics, drop-in centres and outreach schemes. While for the most part new services seem to be community orientated there is still thought to be a need for hospitalisation in some cases. Admissions are generally of a shorter duration and are followed up with planned rehabilitation programmes which may include therapeutic residential programmes and rehabilitation halfway houses. Health workers have begun to organise individually tailored rehabilitation programmes around the biological, psychological and social factors that shape each person's addiction needs, behaviours and associated problems.

UNDERSTANDING SUBSTANCE ABUSE

Regardless of the causes there has been a gradual transformation in society's general attitude towards substance abuse, from regarding it as a sin or crime to considering it as a sickness or disease. For some such a shift is seen as nothing more than another example of the medicalisation of social problems. However, the logical argument presented by Conrad and Schneider (1980) that to abuse substances one somehow has to get the substance into one's body immediately legitimates medicine's concern with the problem.

The psychiatric disease model applied to substance abuse in which addiction is seen as an uncontrollable symptom of an underlying disease has been severely criticised over the years. Although medical intervention and detoxification often remain central to the treatment of people who abuse substances it is now generally regarded in terms of a health problem rather than a strict medical problem, addictive behaviour being regarded as within the individual's control. It is more commonly accepted that biological, psychological and sociocultural factors contribute to both alcohol and drug problems. Psychiatrists have begun to emphasise the increasingly complex nature of individuals who abuse substances. Frosch (1990) suggests that one of the important contributions of

DSM III (1980) is the introduction of multiple axes, which has enabled psychiatrists to think of personality as well as disease, of physical illness as well as mental illness, of external stressors and functional abilities and of the social cultural context.

There are numerous theories and models which have been proposed to explain substance abuse. While each adds to our general understanding of the concept they also direct our beliefs and subsequently determine the basis of treatment and rehabilitation programmes (Shaffer et al 1989). Some of the theories proposed are so strongly held that despite research evidence to the contrary they remain entrenched beliefs. Examples include the proposition that people who abuse substances have predisposing characteristics that consistently differentiate them from those who are not substance abusers. Since theory determines the nature of potential solutions then it also affects whether a substance abuser will accept or reject the service offered and their lay explanation of addiction. The absolute necessity of abstinence from alcohol has been the guiding principle of many treatment programmes, based on the belief that once an alcoholic always an alcoholic, or once a drug user always a drug user. The idea of a patient returning to controlled drinking becomes a practical impossibility. Until recently this was the basis of all treatment offered, and thereby excluded the possibility of teaching controlled drinking or controlled drug use and individually tailored treatment and rehabilitation programmes. Miller (1990) discusses some common beliefs about alcoholism treatments that are not substantiated by research findings. He suggests that a large number of alcoholics recover without ever undergoing treatment. This is consistent with the research finding that long-term recovery is much less influenced by treatment events than by experience and conditions in the individual's life following treatment and therefore strengthens the case for rehabilitation. Currently universal explanations are continued against; it seems that no single treatment and rehabilitation approach is optimal for all or even most people who are substance abusers. The pervasive and diffuse nature of substance abuse ensures that responding to such problems requires an active and extended process.

REHABILITATION

It is generally accepted that ideally treatment and rehabilitation should occur concurrently. Traditionally in the United Kingdom this seldom occurs since treatment is the responsibility of the health service while rehabilitation is a statutory provision of social services. The introduction of the Health Service and Community Care Act (1990) is designed to bring about more effective collaboration and co-operation between these services for the benefit of those people requiring help. Rehabilitation attempts to maximise on an individual's functioning in a supportive manner, while acknowledging that there may be persistent disabilities. It is a continuous process of interaction between the person's disabilities and the social environment. This is very different to the previous notion of treatment which is seen as short-term concentrating on the amelioration of symptoms. Previously rehabilitation, if it occurred at all, was something only added on when the patient was symptom free, aimed at assisting them to return to independent functioning. The Report of the Advisory Council on the Misuse of Drugs 'Treatment and Rehabilitation' (DHSS 1982) criticised the dichotomy between treatment and rehabilitation as counter-productive. The report suggests that a long-term response is required, related to the learning of new skills and coping mechanisms. Ideally the overall care of substance abusers requires the integration of treatment and rehabilitation in a co-ordinated manner which tries to meet patients' needs by limiting their problems, utilising their personal resources and building on their competencies.

Thorley (1983) suggests that rehabilitation can occur from a basis of abstinence or of harm-free alcohol or drug use. In the past too many patients have inevitably failed because of unrealistic goals imposed upon them by professionals. It is important, therefore, to determine mutually acceptable goals which can be structured on a short-term to long-term basis.

Inclusion of the individual in the planning of a rehabilitation programme is essential, and the starting point is a basic understanding and acceptance between the professional and the patient about the meaning and basis of the problems. Assessment should be directed towards understanding the causes and consequences from biological, psychological and sociocultural perspectives. Ghodse (1989) suggests that careful, detailed and thorough assessment of individuals is essential if they are to receive effective help. As well as identifying the causes and consequences of the problem, it is necessary to establish the nature and severity of the problem and the strengths and weaknesses of the patient and his life situation. Kaplan (1990) suggests that help must be based upon an understanding of the symbolic significance of substance abuse for the individual. Programmes have a low probability of effectiveness if they do not take into account the meaning of substance abuse to the individual. The programme should involve an understanding of why an individual adopted the substance abuse to begin with, what functions the substance abuse serves and what loss would be created by the absence of this response.

MULTIDISCIPLINARY TEAMWORK

The variety and complexity of the problems encountered by substance abusers require a multidisciplinary response. A multiple drug user may have psychological, physical, financial, legal and social problems and no single discipline can deal with all these problems. Multidisciplinary teamwork is described fully in Chapter 8. Co-ordinated team functioning is particularly important with substance abusers to provide continuity over time and to ensure close liaison with the numerous agencies which may be involved. It is important that team members share the same philosophy and approach and are not at variance with each other and with the defined programme. The lead should be taken by the professional or discipline most appropriate to the individual concerned.

REHABILITATION FACILITIES

Rehabilitative care will vary according to the underlying service philosophy and whether the aim of the programme is for total abstinence or support, harm reduction and risk minimisation. The needs of the individual are paramount and should determine the services provided. Some patients may require information and advice, others may require in-patient hospital care or enter into drug and alcohol treatment facilities. Others attend out-patient departments, and some may require partial hospitalisation or placement in a residential home. The nature of substance abuse requires a flexible approach and a continuum of rehabilitative programmes. Thorley (1983) suggests that each individual will need a specific response and perhaps a long-term perspective. Short-term prison or hospital-based enforced abstinence almost always leads to relapse whereas long-term out-patient treatment allowing growth of personal responsibility and choice seems to have a better success rate.

Meeting the patient's long-term needs will inevitably involve community care and often includes the use of voluntary organisations, support groups and the primary health care team. Much of the work involved in rehabilitation of substance abusers includes assisting with practical issues such as housing problems, welfare benefits and employment. The Health Service and Community Care Act (1990) involving joint commissioning is meant to diminish the liaison difficulties experienced between health care services and social services' departments. The development of case management is expected to provide effective co-ordinated arrangements between health and social services, primary health care teams and the voluntary agencies and a more comprehensive approach incorporating health and social needs.

The task of providing adequate community care for substance abusers must not be underestimated. In 1989, The Advisory Council on the Misuse of Drugs recommended that general practitioners take a more active role in the care of drug users. However, research has continually shown that general practitioners often feel poorly equipped to treat drug users and are therefore reluctant to take an active role in their care. A study which examined the attendance of heroin users at general practice surgeries demonstrated that opiate users had significantly more 'did not attend' episodes than the control group. Although the total general practice consultation rate for heroin was high, the rate for routine or general medical care was lower than expected (Neville et al 1988). Milne & Keen (1988) conducted a postal survey involving 5% of GPs in England and Wales. Their results suggest that although most GPs considered opiate misuse to be a priority concern, they regarded users to be difficult to manage, beyond their level of competence to treat and less acceptable as patients than others in need of care.

The advent of HIV has clearly identified the need to provide primary health care for, and to give health education to, drug users. Datt & Feinmann (1990) describe the setting up of a team consisting of a doctor, two nurse specialists and a psychologist whose intention was to provide primary health care and health education about the spread of HIV to drug users. Over a period of 12 months they saw 171 patients. A total of 35% of the patients were transient either living with friends or of no fixed abode, and only 38% of the patients were registered with a GP. The majority of referrals (77%) were made by prescribing drug agencies and 13% were made directly by the patients. Datt & Feinmann suggest that their results may reflect the drug users' contact with various services which depends upon their ease of access to the services.

Although there will never be adequate resources or responses to meet the need of substance abusers, there are a variety of treatment and rehabilitation options available to help individuals with their particular dependency problems. Some are directed at the underlying causes which may have led to substance abuse or its continuation. Some help to resolve the problems associated with substance abuse and others deal more directly with the substance abuse behaviour, aiming to reduce or stop the behaviour regardless of associated problems. Not all programmes or interventions are suitable for every individual and many individuals require a mix of approaches. Rehabilitation is generally regarded as consisting of long-term change and this is thought to be particularly pertinent for substance abusers. This is not to deny the importance of short-term intervention but rather to emphasise that the two types of intervention should be initiated concurrently. Many of the interventions often collectively described as rehabilitation include counselling, psychotherapy, cognitive therapy, family therapy, group support, vocational training and behavioural therapy. Two psychological approaches identified as being superior to traditional in-patient treatment are 'community reinforcement' (Azrin et al 1982) and 'relapse prevention' (Chaney et al 1978). The community reinforcement approach involves patients being trained in the skills needed to function effectively in their social environment. Reasons for relapse prevention amongst alcoholic patients have been categorised by Marlatt (1978). Using this categorisation, the study by Chaney et al (1978) evaluated a short-term skill training intervention that taught male alcoholic patients appropriate behaviours in problematic situations. The group exposed to skill training showed considerable performance improvement in response to situations associated with drinking behaviour and relapse compared with control groups. A one-year post-treatment follow-up indicated that skill training decreased the duration and severity of relapse episodes. While having limitations, skill training is used as one component of a multimodal approach to relapse in problem drinking and drug addiction.

SERVICES FOR PEOPLE WHO ABUSE ALCOHOL

The Government report 'The Health of the Nation' (HMSO 1991) suggests that in the UK one in four men, and one in 12 women are drinking more than the recommended sensible drinking limits, the sensible limit being 21 units of alcohol per week for men and 14 units per week for women. The increasing rise in alcohol consumption is accompanied by a rise in alcohol-related problems.

Detoxification and in-patient services

Traditionally, the main approach to alcohol problems has been the medical treatment of alcoholism linked to the goal of abstinence. The main thrust has been detoxification services, whose aim is to remove alcohol from the patient's body or, as it is more generally referred to, 'drying out'. A number of specialised detoxification centres have been established but this process also occurs within hospital-based services. Lack of counselling, rehabilitation and inadequate follow-up have resulted in such services being seen in terms of 'patching up' patients. Similar problems were identified in general psychiatric hospitals which eventually led to more specialist alcoholism treatment units. By 1975, there were more than 30 such units throughout England and Wales. Alcoholism treatment units have recently been criticised because of their emphasis on in-patient status, the narrow range of treatments they offer and failure to demonstrate their effectiveness (DHSS 1978).

Miller (1990) refutes the widely held belief that the hospital is the only or most effective way to address alcohol problems. He finds no reasonable support for this notion among the controlled studies on treatment outcome. There seems to be no overall advantage for residential, intensive or longer treatment over less expensive alternatives. Those with more severe alcohol problems and limited support systems, however, may fare better with an abstinence goal and may have increased benefit from intensive treatment.

Out-patient care

A growing body of work has begun to demonstrate that out-patient treatment and rehabilitation are therapeutically more beneficial and cost-effective than in-patient services. Day hospital and day centres have been developed in the belief that rehabilitation and treatment can be provided just as easily and effectively as in-patient services, but with the added advantages of not artificially removing the patient from his home environment and natural community. While some units continue to emphasise intensive in-patient programmes, day care or community-based services including domiciliary detoxification are becoming increasingly popular (Stockwell 1987) and some have abandoned residential services altogether (Ettore 1988).

Community alcohol teams

In the UK, the Advisory Committee on Alcoholism has produced a model of an integrated pattern of service provision for people who abuse alcohol (DHSS 1978). Community alcohol teams were established to provide such an integrated service by forming the middle ground between primary health care and specialist services. Primary health care workers' reluctance to work with people who abuse alcohol originates from role inadequacy and lack of support. Clement (1987) suggests that community alcohol teams can be effective in enhancing the therapeutic commitment to primary health care workers but this change is often frustrated by lack of interest and support from service managers.

SERVICES FOR PEOPLE WHO ABUSE DRUGS

As with people who abuse alcohol, drug abusers may require a range of services including in-patient drug units, specialist drug clinics, community projects, primary health care and voluntary agencies. Drug treatment facilities can be broadly divided into prescribing and non-prescribing agencies. Prescribing agencies will offer a substitute to heroin, most commonly oral methadone and occasionally injectable methadone. Non-prescribing agencies are often street based and offer support, advice, counselling and sometimes referral for treatment. Contemporary services employ an integrated approach which is user-friendly, locally based and easily accessible. Historically this was not always the case; the treatment and rehabilitation of people who abused drugs were regarded as specialist areas. Strang (1991) suggests that up until the 1980s drug services in the UK conformed to the 'specialist model' where one agency was usually responsible for the service provision, and all other doctors regarded drug takers outside their remit and would refer such cases on to the specialist agency. While specialist services continue to exist, there is a much more integrated approach which enables a filtering out of users and a more efficient and effective use of resources. Users who present to a member of the primary health care team are assessed and may receive care at this level while others may be referred on to a specialist service according to need.

Community drug teams

The development of community drug teams has assisted in this approach and provides support and competence at district level. Such teams consist of two or three full-time workers including a community psychiatric nurse, a social worker and sessional medical input. The rationale behind their introduction was to encourage local practitioners to become more involved in the provision of care to drug users. Important aspects of the role of community drug workers include liaising with other agencies, educating and training other professionals and establishing supportive professional relationships.

In-patient units

Many users referred to the community drug team require residential treatment. The community drug team worker assists the user to explore available options and choose the most suitable. While awaiting admission support is provided by the community drug team worker. In-patient units provide a safe environment in which patients can be detoxified from drugs and engage in treatment within a residential setting. Patients may be admitted for a variety of reasons including assessment of a drug abuse problem, for stabilisation of the dose of their drugs, for detoxification, for secondary complications either physical, mental, or both, and sometimes to assist in the general sorting out of their chaotic life-style. Rehabilitation forms part of the programme from the outset and the aim is to help patients make positive steps in improving their life-style while becoming and remaining drug free.

To encourage easy access many services have adopted a flexible approach, for example the City Roads Project in London offers a 24-hour service. After initial assessment, the project offers a 3-week residential stay when detoxification takes place. During this time, patients are supported by counselling and social work input. Many patients are referred on to therapeutic communities or other residential rehabilitation hostels.

Therapeutic communities

Therapeutic communities have a long tradition both in the USA and the UK. Their use for substance abusers has long been recognised as a response to helping people who have undergone detoxification from relapsing. Within a closed community they provide structure and support, time and space for individuals to adapt to their new life-style and to learn to live without drugs and alcohol. The basic rehabilitative model employed is a 24-hour residential programme with daily schedules involving various activities. Emphasis is on the integration of residents into society. Mainly through the use of group processes, therapy involves motivating residents, changing negative attitudes, values and behaviour, and the acquisition of social and vocational skills. Programmes vary both in their length of duration and the amount of structure provided. Traditional programmes usually consider the optimal length of treatment to be at least 15 months. Deleon and Andrews (1978) found favourable treatment outcome related to time in treatment. The longer residents stay the greater the likelihood of sustained post-treatment success. Presently there are no longer any minimum time requirements and Phoenix House, probably the most well-known therapeutic community, now operates a special programme for employed people that involves only an initial three months of residential care, followed by a year of out-patient treatment.

Hostels

Recognition that newly abstinent drug-dependent individuals often return to their previous life-styles and situations, which put them at risk of relapsing, also led to the development of hostel accommodation. This type of accommodation provides the opportunity for ex-users to consolidate their positive experience of withdrawal. The pressures and worries of daily life are removed; however, staff supervision is minimal enabling residents to gradually regain independence and prepare for their life in the outside world. Hostels provide a bridge between more structured residential care and the world outside. Residential rehabilitation houses have been criticised because most houses are only prepared to accept drug-free clients and often those who are drug free are not able to take up residential places because of personal circumstances. Most houses refuse to take couples, have no facilities for children and require that the resident gives up full-time employment.

The ROMA (Rehabilitation of Metropolitan Addicts) drug project offers an alternative approach. Its aim is to provide a stable environment for people taking opiates on a long-term maintenance basis, assisting them to establish a more settled existence while still taking drugs. The project provides accommodation specifically for drug users notified to the Home Office and receiving a regular prescription for opiates from a drug treatment clinic or general practitioner. It provides support in the form of group therapy, counselling and outside activities.

Outreach programmes

Drug treatment services are in contact with only a small proportion of drug users. People who abuse often have a very chaotic life-style and are suspicious of professional and statutory agencies. Watters et al (1986) found that 53% of drug users contacted in the community would not enter treatment 'even if it was available tomorrow'. The advent of HIV has prompted many drug services to explore alternative ways to make contact with as many of these users as possible to ensure they have access to advice and counselling on risk reduction and treatment services. Many authorities now employ outreach workers in an attempt to find ways of making contact with drug users who are unwilling to attend or use formal drug services. A number of different approaches are being tried, and many outreach programmes distribute bleach to drug users with advice on the procedure to follow for sterilising injecting equipment. Many agencies target people with different needs, for example, the increasing homeless population and inner-city prostitutes. This type of work is a major departure from the more traditional role played by agency-based services but the success of this method of working relies heavily on the skills of the outreach worker. A number of programmes are now using ex-users for outreach work (Friedman et al 1988).

Needle and syringe exchange schemes

The recognition of the spread of HIV among intravenous drug users has produced a variety of measures to try and prevent further transmission. One of the most effective ways has been to increase the availability of sterile needles and syringes to discourage sharing of injecting equipment. A number of needle and syringe exchange schemes have been implemented with a subsequent decrease in behaviours associated with risk of HIV infection (Watters et al 1988), although causality has been difficult to determine. The range of services offered by needle and syringe exchange schemes varies considerably. Some include drug counselling referral for treatment and detoxification, information on legal matters, housing and welfare benefits, free condoms, health education and advice on safer sex practices.

One of the major problems in setting up needle and syringe exchange schemes is finding suitable venues. Because of their contact with large numbers of intravenous drug users, staff of drug and alcohol treatment units would be ideally placed to carry out this work. However, they often subscribe to a treatment philosophy emphasising the promotion of abstinence as the main goal. The provision of sterile injection equipment is often regarded as irreconcilable with this philosophy since it undermines the therapeutic success of treatment programmes and condones further use of illicit drugs. Nevertheless, drug dependency clinics are under considerable pressure to adopt more flexible approaches to encourage injecting drug users to adopt safer practices.

THE ROLE OF COUNSELLING AND EDUCATION

All health care workers involved in rehabilitation require the ability to engage the patient, place them at ease, communicate with the patient effectively, counsel the patient and provide health education. They often need to perform these skills with the patient's relatives and carers. The effectiveness of these basic interpersonal skills makes a significant contribution to the overall success of the rehabilitation programme and the quality of the service.

Alcohol and drug counselling has primarily been concerned with providing advice. This usually occurs on an individual basis and has now been extended to include telephone help lines. There are of course different models of counselling, and according to the approach the counsellor helps the client to identify problems and needs and then explores the various options available to the client and the consequences of such action. The client is helped to decide the best course of action and supported in following the chosen course.

A whole range of problems may be dealt with in counselling sessions including relationships with family and friends, work and study issues and more recently risk behaviours associated with HIV infection. Commonly encountered problems include denial, dependency and low self-esteem. Most patients at some stage deny they are unable to control their substance abusing behaviour. The denial is often related to the stigma attached to alcohol or drug abuse. Denial also protects the person from admitting that he is unable to control his behaviour. It seems essential that denial be overcome and that the patient admits to the problem as the first step towards making the decision to seek help and support. Many health care workers now use a behavioural contract when working with substance abusers. The health care worker and the patient discuss and agree on realistic behavioural objectives for the patient, which are then written down and signed by the worker and the patient. Most workers insist that the patient is drug- and alcohol-free at the time when they attend a counselling session. This communicates the belief that the patient is able to control his behaviour and take positive action on his own behalf.

Patient education is an essential component of all rehabilitation programmes. Substance abusers should be well informed about the drug they have used, the biological and psychological effects on the person. Health education material has come under critical review with the scaremongering tactics of the early AIDS warning campaigns. Broadly based health campaigns have been found to be the most effective. Such approaches concentrate on positive messages which encourage healthy life-styles rather than concentrating on what is dangerous or forbidden. Recognition that intravenous drug users are at risk of HIV transmission has added weight to the argument that greater emphasis should be placed on the need to prevent or reduce the harm associated with drug use and dependence. It is argued that supplying intravenous drug users with sterile needles and syringes will encourage safer injecting practices and prevent sharing injection equipment, thereby reducing the likelihood of transmission of HIV between users and from them to their sexual partners. Stimson et al (1988) have reported that many intravenous drug users have sexual partners who are non-drug users and there is an increase of HIV transmission amongst this population. As previously discussed this preventative campaign remains controversial. The advantages and disadvantages have been widely debated and well documented. Research results available so far suggest that substantial numbers of intravenous drug users have modified their injecting behaviour (Mulleady & Sherr 1988). More research is required to substantiate these findings and to establish if the changed behaviour is maintained. However, such research is problematic because HIV is not exclusively transmitted by sharing contaminated injection equipment and because of the long time-lag between infection with HIV and seroconversion.

SUPPORT GROUPS AND VOLUNTARY ORGANISATIONS

The previous lack of adequate statutory rehabilitation services gave rise to the interventions of charitable organisations many of whom were of religious origins. The self-help movement provides non-professional support and has developed according to local needs. A number of support and self-help groups have been formed in response to a variety of drug problems, such as tranquilliser dependence and opiate dependence. In recent years, groups of HIV-positive intravenous drug users have developed in some parts of the United Kingdom. The commonality of all self-help groups is of mutual aid and support. They provide an essential forum for sharing information and common experiences. Furthermore they provide social acceptance and social identity for people who have become isolated because of their addiction problems.

The most established support groups are Alcoholics Anonymous and Narcotics Anonymous. Both organisations provide a caring supportive structure and are run by ex-users, carefully preserving the anonymity of members. Open to all those who seek help, participants follow a 12-step programme that insists upon total abstinence. They share a common philosophy which has been adopted by other organisations, of encouraging people to take one day at a time and to acknowledge and accept their powerlessness over addiction. Although reported correlations between attendance at Alcoholics Anonymous and abstinence are common, casual interpretation is difficult. Miller's (1990) survey of research which addressed the treatment strategies of Alcoholics Anonymous, reports that not one of the four studies that qualify as controlled studies found a beneficial treatment effect efficacy of Alcoholics Anonymous.

The most widely adopted model of treatment in the USA is called the Minnesota method. This consists of a programme that adopts Alcoholics Anonymous/Narcotics Anonymous ideology. Treatment is based around the first five steps and attendance at meetings is an essential component of aftercare. It provides a programme that is tailored according to individual needs and care is provided by members of the multidisciplinary team. A number of houses have recently been established in the UK either based on this approach or using some elements of the method. People usually live in these houses for three to six months; however, day attendance is also available in some cases. Examples in the London area include Headway Halfway House which has 10 beds for women only, and Thurston House which has 21 beds for men only. The Standing Conference on Drug Abuse (SCODA), a voluntary organisation centrally funded, acts as a co-ordinating body for all voluntary services dealing with drug abusers.

TRAINING IN SUBSTANCE ABUSE

The provision of suitable training is essential for the wide range of professionals involved in the rehabilitation of substance abusers. However, research into the training on substance abuse amongst various professional groups has demonstrated that while this is an increasing health problem it is hardly touched upon in most curricula. In a survey of medical schools in the United Kingdom, Glass (1989) found that on average only 14 hours were spent in formal education such as lectures and seminars on substance abuse amongst medical students in a five- or six-year course. The lack of significant training has been continually highlighted in a series of reports by the Advisory Council on the Misuse of Drugs. Glass & Strang (1991) suggest that there are a number of limitations to overcome when considering how to go about implementing a training programme. Negative attitudes to substance abusers is one such barrier. Many people still hold stereotypical views of substance abusers which see them as useless, destitute individuals. Secondly, response to treatment is thought to be so poor that it is hardly worth trying to treat substance abusers and thirdly, those treatments which have been shown to work have often emanated from non-medical disciplines.

In its latest report 'Problem Drug Use: A Review of Training' (HMSO 1990), the Advisory Council on the Misuse of Drugs suggests that wherever possible future training should be conducted on a substance problems basis rather than either drug or alcohol problems alone. The report recommends that each specialty should define minimal standards, that basic training should cover substance problems and that there is a need for standardisation and thorough evaluation of all training activities. The committee recommends the establishment of a National Drug

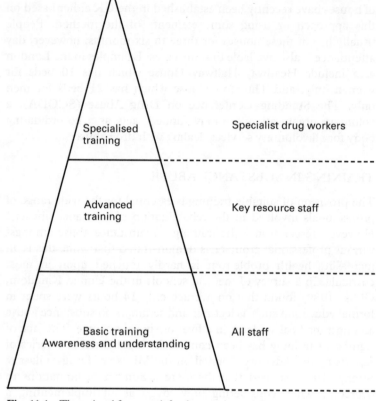

Fig. 11.1   Three tiered framework for drug worker training.

Training Development Agency and proposes a three-tiered approach to future training (see Fig. 11.1).

Farrell (1990) is critical of the report and compares the recommendations made to previous reports published in the last decade. He agrees that training requires a careful analysis of the attitudinal barriers of each discipline but suggests that it also requires a recognition of the genuine difficulties of incorporating change into existing treatment services. He argues that much of this will only be changed by the actual execution of good models of practice. Farrell suggests that the best way forward is to establish a strong network of national trainers, which will form the basis of an effective and organisationally coherent training system. Cranfield & Dixon (1990) examined in-service training courses in England, Scotland and the United States relating to HIV and AIDS and drug specialists. They provide a detailed analysis of current courses and examples of training techniques in 19 subject areas, including harm minimisation, safer sex, pre- and post-test counselling and bereavement. They suggest that drug services are experiencing rapid and radical changes and that training has a catalytic role to play in helping planners, managers and staff to cope with these changes. They identify key issues which trainers, agencies and funders need to address to enable professionals to cope with the impact of HIV and AIDS on their work with drug users and suggest that trainers need to examine ways of helping staff to integrate these themes into their daily practice.

CONCLUSION

From the discussion, it is evident that there is no universal treatment and rehabilitation approach that is solely the correct one in the drug and alcohol field. Providing rehabilitation for people with substance problems is a complex business. People who abuse substances are no longer regarded as a homogeneous group. It is recognised that they are a diverse group whose dependence needs differ and whose psychological, physical and social problems related to their dependence are extremely variable. Different interventions are needed to deal with specific problems and the preferences and needs of individuals. Services should be accessible, user-friendly, non-stigmatising, flexible and responsive to people's needs. In developing new services, innovation and imagination are required; old stereotypes of traditional roles must give way to more inter-agency respect and sharing of skills. Services should be provided by an integrated group of co-professionals in collaboration with voluntary agencies.

REFERENCES

Advising Council on Misuse of Drugs 1989 AIDS and drug misuse: report by the Advisory Council on Misuse of Drugs, Part 2.

Allsop S J, Saunders W 1988 The effectiveness of relapse programs. Cognitive-behavioural approaches to the treatment of drug and alcohol problems. In: Grenyer B F, Solowij N (eds) Monograph No. 7 National Drug and Alcohol Research Centre, University of New South Wales

Azrin N H, Sisson R W, Meyers R, Godfrey M 1982 Alcoholism treatment by disulfiram and community reinforcement therapy. Journal of Behavioural Therapy and Experimental Psychiatry 13: 105–112

Chaney E F, O'Leary M R, Marlett G A 1978 Skill training with alcoholics. Journal of Consulting and Clinical Psychology 46: 1092–1104

Clement S 1987 The Salford Experiment: an account of the community alcohol project. In: Stockwell T & Clement S (eds) Helping the problem drinker: new initiatives in community care. Croom Helm, London

Conrad P, Schneider J W 1980 Deviance and medicalization: from badness to sickness. CV Mosby, St Louis

Cranfield S, Dixon A (1990) Drug training, HIV and AIDS in the 1990s: a guide for training professionals. Health Education Authority, London

Datt N, Feinmann C 1990 Providing health care for drug users? British Journal of Addiction 85: 1571–1575

Deleon G, Andrews M 1978 Therapeutic community dropouts five years later: preliminary findings on self reported status. In: Smith U (ed) A multi-cultural view of drug abuse. Schenkman, Cambridge, Massachusetts, pp 369–378

DHSS 1978 Advisory Committee on Alcoholism: the pattern and range of services for problem drinkers. Department of Health and Social Security, London

DHSS 1982 Treatment and rehabilitation. Report of the treatment and rehabilitation working group of the Advisory Council on the Misuse of Drugs. HMSO, London

Ettore B 1988 A follow-up study of alcoholism treatment units: exploring consolidation and change. British Journal of Addiction 83: 57–65

Farrell M 1990 Beyond platitudes: problem drug use: a review of training. British Journal of Addiction 85: 1559–1562

Friedman A S, Grannick S 1990 Family therapy for adolescent drug abuse. Lexington Books, Massachusetts

Frosch W 1990 Multiproblem patients. Prologue to part III. In: Milkman H, Sederer L, (eds) Treatment choices for alcoholism and substance abuse. Lexington Books, Lexington, Massachusetts

Ghodse H 1989 Drugs and addictive behaviour: a guide to treatment. Blackwell Scientific Publications, Oxford

Glass I B 1989 Undergraduate training in substance abuse in the United Kingdom. British Journal of Addiction 84: 197–202

Glass I B, Strang J 1991 Professional training and substance abuse: the UK experience. In Glass I B (ed) The international handbook of addiction behaviour. Routledge, London

HMSO 1989 Caring for people: Community care in the next decade and beyond. HMSO, London

HMSO 1990 Problem drug use: a review of training. Report by the Advisory Council on the Misuse of Drugs. HMSO, London

HMSO 1991 The health of the nation: a consultative document for health in England. HMSO, London

Kaplan H 1990 From theory to practice: the planned treatment of drug users. A series of interviews. The International Journal of Addiction 25: 957–981

Marlatt G A 1978 Craving for alcohol, loss of control, and relapse: a cognitive behavioural analysis. In: Nathan P E, Marlatt G A, Loberg T (eds) Alcoholism: new directions in behavioural research and treatment. Plenum Press, New York

Miller W R 1990 Alcohol treatment alternatives: what works? In: Milkman H, Sederer L (eds) Treatment choices for alcoholism and substance abuse. Lexington Books, Lexington, Massachusetts

Milne R, Keen S 1988 Are general practitioners ready to prevent the spread of HIV? British Medical Journal 296: 533–535

Mulleady G, Sherr L 1988 Lifestyle factors for drug users in relation to risks for HIV and AIDS. British Journal of Clinical Psychology

Neville N G, McKelligan J F, Foster J 1988 Heroin users in general practice: ascertainment and features. British Medical Journal 296: 755–758

Shaffer D et al (eds) 1989 Prevention of mental disorders, alcohol and other drug use in children and adolescents. Office for Substance Abuse Prevention: US DHSS, Rockville M D

Stimson G V, Aldritt L, Dolan K, Donoghoe M 1988 Injecting equipment exchange schemes: a preliminary report on research. Monitoring Research Group, Sociology Department, Goldsmiths College, University of London

Stockwell T 1987 The Exeter home detoxification project. In: Stockwell T, Clement S (eds) Helping the problem drinker. Croom Helm, London

Strang J 1991 Service development and organisation: drugs. In: Glass I B (ed) The international handbook of addiction behaviour. Routledge, London

The Royal College of Psychiatrists 1987 Drug scenes: a report on drugs and drug dependence. The Royal College of Psychiatrists, London

Thorley A 1983 Problem drinkers and drug takers. In: Watts F N, Bennett D H (eds) Theory and practice of psychiatric rehabilitation. John Wiley, Chichester

Watters J K, Lura D M, Lura K W 1986 AIDS prevention and education services to intravenous drug users through the mid consortium to combat AIDS: administrative report on the first six months

Watters J K, Case P, Haung K, Cheng Y T, Lovrick J, Carlson J 1988 HIV seroepidemiology and behaviour change in intravenous drug users: progress report on the effectiveness of street-based prevention. IV International Conference on AIDS, Stockholm, Sweden, Abstract 85243

12. Old age

Ian Pullen

Old age is the most unexpected of all things that happen to a man.

Lev Trotsky **Diary in Exile 1935**

In most societies, one's age is of great importance both socially and legally. In Britain, it is illegal to leave school, have heterosexual intercourse or marry before the age of 16. We may not drive a car before 17 or vote before the age of 18. Much advertising is aimed at younger people who, because of their disposable income, are therefore 'important'.

At the other end of the scale, age is also important. At present in Britain, most women retire at 60 and men at 65. At these ages we are entitled to a state pension and, together with the very young and the handicapped, are exempt from certain payments. Like the handicapped, old people tend to be treated as a homogeneous group, the elderly.

Yet increasing numbers of people in the world are old. In Britain today, more than 10 million are over retirement age. The phenomenon of the bulk of the population surviving infancy and living well into their 70s and 80s is quite new and something to be proud of. Current negative attitudes to ageing may, in part, be the result of the time-lag between social change and a change in people's attitudes (Marshall 1991).

MYTHS OF OLD AGE

'Last scene of all.
That ends this strange, eventful history,
Is second childishness and mere oblivion,
Sans teeth, sans eyes, sans taste, sans everything.'

The traditional view of old age is spoken by Jacques in the familiar 'Seven Ages of Man' speech from *As You Like It* quoted above. In

181

other words, as people get older their 'minds go'. This is not the case. Even the very old, those over the age of 80, have only a one in five risk of having dementia. The vast majority of people will retain their faculties throughout their life.

Other myths dealt with in this chapter include:

'There are more old people about now because modern medicine is keeping them alive longer';
'Few people now look after their elderly relations';
'There is nothing that can be done for the person with dementia.'

But first, we must consider what happens normally as a person gets older.

NORMAL AGEING

Ageing is a normal biological process that happens to everyone. The rate of progress is very variable and is dictated largely by inherited genetic factors, but may be modified by factors such as trauma or illness.

Physical changes

Many physical changes, which have been happening slowly over decades, become more noticeable in the seventh decade. Drive and energy will be reduced from their peaks earlier in life. Appearance will change under the influence of reduced tissue elasticity and muscle bulk, and altered hormone levels. Bone resilience declines and joints may show signs of wear and tear. Chest movements and cardiac output are reduced.

Some of these changes may be masked by plastic (cosmetic) surgery or minimised by diet, exercise or hormone replacement therapy (HRT). The ageing process cannot be slowed down, but people can be encouraged to make the best of what they have got.

Sexual activity in old age was for a long time a taboo subject. Kinsey, in a small sample, found that a fifth of men over 60 were unable to manage sexual intercourse, and that this increased to four-fifths by the age of 80 (Kinsey et al 1948). Masters and Johnston (1970) considered a 'large part of post-menopausal sex drive in women is related directly to sexual habits established earlier in life'.

Psychological changes

These changes are even more variable. The quotation cited earlier from Trotsky's diary highlights how many people view old age as something that happens to other people.*

What is the attitude of older people to ageing? A Gallup poll survey of nearly 1 000 people aged over 60 reported that 78% agreed with the statement 'I never think of myself as old', with only 14% disagreeing (Gallup 1984). If you ask old people if they ever feel old, they tell you it is only when they are ill or feeling very unhappy (Marshall 1991).

Emotions are usually less turbulent and impulses slower, which may give rise to fewer ill-considered actions. Intellectual processes are slower and old people take on new information or ways of looking at things with less enthusiasm than is characteristic of youth, yet performance in the face of problems may remain excellent, supported by a wealth of accumulated experience (Bromley 1966).

With increasing age memory may be affected. For simple recent memory, this tends to be minimal, but may be greater for complex recent memory. The common belief that old people have an excellent memory for events of long ago may be illusory. Apparently good recall of past events may arise in part from skilful use of visual memories, and the old person's ability to make detailed statements about past events may be limited to selected topics of emotional significance or topics frequently rehearsed.

The problems of measuring intellectual functioning in older people are complex as many tests are weighted in favour of younger people. Older people tend to score better on tests which reflect educational attainment (verbal skills) than those measuring performance (coping with new material).

Social changes

While a society's attitude to old people varies from culture to culture, it is still the norm in most societies for old people to be

---

*Trotsky wrote this entry in his diary in May 1935 when he was 56. He was not to live to see old age as he was assassinated five years later.

looked after by the family until death. In the UK, 94% of old people live in private households; 40% are alone, and the same proportion live with one other person, often an elderly spouse (CSO 1979). Old people occupy a disproportionate amount of old and unimproved housing, often having lived there all their married life.

In the West, old age brings retirement with loss of income and status. By contrast, 12% of the oldest men studied in Greece were still working, yet they were more likely than those elsewhere to complain of feeling lonely (WHO 1983). Pensions rarely keep pace with inflation, so many old people live close to the poverty line.

Loneliness, isolation and boredom are common complaints amongst old people. The number of contacts with other people that are sought and achieved is reduced, whilst the quality of established relationships may become more intense and important (Jolley & Jolley 1991). Isolation may result from reduced mobility and may be exacerbated by the death of a spouse or friends, and children moving away. Many very old people feel tired and may be poorly motivated to carry on looking after themselves.

Two main theories set out to describe why old people tend to become socially isolated. They are the disengagement theory and the activity theory.

Disengagement theory (Cumming & Henry 1961)

This theory suggests that old people cope best if they accept the inevitability of reduced contact with others, particularly the activities of younger people, and manage to enjoy their retreat from the hurly-burly of everyday life.

Activity theory (Maddox 1963)

Older people, aware of certain failing skills, must make an effort to counteract this deterioration in order to maintain a sense of purpose and satisfaction.

It appears that each theory is correct, but for different groups of old people. The disengagement theory suggests an acceptance of decline and detachment from the world. Supports should allow the old person to withdraw from social contact and do what she wants. On the other hand, the activity theory suggests a more active approach, stimulating the individual to remain sociable, in touch with current affairs and mixing with all age groups.

The growing numbers of newly retired and relatively affluent people have brought about a change in attitude in that magazines, holidays and insurance specifically designed for older people have been marketed. In spite of their being only a minority of the pensioner population, affluent, active, newly retired people are slowly changing public attitudes. They are not seen as 'old' (Marshall 1991).

Management of normal ageing

The population of any country depends on the balance between births, deaths, immigration and emigration. In the United Kingdom, since the beginning of this century, births have exceeded deaths, and with the exception of the decades either side of World War II and the late 1950s, emigration has exceeded immigration. Not only has the population grown, but the balance of the population has shifted. Since 1900, the numbers of older people (aged 65 and over) have increased by over 400% (Table 12.1), and now account for about 15% of the population.

In Australia, Canada, USA and the former USSR, the proportion of old people is about two-thirds that of the UK. In the poorer countries of Asia, South America and Africa, the picture is similar to that which prevailed in Europe 90 years ago, only 5% of their populations being old. However, the predicted increase in the numbers of old people in the Third World over two decades is 40% (CSO 1986, Arie & Jolley 1982).

These changes are not a result of improved medical care extending the life of very old people.

Table 12.1 Numbers of elderly (in millions) in the UK.
(Source: CSO 1982 Social trends No. 12. HMSO, London. Reproduced with permission.)

Year	Age: 65–74	75–84	85+
1901	1.3		0.5
1971	4.7	2.1	0.5
1980	5.2*	2.6	0.6
1991	4.9	2.9*	0.8
2001	4.5	2.8	0.9 (still rising)

* = peak

The life expectancy today of a person of 80 is little different from that at the turn of the century. So what has been responsible for the change? In the early decades of this century in the UK and Europe, improved sanitation and food supplies reduced the infant mortality rate. So, quite suddenly, many more children survived childhood. The last two decades have brought further changes. Improved contraception and more permissive abortion legislation have reduced the growth in the birth rate.

The future

In the UK, while the 65–74 age group reached its peak in the early 1980s, and the 75–84 age group peaks about now, the very old, those over 84, will continue to increase into the next century. The rate of change in 'Third World' countries is expected to be very rapid with the numbers of old people increasing by 40% over two decades (CSO 1986, Arie & Jolley 1982).

With advancing age and frailty, old people need more support and practical help with routine day-to-day tasks. The choice lies between maintaining independence with support at home (for the majority), sheltered housing (only 5%), or relinquishing independence for the security of residential accommodation. The recent UK community care legislation should ensure better needs' assessment (see Ch. 5), but many residential facilities provide care that may treat residents as

'less than fully human ... with the prospect of having our bodies cared for but our personal and social lives neglected or even dismissed as irrelevant' (Hepworth 1988).

Support

As an old person becomes more frail, she must rely increasingly on outside support. Usually this will be provided by family and friends, and the amount of support required varies from person to person.

Informal support

Most old people will have a number of people who support them. Mostly these will be spouses and children (female relatives often bearing the brunt), who might themselves be elderly. Additional support will come from neighbours, friends and grandchildren who may do some shopping, provide the occasional meal, collect their pension or take them for a social outing.

Formal support

Old people are high users of medical and personal social services. Many old people will be experiencing physical illness for the first time. This will be stressful and may be complicated by anxiety or depression (neurotic disorders are much more common in old age than dementia). Most general practices in the UK now have attached health visitors and a few have social workers. Old people are more likely to be visited at home than younger people, and GPs are now required to see every patient over the age of 75 for an annual medical check (admittedly of a rather rudimentary sort). Even before this became a requirement 90% of the over 75s were seen at least once each year (Williams 1984), the remainder being fit. About 30% of the workload of an average practice is with old people (Williamson 1985). Ready access to specialist services (geriatric and psychogeriatric) and paramedical services, such as chiropody and physiotherapy will provide appropriate treatment and advice.

Social services provide home helps to give practical help for old people (cleaning, shopping, etc.), as well as 'meals on wheels' (lunch delivered to the person's home by volunteers), lunch clubs (meals and social contact for old people locally) and day centres for the frail and confused. A community occupational therapist may suggest aids for the home, such as large-handled cutlery for weakness of grip. The provision of a trolley to act as a walking frame and to carry things about may make it possible for the old person to move about in safety and with greater confidence.

Other services may provide simple, but extremely useful, help. Correction of physical and sensory problems is of vital importance. Spectacles or a hearing aid, where appropriate, will make communicating easier and may ease the sense of isolation. A simple alarm system may remove the fear of being taken ill and being unable to summon help.

Many old people will benefit from a mix of informal and formal support. Current UK government policy is aimed at encouraging and complementing informal support.

RMAL AGEING

...hing so far considered in this chapter relates to the normal process of ageing, not to illness. Abnormal ageing (dementia or 'chronic brain failure') is a disease process which runs a progressive course over a number of years, leading ultimately to death. It is quite different from normal ageing.

Although the older a person gets, the higher the likelihood of dementia, only 3% of those aged 65–70 are demented, rising to only about a fifth of those over 80. Thus the vast majority of old people, including the very old, are not, and never will become, demented.

Dementia (chronic brain failure)

Dementia is a global deterioration affecting personality, intellect, memory and cognitive functioning. Alzheimer's disease, the most common form of dementia, results in a reduction in the number of neurones in the brain and reduced brain size. Less common forms of dementia include arteriosclerotic or multi-infarct dementia, caused by vascular changes to the brain and ensuing damage, and Pick's disease which affects mainly the frontal and temporal lobes of the brain.

Dementia occurring before the age of 65 is called 'pre-senile', while that occurring after that age is 'senile'. So these terms relate to age of onset, not aetiology.

Symptoms of dementia (see Table 12.2)

Table 12.2 Symptoms of dementia. (Taken from Moyes 1980 The Psychiatry of Old Age. S, K & F Publications, London, with the permission of the late author and the publisher)

Personality	Intellect	Memory	Cognitive function
Personal neglect	Difficulty in abstract thinking	Poor short-term memory	Poor comprehension
Loss of interest and drive	Poor reasoning and judgement	Poor acquisition of new material	Loss of fluency
Blunting of emotions	Inability to plan ahead	Disorientation in time and space	Inability to carry out instructions
Social misbehaviour	Poor concentration		

Memory

There is a progressive impairment of memory. At first, this is only for recent events, so a shopper may return home without items she set out to buy. This is largely a deficit of registration rather than of recall, and a simultaneous decline in cognitive function and intellect makes new learning difficult.

The first indication of dementia might be the failure to learn the layout of a hotel while on holiday, or inability to locate the toilet when her son moves to a new house.

Disorientation in place (getting lost) may be followed by disorientation in time (not knowing the year, month, day or time of day). Later, memory for more distant events is lost and finally memory for self (name).

Cognition and intellect

Poor comprehension and reasoning ability make it difficult to cope with new situations, although regular routines may be unaffected.

Mrs A coped well with shopping daily at the corner shop where she was well known. She bought the same items each day, handing her purse to the shopkeeper who would take out the correct money. She managed by cooking the same meal each day. Then one day the local shop changed hands and was turned into a supermarket. Mrs A could not understand the new system and became confused and frightened. She stopped buying food but, fortunately, this was noticed by a neighbour, and a home help was organised.

It took only one change to tip the balance with the result that Mrs A failed to cope. Larger changes, such as a move of house, will have even greater impact.

Poor comprehension may lead to misinterpretation of events, especially when memory is poor.

A lady with early dementia may sit down in a chair placing her handbag at her feet. When she wanders off to another chair she forgets to take her handbag with her. Looking at her feet, she finds her handbag is not where she expects to find it. Mistakenly, she is quite convinced that it has been stolen.

Although insight may be maintained for some time, with a recognition that memory is impaired, eventually it will be lost.

Personality and social functioning

Personality becomes coarsened and self-control and social façade declines. There may be a loss of interest and drive, and socially embarrassing situations may arise.

Mood is variable and may be blunted or swing rapidly. The frustration threshold may be lowered, leading to verbal or physical aggression if thwarted. This behaviour may endanger others, for example, crossing roads without looking or dropping lighted matches or cigarettes.

Physical changes

Most bodily functions are ultimately controlled by the brain. As deterioration proceeds there may be unsteadiness (ataxia), cardiac arrhythmias, fits and sometimes weight loss. Urinary and faecal incontinence reflect a lessened ability to recognise and interpret bodily sensations (as well as difficulty finding the w.c., or inability to walk fast enough). Sleep patterns are upset so that more of the night might be spent awake.

Dementia is a terminal illness, death occurring usually after three to five years, although occasionally progression is much slower.

Management of dementia

The first task is to confirm the diagnosis. A careful history must be obtained from relatives and friends. Mental state examination, especially tests of memory and cognitive function, must be undertaken together with a careful physical examination. Routine blood testing should exclude treatable causes of a dementia-like picture (such as thyroid disease). In some cases, further tests (e.g. CT brain scanning) will be indicated.

As yet no specific treatment has been found which will even modify the progress of dementia, let alone offer any hope of cure. Nevertheless, trials of possible treatments continue (see Rabins 1991 for recent review). Management must therefore be aimed at minimising handicap and distress, and in common with other forms of rehabilitation, maintaining the best possible level of functioning for as long as possible. The emphasis is on maintenance rather than rehabilitation in the sense of making progress.

Planning

The cornerstone of management is assessment and reassessment. With much of psychiatry the focus of assessment is the pathology; the abnormal symptoms and signs, the positive family history of illness and disturbance, and the problems encountered in the patient. With dementia the focus lies not with what is going wrong, but what has been preserved. Of crucial importance is how much healthy function remains.

Where?

Accurate assessment of an old person should begin in her own home. Even a normal old person may perform less competently in strange or intimidating surroundings, such as in a day centre. The performance of an old person with impaired comprehension and memory disturbance will deteriorate in unfamiliar surroundings. Assessment should always be aimed at judging how well a person is able to cope in the familiarity of her own surroundings using her own equipment and local shops. Any assessment away from these surroundings will be of questionable validity.

By whom?

Under the new community care arrangements in Britain, assessment will be co-ordinated by the local authority social services department. Detailed planning is still underway, but it is envisaged that the assessment arrangements should be effective and simple. The object should be to obtain a well-targeted, concise report of the old person's circumstances by gathering information from the old person, carers, GP and other services involved.

Needs should be assessed by someone who is not involved with the provision of services, so that a lack of provision of particular services will be identified and this information passed on to planners.

What to assess?

A general outline is shown below:

1. Psychiatric status
   — history
   — memory
   — reasoning
   — misinterpretation   } leading to diagnosis
   — psychosis
   — suicide risk
   — insight
   — physical status

2. Abilities for daily living
   — shopping, cooking, cleaning, organising meals
   — managing money, bills, rent
   — orientation, house and surroundings
   — mobility, public transport, walking
   — self-care, washing, clothing, dressing, taking medication
   — care of pet, feeding and exercising dog, etc.
   — identify any dangers
3. Informal support—who is doing what, how often and their ability and willingness to do more
4. Formal support—all those at present professionally involved and their roles
5. Further investigations—specific physical investigations may be indicated to exclude other physical disorder. These may include simple blood investigations (to exclude anaemia, abnormal blood chemistry or hormone function), or more complex tests such as CT brain scanning.

Rating scales are now available for the assessment of mood, cognition and behaviour, including those considered 'activities of daily living'. The Informant Questionnaire of Cognitive Decline in the Elderly (IQCODE), a 26-item questionnaire, asks informants about changes over the past 10 years in the old person, and the Mini-Mental State Examination (MMSE) is widely used because of its brevity.

Assessment of depression in elderly people with cognitive impairment can be difficult and may be facilitated by the use of the Geriatric Health Scale (GHS). Behaviour may be reliably assessed using the Clifton Assessment Procedures for the Elderly (CAPE) (Pattie & Gilleard 1979) which include a behaviour scale as well as a cognitive scale. (For an up-to-date review of these procedures see Folstein 1991).

Assessment should not be rushed. The person being assessed must have time to get to know the assessor before attempting any task. Even then the results of the assessment require interpretation. Performance may vary at different times of the day and must be set in context. For example, it does not matter that an old woman is unable to name correctly the Prime Minister or the day of the week if she is generally able to look after herself. In other words, there are no absolutes: it is a matter of weighing up abilities and risks.

Therapies for elderly people

The established approaches include reality orientation and reminiscence therapy. They have no formal theoretical basis, but offer staff and carers frameworks to help them work with and relate to older people (Little 1991).

Reality orientation is a basic technique used for people who are disorientated in time, place or person. The aim is re-orientation by repeatedly reminding the old person who she is, where she is, the time of day and season of the year, etc. Two methods have been used: classroom reality orientation, using 30-minute sessions; and 24-hour reality orientation, where cues in the environment and contacts with other people (carers etc.) throughout the 24 hours are used to reinforce orientation. The efficacy of these approaches has been disputed. Some studies have shown that classroom reality orientation can improve cognitive functioning, but that 24-hour reality orientation may also improve behaviour (Hanley et al 1981); however many attempts to use reality orientation are inadequate (Hanley 1984).

Reminiscence therapy may act as a stimulus for 'life review' for any elderly person. Memories are prompted in a variety of ways making use of old photographs, magazines, records and films. Both old people and carers enjoy such sessions, but evidence to support its therapeutic value is lacking. At very least it improves interaction between staff and clients and helps staff to learn more about their clients.

The family

Any change in relationships requires adjustment. It can be painful to see a relative or friend change mentally and deteriorate. It can be a frustrating experience trying to communicate with a relative who fails to understand. It may be embarrassing or even offensive to have to wash and clean up after an incontinent parent. Guilt may arise from several sources simultaneously. The guilt at not being able to cope with an elderly parent, the lack of time available for one's own children and the guilt associated with resentment are all difficult to cope with. The move into respite or permanent institutional care and eventual death are further major stresses.

How best can we help with these problems? Individual counselling is aimed at allowing the carer, or other relative, to speak about both the acceptable feelings that they experience and the unacceptable. This includes the dreadful thoughts and feelings that so commonly occur in these situations, but which seem so alien and terrible to those experiencing them for the first time. These may include feelings of hate, anger, despair, and the thought that the old person might be better off dead. They are grieving for the loss of the healthy person that they knew and, like any grief, it may be intense and painful. The family must be helped to see that this is a normal, healthy reaction to a distressing change in their lives, and be supported through this grieving process.

Sometimes it is difficult for carers to understand why the aggressive, demanding and frustrating old person who has caused them so much difficulty and distress is apparently so well behaved and easily managed by staff when admitted to a home or hospital. It is all too easy for them to interpret this as confirmation that they have failed personally. The staff must help them to understand that it is often easier to cope with troublesome people who are not relatives and with whom one does not have the same emotional ties. Also, the staff are only in contact with the old person for a maximum of an 8-hour shift, and frequently this will be shared with a number of staff. The relative has been in contact with the old person 24 hours out of 24. No wonder it was difficult.

Relatives' groups

Individual counselling of relatives is always useful, but it is helpful for them to meet others in the 'same boat'. It is good to know that the problems, feelings and experiences that seemed so unique to them, are in fact shared by others.

Voluntary support groups, such as the Alzheimer's Disease Society in England, provide this sort of support as well as education, advice and fund-raising activities to fund research.

Problem behaviour

The behaviour often described as being most difficult for carers to cope with is the restlessness, repetitive questions or actions, wandering and incontinence of the old person. Other problem behaviours include dangerousness, violence, drinking, suicidal actions and Capgras syndrome (see below).

Antipsychotic drugs (see Ch. 6) may reduce agitation, aggression and, given at night, may help the old person to fall asleep at the normal time. She should not be allowed to sleep during the day as this will reduce the amount of sleep required at night. Incontinence may be helped by a variety of devices, pads and waterproof garments, but the development of a regular routine and clear labelling of toilet doors will undoubtedly be of help.

Dangerous behaviour, such as not lighting the gas cooker reliably or forgetting about burning cigarette ends, is a constant source of concern for relatives and neighbours. Old cookers and heaters should, where possible, be replaced by modern appliances with built-in safety devices. The hazards of smoking may be reduced by limiting smoking to when another person is present and installing smoke alarms.

The Capgras syndrome is a not uncommon symptom of dementia. The old person becomes convinced that her relatives have been replaced by people who are only pretending to be relatives. She sees these bogus relatives as evil and will address all manner of dreadful and hurtful remarks to them. It can be very difficult for the carer to cope, especially if she does not recognise that this is part of the illness and not addressed to her personally. Unfortunately there is no specific treatment for this syndrome and considerable support and explanation must be given to the family.

OTHER PSYCHIATRIC DISORDERS IN THE ELDERLY

Any of the disorders of earlier life may continue into old age, or return then. Thus, neuroses and personality disorder, which always manifest themselves earlier in life, may cause problems into old age, but will never appear for the first time at that stage.

Depressive disorder

Depressive disorder (illness) is a condition which is most common in middle and old age. In the elderly, agitation and delusions may be prominent, leading to a failure to eat and drink and a rapid deterioration of physical health. Hypochondriasis and other 'neurotic' symptoms (e.g. obsessional rituals) may occur as part of the illness.

Depressive disorder requires appropriate physical treatment: antidepressants or electroconvulsive therapy (ECT). The newer antidepressants (SSRIs) (see Ch. 6) have fewer side-effects and therefore are better tolerated by older people. ECT has a more rapid onset than medication and should be considered especially where the patient's physical state is deteriorating.

Common delusions in the elderly are:

Delusion	Example
Paranoid	Convinced that food and water are poisoned
Guilt	Convinced that she has committed a crime or does not deserve food, etc.
Poverty	Thinks she is unable to pay for food or keep
Nihilistic	Convinced her insides are rotting away

Pseudo-dementia

This occurs occasionally in severely depressed old people. Over a relatively short period of time, the old person changes from being normal to appearing quite demented: perplexed, forgetful, unable to grasp what is happening about her. The clues to the diagnosis are the rapidity of change, which is far faster than is usual for dementia; a past history of depression; or symptoms and signs suggestive of depression such as early morning wakening or diurnal mood variation.

In cases of doubt, a sodium amytal interview may be helpful. An interview after the administration of the barbiturate has been given, either intravenously or by mouth, may enable a patient suffering from depressive pseudo-dementia to communicate more freely or to talk about worries or delusions. In the case of dementia, the barbiturate will have no effect on performance. Once identified, the depression should be treated.

Acute confusional state (delirium)

Acute confusional states may occur at any age, but are most common in the very young and the very old. This always occurs secondary to some other condition. Common causes are acute physical illness such as pneumonia or urinary tract infections, prescribed medication, especially sleeping tablets and tranquillisers, withdrawal from alcohol or drugs, and metabolic conditions such as uncontrolled diabetes.

The old person is confused, has clouding of consciousness and may hallucinate (usually visually) or misinterpret what is happening about her (illusions). She appears anxious, perplexed and frightened, and this is usually worse at night. The treatment is that of the underlying cause. During the acute phase, the patient may be helped by being nursed in quiet, well-lit surroundings, with the minimum of staff changes.

Paraphrenia

The paranoid psychosis of old age has a variable response to treatment with antipsychotic drugs. After an adequate trial, if no improvement is seen, the drugs should be withdrawn.

Many old people can live comfortably in the community harbouring many strange ideas as long as they can be encouraged only to talk to the care staff, and not to bother neighbours, friends, carers and the police. Intellectual functioning and memory are not affected by this illness.

Mrs X, a 70-year-old widow, became convinced that local policemen visited her nightly and sexually assaulted her with their truncheons. Her frequent complaints to her neighbours and the local police made no difference to her delusions, but caused her to be ostracised. Slowly, over a period of time, a community psychiatric nurse gained her confidence. Mrs X agreed to save up all her worries until the weekly visit from the nurse. Having a regular opportunity to talk about her (false) beliefs, she did not need to mention them to the police or her neighbours. Although the delusions persist, she is again an acceptable member of the local community.

Unidentified physical illness

Psychological change in an old person should not automatically be attributed to a psychiatric disorder just because no obvious physical condition has been noted. There must be a full psychiatric assessment with sufficient grounds to justify a positive psychiatric diagnosis, not just the absence of obvious physical illness. In any case of doubt, routine physical screening tests should be carried out, including full physical examination, routine haematology including ESR, liver and thyroid function tests, urinalysis, and chest and skull X-rays. Further specific tests may be indicated.

Specific problems—abuse, suicide and the law

Elder abuse

Although there have been anecdotal reports of old people being abused, the extent of the problem has only recently been studied.

A figure of about 4% of old people has been widely quoted (Block & Sinnott 1979). The abuse might be physical (e.g. assaults or neglect), psychological (e.g. threats and intimidation) or financial (e.g. theft of money).

Risk factors for being a victim of abuse include being: female; over 75; physically frail; mentally incompetent; socially isolated; and an abusing parent in the past (see Fisk 1991 for an excellent review). It is important for everybody who is involved with old people to be aware that abuse is a possibility, both for people living at home as well as those in institutions.

Suicide

Successful suicides in Britain peak at 75. Risk factors for suicide include being old, lonely and recent loss. The risk is especially high during the year following the loss of a spouse, in all divorced and widowed people and those with physical illness. Alcohol abuse and lack of social ties further increase the risk.

Suicide in the old, as in any other age group, is closely associated with depressive illness. The survivor of any suicidal behaviour should be carefully screened for depression which, if found, should be treated vigorously.

Capacity to manage affairs

Mental deterioration may render a person quite incapable of understanding or managing financial or legal affairs. Thus an old person may get into financial difficulties through incompetence or be at risk of exploitation (see abuse earlier). In order to protect the muddled person, it may be necessary for someone else to take over the management of her affairs. The legal systems vary from country to country; for example, the Court of Protection in England and Wales and the Sheriff Court in Scotland. The court may appoint a relative, lawyer, accountant or other professional person to administer the patient's affairs on her behalf.

These legal procedures are by no means a recent invention but date back to ancient Greece. Sophocles' son applied to the court for the appointment of a 'Committee of the Person' on the grounds that, owing to old age, his father was unable to manage his affairs. Sophocles is supposed to have said the following to the court: 'If I am Sophocles, I am not beside myself; if I am beside myself, I am not Sophocles'.

Enduring power of attorney

The enduring power of attorney was introduced in England and Wales in 1986. This has to be arranged before the person becomes impaired, but allows the old person to chose who should act on her behalf. Thus, a person who is becoming physically frail may wish her daughter to take over her financial affairs. When later she becomes demented the arrangement continues.

Testamentary capacity

For a will to be valid the testator must have been in sound mind at the time that the will was prepared and signed; that is she should understand that she is giving the property, know the extent of her property and the claims upon her. The later development of a psychiatric condition (e.g. dementia) that renders her incapable of fully understanding the above will not invalidate her will, but would make any new will invalid.

Where a person with some degree of confusion or memory disturbance wishes to make a new will, it is advisable to obtain a medical opinion as to the person's ability to understand and know what she is doing.

DEATH, DYING AND BEREAVEMENT

Thoughts of death tend to increase with age and, in general, most old people come to terms with and accept the inevitability of their own death and the deaths of elderly friends and relatives. In fact, many lonely old people, especially those with chronic physical disorders, look upon death as a welcome relief. Despite these attitudes, deaths will bring a period of grief, bereavement and adjustment to the changed situation.

Lindemann (1944) in his classic study of grief pointed out that grief is a normal, healthy response to a distressing situation. Although the detailed manifestations of grief vary from person to person depending on circumstances, most people will pass through the three phases of grief set out below.

The stages of grief

Stage 1—shock, numbness, disbelief—lasts for a few hours to a few days.

Stage 2—full grieving: ruminations about the death and the dead person, tearful, socially withdrawn, loss of appetite, difficulty sleeping, frequent anger and guilt, a need to talk about the dead person, separation anxiety (the anxiety associated with being left alone) and recurrent grief pangs.

Stage 3—resolution: accepting the death, separating from the dead person, becoming able to make new relationships and plans without devaluing the dead person.

The duration of stage 2 (full grieving) is extremely variable, but probably understated by many authors. Some elderly people who lose their partner of half a century or more will never accept the loss.

Lindemann (1944) suggested that appropriate help at times of crisis, such as grief, could reduce the incidence of pathology. It is to be hoped that by promoting healthy grieving, fewer people will go on to develop abnormally prolonged grief reactions or even mental illness.

Simple guidelines to promote healthy grieving

These simple measures may be applied by care staff and, better still, can be taught to relatives and friends of the bereaved.

The bereaved person:

1. must be allowed/encouraged to talk about the dead person and to express her grief without embarrassment and without fear that others will be unable to cope with this show of emotion;

2. must be encouraged to see grief as a normal, healthy response which will not be helped (and almost certainly will be hindered) by the use of minor tranquillisers or antidepressants;

3. must understand that the grieving is a necessary part of the process of coming to terms with what has happened in her life;

4. many bereaved people are terrified that they are 'going crazy' because of the bizarre experiences following the death. The majority will feel that they see, hear or feel the presence of the dead person during the weeks or months after the death. They are often terrified to mention this, even to their closest friends. They may be greatly relieved to be asked if they have had any of these experiences and to be told that they are very common and normal.

Relatives must be encouraged to follow these guidelines and especially not to try to distract the bereaved person from her grief.

With the best of intentions relatives frequently try to talk about anything but the death and may suggest an immediate move of house or a holiday to make the person less distressed. Attempts to deny the impact of the death may leave the bereaved unable to express the appropriate emotion.

Mr G was on holiday with his wife in a remote Third World country when she was suddenly taken ill and died. For the next few days, he was totally occupied with completing the complex arrangements to register his wife's death and organise her cremation prior to his return to Britain. He was surprised to note that he felt and showed no emotion at his wife's death. It was only three months later when, waking out of a sleep in front of the television, he thought he heard his wife moving about the house. Almost immediately, he became aware that this was impossible and that she was dead. For the first time, he felt the desolation and distress and wept. The delay in grief could perhaps have been prevented if there had been someone with whom he could have shared his distress at the time of the event.

Dying

It is not only bereaved relatives who experience grief, but also the dying. They are grieving for the loss of health, loss of life and loss of a future. The process is very similar to the grief experienced by relatives and the dying must be allowed, if they wish, to talk about and freely express these emotions. Frequently, they are encouraged not to show emotion and are praised by care staff and relatives for having a 'stiff upper lip' and coping so well with the knowledge of their terminal illness. This manoeuvre to prevent the show of emotion is often to help relatives and staff cope at the expense of the dying person.

The dying must be given the time and opportunity to talk about what is happening to them. This requires a sensitive counselling approach with privacy and time.

Death and the care team

The impact that a death has on professional carers is often under-estimated, particularly where the person is well known to the staff, or where the death is sudden or in some other way traumatic (such as a suicide or a painful cancer). The team should have a built-in opportunity to discuss the emotional impact of such an event at a regular team meeting or sensitivity group. All team members should be sensitive to the impact such an event has on

themselves and on individual colleagues who might need particular support.

CHALLENGES OF WORKING WITH THE ELDERLY

Fortunately, a large number of people positively enjoy working
with elderly people. However, this is by no means universal. The
Group for the Advancement of Psychiatry (1971) identified several
reasons why many people are reluctant to deal with the elderly.
The main points of this report may prove useful in team discussion
and in sensitivity meetings.

The main findings are:

1. old people stimulate the therapist's/helper's fears about her
own old age;

2. they arouse conflicts about her own relationships with
parental figures;

3. the therapist believes she has nothing useful to offer old
people because she believes they cannot change their behaviour or
that their problems are all due to untreatable organic brain
disease;

4. the therapist believes that her skills will be wasted if she
works with old people because they are near death and not really
deserving of attention;

5. the therapist's colleagues may be contemptuous of her efforts
on behalf of old people.

In Britain, the Royal College of Psychiatrists set up a Section for
the Psychiatry of Old Age in 1978, and in 1988 the specialty of old
age psychiatry was officially recognised. This has stimulated
improved training, research and improved standards of care.
These changes have also occurred in the USA and elsewhere.
Organisations such as Age Concern and the Alzheimer's Disease
Association have highlighted the consumer and carer interest.
Increasingly, social services, voluntary organisations and the
private sector are taking an interest in the growing numbers of old
people.

CONCLUSIONS

This chapter has not attempted to provide a comprehensive review
of rehabilitation with elderly people. It has focused on the
problems of normal ageing in order to help identify what is due to

illness and what is an accepted part of normal ageing. Attention should also be drawn to the dangers inherent in treating old people. In particular, an over-zealous attempt to treat all physical illnesses may lead to a poorer quality of life due to drug side-effects, especially since old people tend to be more sensitive to medication. It is worth remembering Napoleon's statement, 'I do not want two diseases — one nature-made, one doctor-made.' (Napoleon Bonaparte 1820).

REFERENCES

Arie T, Jolley D J 1982 Making services work; organisation and style of psychogeriatric services. In: Levy and Post F (eds) The psychiatry of later life. Blackwell, Oxford

Block M R, Sinnott J D 1979 The battered elder syndrome. MD thesis. Centre on Aging, University of Maryland

Bromley D 1966 The psychology of human ageing. Penguin, Harmondsworth

CSO (Central Statistical Office) 1979 Social trends No. 9. HMSO, London

CSO 1982 Social trends No. 12. HMSO, London

CSO 1986 Social trends No. 16. HMSO, London

Cumming E, Henry W E 1961 Growing old. Basic Books, New York

Fisk J 1991 Abuse of the elderly. In: Jacoby and Oppenheimer (eds) Psychiatry in the elderly. Oxford University Press, London

Folstein M F 1991 Rating scales for use in the elderly. Current Opinion in Psychiatry 4: 591–595

Gallup Poll 1984 (conducted for Sidartha Films Ltd) The elderly. Gallup Polls Ltd, London

Group for the Advancement of Psychiatry 1971 The aged and community mental health. Mental Health Materials Center, New York

Hanley I G 1984 Theoretical and practical considerations in reality orientation therapy with the elderly. In: Hanley, Hodge (eds) Psychological approaches to the care of the elderly. Croom Helm, Beckenham

Hanley I G, McGuire R J, Boyd W D 1981 Reality orientation and dementia: a controlled trial of two approaches. British Journal of Psychiatry 138: 10–14

Hepworth M 1988 Age conscious: an illustrated look at age prejudice. Age Concern Scotland, Edinburgh

Jolley D J, Jolley S P 1991 Psychiatric disorders in old age. In: Bennett D H and Freeman H L (eds) Community psychiatry. Churchill Livingstone, Edinburgh

Kinsey A S, Pomeroy W B, Martin C R 1948 Sexual behaviour in the human male. Saunders, Philadelphia

Lindemann E 1944 Symptomatology and management of acute grief. American Journal of Psychiatry 101: 141–148

Little A 1991 Psychological treatments. In: Jacoby and Oppenheimer (eds) Psychiatry in the elderly. Oxford University Press, London

Maddox G L 1963 Activity-morale: a longitudinal study of selected elderly subjects. Social Forces 42: 195

Marshall M 1991 Proud to be old: attitudes to age and ageing. In: Age: the unrecognised discrimination. Age Concern, London

Masters W H, Johnson V E 1970 Human sexual inadequacy. Little Brown, Boston

Moyes I 1980 The psychiatry of old age. S K & F Publications, London

Rabins P V 1991 Treatment by physical methods—medication. Current Opinions in Psychiatry 4: 584–586

Williams E I 1984 Characteristics of patients aged over 75 not seen during one year in general practice. British Medical Journal 228: 119–121

Williamson J 1985 Preventive aspects of geriatric medicine. In: Pathy (ed) Principles and practice of geriatric medicine. Wiley, Chichester

World Health Organization 1983 The elderly in eleven countries. A sociomedical study. Public Health in Europe No. 21. WHO, Geneva

13. Physical handicap

Clephane Hume   Nicola Stuckey

Life is not a matter of holding good cards, but of playing a poor hand well.

Robert Louis Stevenson

INTRODUCTION

Coming to terms with physical illness or disability can pose great psychological demands on the patient and those around him. It is generally accepted, but not always remembered, that a person's psychological state will influence his recovery. A person who is psychologically healthy yet severely physically disabled may well reach a higher level of independence than his fellow patient who is poorly motivated due to psychological problems. Adjustment to and acceptance of disability are vital if recovery and independence are to be achieved.

Abnormal psychological difficulties can be minimised, if not actually prevented, by the attitudes of the rehabilitation team. Essentially, it is a matter of time, openness, accurate information, honesty and encouragement to the patient to express his worries and fears, however embarrassing or ridiculous he may feel these to be.

It is easy for staff to forget how strange, impersonal and frightening most hospitals are. The patient requires straightforward information and non-technical explanations. If patients feel that staff have time to listen, and will not regard people—patients and relatives—as stupid if they ask apparently trivial questions, that in itself is reassuring. Patients are often reluctant to raise emotionally loaded or embarrassing questions. Staff must learn to broach these topics in a sensitive but matter-of-fact way when a suitable opportunity presents itself. It is necessary to be sensitive to any hints the person may give, since even an apparently small item of self-disclosure may feel enormously self-revealing to the patient. This applies particularly to marital and sexual problems and life-threatening illness. Simple information may be enough, but further counselling may be required.

The concept of handicap is described in Chapter 1 and the same ideas can be applied to physical disorders — those disabilities which arise as part of the illness and the secondary handicaps which are the result of having been ill (patient's own or other people's reactions to the illness). This must be seen in the context of the individual. The level of handicap may be very different from the level of measurable physical disability. A minor impairment such as stiffness in one finger caused by arthritis could put an end to the career of a concert pianist, whereas a gardener with a similar problem might not consider himself to be disabled in any way.

This chapter will consider reactions to physical disability, links between psychiatric and physical illness, and ways in which people can be helped to adjust to physical disability and thus maximise their independence.

REHABILITATION IN PHYSICAL DISABILITY

Where do psychological issues apply?

A common observation made by those with psychological expertise of staff involved with the rehabilitation of the physically disabled is that psychological issues are ignored or at best dealt with in a cursory manner. Note is also sometimes made of the fact that patients are distrustful of a member of staff bringing up psychological issues, particularly if they introduce themselves as a psychologist or psychiatrist, e.g. 'there is nothing wrong with my brain, do you think I'm going round the twist?' Concern is also sometimes noted that bringing up the issue of feelings with patients is going to upset them when they appear to be making a good recovery and have already come to terms with their disability.

How true is this and does it matter?

Units and staff teams vary enormously in the amount of time and resources that are addressed to psychological issues. This will often be related to the level of staffing within the rehabilitation team, the interests of the staff members and perhaps most importantly, how comfortable the staff feel in tackling psychological issues and the training they have in how to handle them.

We hope that this chapter goes some way to looking at:

- what are the common psychological issues in rehabilitation of physical disability?
- how can these issues be best handled both by those working in a rehabilitation team and those with more specialist psychological knowledge?

THE COPING PROCESS

How one copes with a physical disability depends on a variety of factors, some of which will be those which allow someone to cope with a psychiatric problem. These factors are broadly:

- the nature of the onset of the disability
- the nature of the disability itself
- what the disability means for that person
- the reaction of others to the disability.

Theories of adaptation

Psychoanalytic ideas

Some have likened the process of adapting to physical disability to that of bereavement, as there are obvious parallels in terms of loss. This is sometimes described as the 'requirement for mourning model' borrowed from Kübler Ross (1970), and people are thought to need to progress through a series of stages before they can adjust to their disability. These stages are:

- shock
- denial
- depression
- anger
- conflict resolution and acceptance.

Someone who has a stroke, head injury, spinal injury or amputation may well feel this sense of loss, although they may not progress through all the stages as described in the model. The 'requirement for mourning model' does not fit very well for those who have a congenital disability such as spina bifida, thalidomide problems, etc., or for those whose disability has a slower onset and the individual has more time to adapt, e.g. multiple sclerosis or rheumatoid arthritis. The model may, however, have some implications for the parents of a handicapped child or spouse and family of the affected individual.

Recent reviewers have found little evidence to support this stage model and it seems that we have to take a wider look at what is involved in rehabilitation and adaptation to physical disability.

Social learning ideas

Trieschmann (1980) and Moos (1984) have suggested alternative models of coping which appear more mentally healthy. Moos suggests that the individual needs to recognize his new situation and learn a series of skills to enable him to cope with it. Trieschmann indicates that the extent of adaptation depends on:

- person variables, e.g. personality, previous coping strategies, etc.
- organism, e.g. type of disability, complications, previous health
- environment—social attitudes, family network, etc.

She adopts an *educational model* where rehabilitation becomes the process of teaching the individual to live with his disability in his own environment. This sounds logical enough, but if one looks at the frequently used medical model for rehabilitation, the patient is dispensed units of treatment and is often left as the passive recipient. If rehabilitation becomes an active educational process where the patient is part of the decision-making process, then this will influence his/her coping response to the disability itself.

IMPORTANT FACTORS IN THE COPING PROCESS

Nature of the onset of the disability

Congenital disability

The way in which a disability first becomes apparent may have considerable bearing on how well someone is able to come to terms with it. Something that one is born with may be easier to accept in that the individual has never known anything else, although they may well feel angry as they grow up and realise they cannot do the same as others. It may be then that they feel a sense of loss at what they will never be able to experience compared with their peers. As mentioned earlier, families may be those who experience a sense of bereavement after the birth of a handicapped child.

Sudden or gradual onset of disability

Those who have become disabled as a result of an accident or unexpected illness will have had no time to prepare for the immense changes and implications that an acquired disability may bring. Examples of this include: head injury, spinal injury, severe problems following a heart attack, amputation, stroke. The change in life-style may range from small to immense, depending on how disabling the condition is and how active a life the person previously led.

Another factor which may be important in terms of adaptation to suddenly acquired disability is the responsibility for the injury. If the individual had some part to play in why he became disabled, he may feel guilt or anger and frustration at not being able to put the clock back to correct an action taken, e.g. head or spinal injury following a motor-bike accident, sporting accident or suicide attempt; having been a heavy smoker or drinker and not heeding medical advice to give up.

Where the 'fault' for the disability lies elsewhere, e.g. injury due to reckless driving on someone else's part, anger is a very common and understandable reaction. If individuals are involved in protracted compensation suits, progression through the rehabilitation process may be affected by waiting for settlement.

A gradual onset of conditions such as multiple sclerosis, rheumatoid arthritis and diabetes may give the person more time to come to terms with the changes that will ensue in their life-style. This does not preclude them from feeling angry or depressed about the prospect of their future potential having narrowed horizons. Conditions that have life-threatening connotations such as cancer, Huntington's chorea and now AIDS, mean that individuals are having to carry on with uncertainty hanging over their heads. What may happen will have a significant effect on the person's view of the future and the level of his mood. It may be very difficult to help someone to think positively about the time they have left when they have insight into a possibly painful and disfiguring time leading up to eventual death.

In conditions where intellectual deterioration is also a component of the disability, the degree of insight and understanding that the person has of this will influence his ability to cope with its prospect. This applies to conditions such as Alzheimer's disease, other dementias, multiple sclerosis, Huntington's chorea, etc.

At what stage in life the disability occurs

Those who become disabled at a young age may be more flexible in their thinking and their approach to adapting to life as a disabled person. An older person may find it very hard to accept and adapt to a newly disabled life having lived a very active life previously.

Conversely, some older disabled people feel that they have achieved most of their major goals in life, e.g. getting married and having children, progressing in their job, taking up sporting activities. They may, thus, find the process of acceptance relatively easy. Younger people may feel very bitter that their chances of finding a partner are limited and that they may be unable to have children. They may feel they will be unable to partake of sports or work activities that they had envisaged.

The most important variable determining adaptation is probably the personality and coping resources of that individual.

The nature of the disability

How disabling is the condition?

The degree to which the disability limits the individual may be very crucial to adaptation. Having to spend a lot of extra time on basic self-care or mobility may become very frustrating. The cost to the person due to the disability is also of great relevance. For instance, the person may have to give up his job and have little prospect of finding an alternative; his spouse may decide that she cannot accept that her partner is no longer the person she married due to personality change following head injury, or not be able to manage the additional burden of care that is asked of her, and consequently seek a divorce.

It is important to remember, however, that some people have such personal drive that they are able to overcome many limitations of the disability, and also some who will enjoy the sick role and allow the disability to limit activities more than necessary. For example, someone may have no control over his bowel or bladder function, but be very adept at methods of managing this aspect of the disability. Others may make no attempt to help themselves and leave it all to their carers and allow it to be a reason for cutting down on activities and possible quality of life. Consequently, the amount that bowel and bladder function limit the person's activities is related to his skill of management rather than to the degree of impairment imposed by the disability.

Whether the disability is progressive (as in multiple sclerosis), or static with perhaps some recovery potential (as in strokes and spinal injuries) may also affect adaptation. This has obvious implications for the person's mood and level of optimism in assessing his prospects for and planning for the future.

The amount of pain experienced may also have a direct effect on mood as chronic pain can be clearly linked with depression and affects the person's tolerance which may in turn determine ultimate limits of ability.

The amount of physical change and disfigurement may well influence the acceptability of the disability both to the affected individual and to others.

How does treatment affect everyday life?

Treatment for a disability may be almost minimal with only a few routine visits to hospital or GP yearly, or may involve considerable medication, invasive treatment and hospitalisation.

There may also be the need for many personnel to visit the person's home to administer treatment or aid in self-care, which can be very invasive to one's privacy.

Medication may have side-effects which add to the burden, e.g. an individual who has had a hypertensive stroke may have dizziness as a result of antihypertensive medication, making regaining mobility and balance more difficult. However, conversely, drug treatment in early Parkinson's disease can virtually alleviate symptoms and greatly increase mobility.

Invasive treatments, for instance in some cancers, can add to the degree of disability and distress which in turn will affect the coping process.

Hospitalisation, whether for treatment or respite care, can be very disruptive to normal life when one is trying to get on with a job and/or family life.

The effect of the disability for one particular individual

Loss

The bereavement model inevitably involves issues of loss. Disability may involve much loss, whether it is of something that has already been achieved, such as a career, or the fact that something may never be possible, such as having a family or to be able to walk.

The range of issues which one could include under 'loss' is immense. Job, spouse/partner, financial security, housing, standard of living, family, mobility (both self-propelled and use of transport), independence, privacy, freedom of choice, control of decisions, sporting and social activities, spontaneity, friends, access to remote places, self-esteem, positive self-image, quality of life—the list is vast.

Adaptation

How one adapts to the loss associated with the disability depends on three main factors:

Flexibility of the environment

● How possible it is to change physical things, such as adapting the house to allow maximum independence, finding alternative systems of transport. This in turn may depend on finance within the local authority social services' budget.

● How possible it is to change organisational issues, such as adapting an existing job, finding alternative employment or leisure activities. Specialist support groups dealing with issues related to disability may be very helpful (those dealing with housing, transport, access, sporting facilities, holidays and similar issues).

● How much support is organised for family members or carers in order to reduce the strain on relationships where a major change in role may have taken place.

● Acceptability to the local community of someone with a disability will be reflected in the architectural design and adaptation of public buildings, and the degree of knowledge and stigma attached to disabilities within communities themselves. Those near a psychiatric hospital or spinal injuries unit may be much more used to seeing people in wheelchairs or behaving slightly differently from others.

Flexibility of the individual

● Personal resources are crucial factors in adaptation and ability to cope with any kind of stress or strain. Disability brings with it changes in self-image and quite probably self-esteem, both of which may be difficult to come to terms with. Factors such as intelligence and personality may be very important features in adapting to disability and getting through the rehabilitation process, e.g. how anxious one gets, how resourceful one is, confidence, extraversion, contemplative, obsessional, striving—all will influence coping style. The belief system of the individual will also be a crucial factor in compliance with and understanding of treatment and preventative issues, e.g. medication, bladder and skin care, dietary and exercise advice. If someone values health as a construct and believes that he has some responsibility for maintaining his health, then compliance and understanding is likely to be greater. Some studies have looked at measures of health locus of control. Where there is a high degree of internal control, i.e. believing that there are ways in which we can influence the state of our health, such studies have found more successful adaptation and compliance with advice.

Flexibility of friends and family

● Personal resources of those who are closely involved with the affected individual will be important in the same way as mentioned in the previous paragraph.

● The meaning of the loss to these people may be different from the disabled individual and they may need their own support system to enable them to adapt to the change and continue to remain in that relationship with the affected person.

● The change in role involved for some family members may be considerable. The difference between being a sexual partner and also having to deal with functions such as excretion may be very difficult for some people. Others may have to become the breadwinner, or perhaps remain as the main carer where an adult child has to return to the parental home to live.

Some examples of how the flexibility of family and friends might influence outcome might be:

Tony who sustained a spinal injury in a motor accident felt that his inability to play football with his sons and their friends would have a disastrous effect on his relationship with them. In reality, it seemed that every child in the neighbourhood was coming round to welcome him back and explore the potential of his newly acquired computer.

In contrast, the complexities of the guilt feelings of the mother who felt responsible for her son's accident and her attempts to make amends created considerable difficulties for them both.

A move to accommodation which provides easier access may entail the entire family learning to adjust to a new environment, neighbours and a change of school for the children.

Common psychological issues in the coping process

Earlier reference was made to the stages of adjustment in the 'requirement for mourning model'. While it may not be the most appropriate model to use in understanding adjustment, the range of emotions described are common following disability.

Shock and denial

These can be felt both at early stages of disability and later. Denial is where the individual chooses not to believe or accept information and/or advice about his condition. This ignoring of the 'truth' is often seen as a self-protective mechanism to cushion against painful information which may be too difficult to assimilate. For example, a person with severe angina following a myocardial infarction refuses to admit that he would be unable to continue his job as a heavy goods driver and to look at alternative ways of using his time.

Anger and frustration

Many may feel the frustration of having to rely on other people to do things which one previously took for granted. This in turn can lead to feelings of anger against oneself and possibly members of staff or family who are in a position of being able to help. There may be anger directed at the doctors who should have done more to care and prevent the onset of the disability, or done more to cure it. A distressing manifestation of anger for the believer is anger with God. 'How can I believe in a God who has done this to me?'

Anxiety and depression

Anxiety may be frequently felt at the prospect of facing the outside world for the first time when one has been cushioned in hospital from the gaze of the public. There are probably other 'danger' spots for anxiety with the newly disabled as they progress through rehabilitation, e.g. first trying transfers, going home for weekends, returning to work, etc. For those who have a progressive condition, anxiety may be common about how long until one's symptoms worsen, or whether or not the odd twinge is the beginning of the deterioration process.

Depression is also understandable where the implications of the disability are great in terms of loss to that individual. It may take time before someone is prepared to look at alternative ways of living life and in that time become quite withdrawn and low. The task of overcoming some of the obstacles placed by disability can seem insuperable. Depression has been noted to be common in stroke victims and other conditions such as cardiac disorders and rheumatoid patients. It is, however, not an inevitable part of adjusting to disability and many do not experience depression at all.

Other issues such as compliance and motivation are dealt with later in the chapter.

PROBLEMS ENCOUNTERED DURING REHABILITATION

As described above, acceptance of disability is the first important step in the rehabilitation process. Having dealt with his own reactions and learned to cope with his physical limitations, the patient has to contend with the barriers to integration imposed by society, and the reactions of his family and friends.

Barriers to integration

Physical barriers such as restricted access to buildings, transport and general restriction on mobility are obvious factors which create obstacles for the disabled person. Smoky environments may cause distress to someone with bronchitis and air-conditioning can make some people light-headed.

There are also economic restrictions — some disabilities force people into having contact mainly with similarly affected people because of mobility problems or need for assistance. (It may also be felt that a disfiguring or potentially stigmatising disability may be more easily coped with in the company of other sufferers.) Special transport services are often expensive for people on a fixed income, and as many handicapped people will not be working, state benefits may permit only limited opportunities for leaving the house.

More insidious are the psychological and social barriers. For people who have 'hidden' or 'invisible' disabilities, there is the additional problem of appearing 'normal' and yet not behaving as expected. It may not be obvious that someone is partially sighted and people do not look deaf. (Modern hearing aids may be unhelpfully discreet.) Speech problems may be immediately apparent, while dietary restrictions may not be noticed for some time if the sufferer is adept at coping.

The greatest of all barriers is, however, the attitude of society. Rejection or revulsion, curiosity, patronising behaviour or effusive and unrequired help all severely hamper the disabled person's integration. 'Does he take sugar?' has become a well-known phrase in the United Kingdom following a radio programme with that title. Despite this, the problems behind the question are still not fully understood by the general public. Education and public relations by a wide number of people, organisations and the media have increased some people's awareness but much ignorance still remains. An obvious disability may have some compensations, but all too often it is the wheelchair attendant who is addressed rather than the user.

People who have deteriorating or terminal illnesses may find themselves being avoided by others who do not feel at ease with the reality of diminishing abilities or approaching death. This context has its own special problems and the reader is referred to specific sources for further guidance (Penson & Fisher 1991).

Psychosocial problems

Within the family, there will often, of necessity, be changes in roles and therefore in status, particularly for someone who is newly disabled. The husband who has been breadwinner, do-it-yourself handyman and financial administrator may find his wife taking over all these tasks. His role as father may be restricted by his inability to enjoy physical recreation with his children, while his role as husband may be altered by difficulty in achieving a mutually satisfactory sexual relationship. He may feel that his status within the family has been devalued.

Obviously this is the pessimistic view of the situation, but it represents some of the obstacles, real or expected. The degree of handicap and the nature of previous family relationships will influence which problems arise. At the time of leaving hospital, even for a weekend out, the realities of the change in circumstances, and the restrictions imposed by the disability can make a depressing impact. It is not possible to join in previous activities and both the disabled person and the family are confronted with the implications for the future.

Difficulties may occur in other aspects of life. A move to accommodation which provides easier access may entail the entire family learning to adjust to a new environment, neighbours and a change of school for the children. Social support may be reduced as people who used to 'pop in' now have to make a planned journey in order to visit. People who visited the patient regularly in hospital may assume that on his return home they can withdraw their attention, which may add to the distress of what feels like a very slow process of rehabilitation. Behind closed doors, the loneliness may be considerable. To have long visits or too many visitors is of course tiring, and also invades the family's privacy.

On a wider level, social activity beyond the home may be severely curtailed. It can be a hindrance and embarrassment to take a disabled person on social outings or holidays and although there may be no malicious intent, the individual may find himself excluded.

For the person who lives alone, the social problems and isolation may be more extreme. For anyone with a physical disability or illness, there is the normal need to maintain control over life, with freedom to make choices, including the acceptance or refusal of help. Everyone can experience the frustrations of the difficulties of coping with previously trivial tasks and the loss of independence which this creates, but having to summon help from an external source can prove highly detrimental to self-esteem. Conversely, a person in this situation may sometimes become the victim of too many well-intentioned offers of help and feel that his independence is threatened.

For all age groups, and particularly for those who live in institutions, sexual needs may be more difficult to deal with because of other people's attitudes. 'They are too old for all that, it isn't nice, he's disabled, he wouldn't be interested', 'what would happen if the papers found out that our residents were sharing bedrooms?'.... The frustration of being in close proximity to others to whom the person feels attracted but without the privacy in which to have a closer relationship may be considerable. Even if sexual intercourse is not physically possible or is taboo within the institution, privacy may allow a degree of closeness and physical contact which can lead to a mutually satisfying relationship. It would also be helpful to remember that amongst the general population in the United Kingdom, sexual relationships outwith marriage, and homosexual relationships are widely accepted. Rehabilitation must reflect the norms of society.

PHYSICAL CONDITIONS PRODUCING PSYCHIATRIC SYMPTOMS

Certain physical illnesses may present with psychiatric symptoms (Table 13.1).

Table 13.1   Psychiatric symptoms related to physical disorders

Physical condition		Psychiatric symptoms
Endocrine	Thyrotoxicosis	Anxiety, overactivity
	Myxoedema	Depression, dementia
	Pituitary	Euphoria, depression
	Diabetes	Confusion
Infections	Virus e.g. influenza or mononucleosis (glandular fever)	Depression (may be profound)
	Infection causing high temperature	Confusion (delirium)
	HIV/AIDS	Anxiety, confusion, dementia
Nervous system	Tumour	Confusion
	Multiple sclerosis	Euphoria, depression
	Myalgic encephalomyelitis (ME)	Anxiety, depression
	Head injury	Personality change, dementia
Cardiovascular	Heart failure	Confusion, paranoia, memory disturbance
Drugs and alcohol	Alcohol withdrawal	DTs (confusion), dementia, recent memory disturbance
Prescribed drugs	Methyl dopa	Profound depression
	Steroids	Euphoria, confusion, paranoia
Illegal drugs		Psychosis, withdrawal

In all cases, the quality of life and benefits of treatment must be weighed against the restriction imposed on the individual and undesirable effects of treatment. 'Treatment at all costs' may make staff feel that they have contributed all that they are able to, but the individual's day-to-day quality of life may be poor. Anyone with a physical disability will experience anxiety and worry about what the future may hold. Sometimes, however, this may become so severe that it interferes with the person's life-style—for example, fear of climbing stairs following a heart attack—and intervention is necessary to allay the person's fears and to allow the rehabilitation programme to continue. (Sometimes the anxiety may be experienced by a relative, who may block the person's attempts to do things for himself, which is equally detrimental to recovery.)

Occasionally, hypochondriasis may develop, so that the person is totally concerned with his state of health, and every minor ache becomes a major symptom. This is difficult to deal with, and may sometimes lead to unfortunate consequences.

Joy who for many years complained about headaches, rheumatic pains and a host of other things developed paralysis of her limbs, with the exception of her right arm. She could thus continue to write letters to relatives, who noted the convenience of this situation. A little later, when she was diagnosed as having motor neurone disease, the relatives felt very guilty about their response to what they had taken to be the exaggeration of yet another physical complaint.

For sufferers of myalgic encephalomyelitis (ME), multiple sclerosis or the unidentified 'virus', there is the uncomfortable experience of feeling that nobody quite believes that there is a physical element in the aetiology of the illness. Vague symptoms may be attributed to neurotic behaviour, and negative test results confirm this, becoming a source of frustration and worry rather than reassurance. A confirmed diagnosis, however serious, may sometimes come as a relief.

Sensory deficits, especially deafness and blindness, which cut people off from the world around them, may be associated with feelings of uncertainty or suspicion as communication is reduced or misinterpreted. Paranoid feelings and even delusions may be created by the sensory deprivation of being confined to bed. People who cannot sit up and observe what is going on in the world around them are deprived of contact with others and this may create feelings of suspicion as well as isolation.

It is well documented (Wright 1983) that certain conditions may result in depression—for example, heart attack ('I'm no longer firing on all cylinders'); cancer, with the loss of control over one's life or the surgical removal of part of the body; or rheumatoid disease, where the continual pain has a wearing effect on the person's life-style. Burns, or other disfiguring accidental injury may have a major psychological impact on the person. The experience of depression may be part of a normal adjustment process (see above) but if it is prolonged, or so severe that it restricts the person's life-style, treatment through supportive psychotherapy or antidepressant medication may be indicated.

If someone has had a head injury or viral infection, the consequent psychiatric problems may outweigh the physical disability, and this situation can be particularly difficult to deal with.

Following encephalitis, Bob had features of personality change, including sexually uninhibited behaviour, and cognitive impairments, which made it impossible to return to his previous highly responsible job. He could see no difficulties, apart from some weakness in his right arm, which had ruined his handicap at golf. His firm retired him on a disability pension and he was quite unable to structure a daily routine for himself.

His wife found it very difficult to cope with the situation and worried about the effects on the children. Respite in the form of a place at a local authority unit was of considerable benefit to all concerned.

Some of the behaviour problems following head injury can be reduced by individual behaviour modification programmes, where the person works to achieve particular rewards. Clear definition of acceptable and non-acceptable behaviour is also of benefit. The long-term effects of living with difficult behaviour are acknowledged, but support services are few. Participation in a self-help group such as Headway is of undoubted benefit (see below).

Other people will have insight into the limitations of their abilities and may become anxious or depressed.

Peter sustained brain damage during surgery and was highly aware of the reduction in cognitive skills which resulted. This made him feel ashamed and unable to go outside and participate in normal social events.

The special needs of young chronically disabled patients may be hard to meet. These people may lack the mobility or communication skills which are required for social relationships to develop. Whilst they may desperately want normal social contact with others, sensitive help may be required if this is to be achieved. Clubs such as PHAB (physically handicapped and able bodied) may seem contrived but can provide fun and participation in a range of activities. It is important that the individual has the choice as to whether or not he seeks social contact with other disabled people.

PSYCHIATRIC PROBLEMS CONTRIBUTING TO PHYSICAL ILLNESS

The psychiatrist working in a general hospital may be asked to consider the situation of a person who shows physical symptoms for which there appears to be no physical cause. Unravelling such problems can be complex and resolving the psychiatric background time-consuming. It is also important to remember that unexplained symptoms may not be due to psychological factors, the cause may be attributable to something as yet undiscovered.

Eating disorders and substance abuse may cause major physical disorder. The gross malnutrition resulting from severe anorexia nervosa will produce widespread physiological changes. In extreme cases, death or permanent impairment, e.g. renal failure, will occur. Likewise the bulimic person will impose severe stresses on her digestive system as she alternately binges compulsively or purges herself.

Alcohol abuse and associated vitamin deficiency produce a variety of neurological changes, including sensory impairment, recent memory impairment and dementia. People with alcohol problems are also prone to accidental injury and gastrointestinal disorder (gastritis, ulcers, liver failure).

Intravenous drug users are at high risk of physical illness. Sharing needles leads to the risk of becoming infected with the human immunodeficiency virus (HIV) and this has been well publicised by the media. There is, however, also the danger of contracting hepatitis. Other problems may include septicaemia, injury caused by poor injection technique, or thrombosis resulting from the injection of 'non-injectable' substances. As more veins become thrombosed, and therefore impossible to use, the addict may resort to the large, but hidden blood vessels in the groin (femoral vein) with disastrous results. Infection, thrombosis or damage to the femoral artery may lead to gangrene and the need for amputation of the leg. In addition, there are the problems of overdose, drug-induced psychosis and withdrawal states (see Ch. 11).

Some psychotic patients are at risk of self-harm in response to hallucinations or delusions.

Terry who suffered from schizophrenia was ordered by his 'voices' to jump off a railway bridge, sustaining multiple fractures and internal injuries.

David cut off his arm because he regarded it as containing all the evil in his body. He had great difficulty in accepting and using a prosthesis.

People with sexual delusions may perform self-castration or other mutilating acts.

The consequences of unsuccessful suicide attempts may be particularly distressing, with the depressed person sustaining multiple fractures or brain damage after jumping from a height. The prospect of continuing life in a wheelchair is not going to alleviate depression and people in such circumstances may be angry with themselves for 'not doing the job properly'. Motivation to participate in treatment can be greatly reduced and it can be difficult for staff in orthopaedic units to treat someone with problems which indicate admission to a psychiatric unit.

It is not only psychotic people who damage themselves.

Mary, who had an impulsive and antisocial personality, swallowed cutlery and a variety of other objects with such frequency that she received a near-injurious dose of radiation from all the X-rays taken.

Progress in physical rehabilitation may depend to a great extent on mental state and personality and the management of patients who sustain major physical injuries may not be possible within a psychiatric unit. In such instances, the psychiatric team should endeavour to maintain close contact with the medical team, as well as with their patient.

REHABILITATION IN PHYSICAL DISABILITY — THE PSYCHOLOGICAL PERSPECTIVE

Goal planning

The rehabilitation process in physical disability inevitably involves many different people: these will be professionals working within the hospital and community settings, and equally importantly, the patient and his relatives, and perhaps also volunteers. Most of this group of people will be very familiar with the components of the task involved in the rehabilitation process, e.g. the way in which one is fitted for and learns to use an artificial limb, how to transfer in and out of bed, car, bath, dressing and eating with limited use of upper limbs, organisation of adaptations to the house. To the patient and family, this process often appears huge, daunting, complex and confusing. This is particularly so if the person concerned has suffered any intellectual damage. It can thus be very helpful to the patient and also to other professionals to approach this task in terms of a collaborative effort, where a series of goals are established and progress towards these is monitored and reviewed. This idea obviously has its roots in psychological theories of learning where positive reinforcement increases the chances of behaviour being repeated. The idea of goal attainment scaling has been outlined by Kiresuk & Lund (1978). Staff often talk about patients in terms of being poorly motivated, and structured goal planning goes a long way to improve compliance with treatment and satisfaction all round. It is also a very effective tool in improving team communication, particularly where many people are involved in care.

Technique of goal planning

1. An initial goal planning meeting is set up with the patient and relevant members of staff. A key family member may also be present. It can sometimes be helpful to appoint a key worker at this stage to co-ordinate and see through any decisions made at the goal planning sessions.

2. The patient and staff look initially at the person's strengths and needs, to give a positive outlook on the tasks which lie ahead.

3. From this list of needs is generated a list of overall goals which can be broken down into smaller and more manageable targets, which are to be worked on over the subsequent period— usually between one week and a month. Frequently, goals emerge which might not have been anticipated in planning therapy on an individual basis and work towards these can be co-ordinated between relevant individuals.

4. Each person present at that meeting receives a copy of the decisions reached at the goal planning meeting and action to be taken is noted.

5. Subsequent meetings can review progress on the targets set, set new ones, and/or change the goals.

The advantages of this system are:

● They allow participation by the patient in planning his rehabilitation so that the all important element of control is retained. Where people feel some responsibility for their decisions, they are more likely to work towards achieving them.

● The patient receives feedback on his progress in tasks which may be repetitive or boring, but are very important in reaching an overall aim, e.g. pulling weights to improve muscle strength in upper arms.

● Team communication and accountability for seeing through action which has been decided upon.

Table 13.2 illustrates how a goal planning chart might look.

Table 13.2   Example of a goal planning chart

Achieved since last meeting	Goal	Current target
—transfers from bed to chair	—to manage all transfers	—work on transfers to bath and car
—now able to speak clearly although rather slowly	—to be able to speak as near to previous ability as possible	—work on speeding up speech to .... words per minute
—visited office and discussed return to work with boss	—to return to work	—to try some bits of work suggested by boss at last visit
—ramp fitted to house. Awaiting hoist for bathroom	—to get house fully adapted	—community OT to be contacted re. date for hoist installation

OT = occupational therapist

Information and education

Rehabilitation usually involves aspects of learning new skills or adapting old ones. Some of these skills may be essential in terms of helping the person remain at home rather than in hospital and prevent further deterioration of the condition. It may become paramount that the individual has sufficient information and understands the relevance of these issues. For example:

1. Regular checking of the skin and pressure lifts are essential in the prevention of pressure sores in those who have reduced sensation, such as spinal injury, multiple sclerosis. It is therefore very important that the person is taught how to do this and why. The consequences of not caring for skin can be very costly in terms of time spent in hospital for pressure sores to heal and the disruption to everyday life.

2. Someone who has had major heart surgery will need to know about diet, smoking, exercise, medication and many other factors. If they do not adhere to the relevant advice, they may be putting their life at risk or severely reducing the quality of life of which they would be capable.

Compliance with advice

Much work has been done by Ley (1988) and others on the way in which compliance with aspects of treatment can be improved by the provision of well-prepared information. This information may additionally increase the patient's feeling of satisfaction with treatment and feeling of being in control (which is positively correlated with successful outcome).

Most of the work in this area suggests that such information can be delivered in *verbal form*, but attention should be paid to the factors which tend to make patients forget this information. These are:

- anxiety level of the individual
- nature of presentation of the information (amount of technical words, speed of presentation, how many things are discussed, how much the person understands the concepts, order in which information is presented, etc.)
- atmosphere of the presentation and who is the giver of the information.

Information can also be delivered in *written form*, when similar considerations apply. Research indicates that due to the high rate of forgetting of verbal information, written information is particularly helpful not only for the patient but also for relatives.

Attention must be paid to the ease of reading of this information and the manner of presentation. It may also be helpful to assess patients' knowledge of key areas by questionnaire or interview methods, and results can be used to target repeat education and also to look at correlations with outcome.

Privacy, time and feelings

Privacy

Anyone who has spent time as a patient in hospital will be aware of the lack of privacy and personal space. This is a problem which is exacerbated if one has to spend many months in hospital and may place additional strain on relationships with family members. Hospital visiting itself is an artificial way in which to continue a relationship. It may be worthwhile staff bearing the issue of privacy in mind and doing what is possible to allow people a chance to have access to space where they know they will not be interrupted or overheard by other patients. It may also be helpful to encourage patients to put aside certain visiting days for close relatives only, so that a financial or personal discussion is not interrupted by a well-wishing neighbour who has just 'popped in to say hello'.

Privacy is also important if patients are to feel able to discuss emotional issues which may well have a bearing on how they progress through their rehabilitation. If the design of a ward or out-patient clinic or surgery has limited numbers of small rooms for one-to-one discussion with patients, try to find some ways round this; for example, arranging to use someone else's room when they will be out, using a treatment room or even a large cupboard!

Time and feelings

We discussed earlier in the chapter how feelings of depression, anger, exuberance, etc., are part of the adjustment to disability. It does not have to be the prerogative of certain members of staff to discuss these issues with patients. It is equally valid for a physiotherapist, nurse, occupational therapist, speech therapist or whoever to discuss feelings with the patient, as it is for the doctor, psychologist or psychiatrist. There must be nothing worse for someone to try to discuss feelings of depression with therapists or nursing staff and be met with a response that indicates they do not wish to listen. It is a valid part of anybody's job to take time to do this. Listening can be just as important as offering a solution to the feelings, and if one feels unsure about how to progress with a patient from there, then one can sensitively suggest asking someone more experienced in these matters to discuss the issues with the patient.

Suicide

Some people may experience suicidal feelings as a result of their feelings about their disability. Some may have incurred their disability as a result of a suicide attempt, e.g. spinal injury, head injury. It may be particularly difficult to discuss this with someone who has intellectual or speech impairment as a result of their injury. However, one must remember that consideration of suicide is probably much more common as a passing phenomenon amongst the disabled population, than the able bodied. This is likely to be particularly so when one is virtually totally dependent on others for care and may not always be part of the adjustment process.

If a patient is expressing suicidal ideas, it is important to let him talk about them and to explore the reasoning behind them. If they appear to be related to a depressive condition, then medical help in the form of medication may well be called for. A newly disabled person or someone with a progressive condition may have a distorted view of what may be possible for them in terms of independence in self-care, sporting and social activities, work opportunities and the chance of developing a sexual relationship. It is then crucial that the therapist is able to correct any of these distortions by presenting the options and exploring with the patient which might be acceptable. These may not match up to satisfaction at first sight, but time and continued discussion about such options may help them be viewed more positively. It is also important not to dismiss such suicidal feelings as silly and irrelevant. No one takes a decision about suicide lightly, and it is often a very painful process to reach the point at which it is being considered. Help to discuss the origin of these feelings, to work on changing distorted or negative thinking and review what positive attributes the future could hold can all be of benefit. In some cases, it may be very difficult to find the positive, particularly in terminal cases such as cancer or AIDS, and one may need to look at other ways of coming to terms with the feelings.

The social skills of disability

History

Anyone working in a psychiatric context is likely to have come across the concept of social skills and perhaps be familiar with the model underlying it. Social skills training developed alongside assertiveness training, as a way of teaching patients skills that would be needed to help integrate back into everyday life particularly after spending long periods in psychiatric hospital. It has broadened into uses with all groups of psychiatric patients as a way of building confidence in self, particularly in relationships with other people in different social settings. A very brief summary of the way in which social skills are taught is that it is usually in a group, with some modelling of the desired behaviour, then role-play by the patients, followed by feedback from the therapists of how well this was done with suggestions for improvement. A further progression is sometimes made to try these behaviours in a real situation rather than a simulated one.

Relevance of social skills training to the disabled

Someone who becomes disabled in whatever way may well need to learn new or adapt old social skills. This may be particularly related to how other people perceive those who are disabled but also related to a changed self-image and the ability to build up confidence.

Examples of situations in which social skills could be considered include the following:

1. Dealing with the 'does he take sugar' phenomenon. This is where someone is speaking to an individual who is accompanying the disabled individual about his requirements. Assertiveness skills may well be called for here.

2. Some may find themselves in a situation where too much help is being offered and one would much rather be left to try to do something independently. This is usually with strangers and can be particularly annoying for someone who has been disabled for a considerable time and has a well-developed system for tackling a

task. It may take longer, and they may seem to an outsider to be struggling, but they may infinitely prefer to do it themselves.

3. If a disabled person is alone while shopping or travelling or a similar situation, they may have to become more assertive in asking for help which they require.

4. Some people assume that all those who are physically disabled must also have a mental handicap. This can be very distressing if it happens frequently and one should develop strategies for dealing with this reaction. One tactic can be to always make the first moves in conversations, so that the other party is aware from what is said that the brain is still well intact.

5. Making new friendships particularly when there may be potential sexual involvement is another very important area. How one feels about one's own body image, how one dresses or manages to have conversations at a party where everyone is standing up and you are in a wheelchair are all fruitful areas for discussion and work. If one has an existing partner when the disability occurs and this relationship is sustained, then attracting the opposite sex may not be an issue. If one does not have a partner and wishes one, the social skills of establishing relationships with a disability may be worth considering.

6. Returning to work or finding a new job can also have its problems in terms of people being over solicitous or potential employers showing prejudice about the implications of the disability for the individual's ability to do the job in question.

Setting up social skills training

If one has worked in psychiatry, most patients are used to the idea of group work. When working with those with disability, it may not be so easy to introduce this idea. Some may see the issues too concretely, some may feel that it is irrelevant and others may feel that all this will get sorted out in time once they have had a chance to try things out from home. This may be true for some but by no means all.

Consequently, how one introduces and puts into practice the idea of a 'social skills training' for those with disability must be done with care and tact. One cannot assume that everyone will be equally ready to talk about the emotional aspect of some of the above examples in a group setting. Timing may be critical—if introduced too early in the rehabilitation process, people may have anxieties raised about further difficulties to be faced once home as well as all the physical problems. Some may not believe that these kinds of situations can occur unless they have had some experience of ordinary life outside the protected environment of the hospital and/or spoken to other people with disability who have been living at home for some time.

OTHER ASPECTS OF MANAGEMENT

Honesty is essential. An honest appraisal of the patient's prognosis may be difficult for everyone to face and distressing to give, but unrealistic expectations and false hopes only lead to disappointment and lack of trust. It is usually possible to give an honest account without totally destroying hope.

It is easier for staff if patients do not express the anger, frustration or distress they feel. Staff may, quite unconsciously, encourage and reinforce stoicism and avoidance of any show of emotion. It is much healthier for the patient to express the feelings he has, however difficult this may be for staff. It is important that all carers learn that anger directed towards them may not be the direct consequence of anything they have done, but is the expression of emotion to a trusted recipient.

Needs of patients cannot necessarily be met through the use of psychiatric models of care and sensitivity of approach is required in order to provide appropriate treatment. For example, group discussion may be an idea which seems unacceptable to people whose disabilities are primarily physical. However, modern trends in society lean toward more self-examination and self-disclosure than have formerly been acceptable. Much informal discussion takes place in the ward, but while a regular problem-sharing group is worthy of consideration, it is not something which can be imposed upon people.

The role played by statutory services is one aspect of care. As the balance shifts towards the community, and hence friends and family, it is important to acknowledge the considerable support provided by voluntary and self-help organisations. Some examples of organisations operating in the United Kingdom are the Spinal Injuries Association, Headway (head injuries) and the Multiple Sclerosis Society. They provide information and advice and may have resources which enable them to provide social activities or sheltered work. Special housing or holidays may also be available and these provide support for relatives and patients alike. Some organisations, e.g. DIG (Disabled Income Group) act as a pressure group, campaigning for the needs of the disabled and for suitable provision of resources.

Relationships between professionals and voluntary groups vary, but it is worth remembering that a fellow sufferer has a credibility that no carer can have. Understanding and valuable support and advice can be provided by someone who has already learned to cope with similar problems.

Another aspect of care is understanding of the needs of different cultures, particularly minority ethnic groups (see Ch. 10). Staff should make it their responsibility to become aware of the needs of the different groups in their locality. If, for example, it is regarded as being the family's responsibility to care for their disabled relative or to make decisions about his future, this has obvious implications for rehabilitation. The team should know where to obtain help and advice, and knowledge of special resources, such as interpreting services, is obviously helpful.

Health education is widely used in the prevention of problems, but education directed at a healthy life-style for patients and carers is becoming more common. Awareness of relaxation techniques and yoga have led to individuals practising these with consequent reduction in stress. In some hospitals, staff and self-help groups run courses which focus on education on how to cope with selected aspects of life-style, including disability management, recreation and welfare rights.

CONCLUSION

It can be seen from the points described above that there is considerable overlap between physical and psychiatric disorder. It is easy for psychiatric staff to be critical of the treatment of physical illness without any apparent recognition of the psychological sequelae. It is, however, important to recognise that while some of the issues in physical and psychiatric rehabilitation are similar, others are very different, and it would be a mistake to try to follow the same style of intervention without giving careful consideration to the individual situation. Helping a person to maximise his abilities and to cope as effectively as possible will always be an aim, but the means through which it is attained will vary according to his environment and resources.

REFERENCES AND FURTHER READING

Goffman E 1968 Stigma. Notes on the management of spoiled identity. Penguin, Harmondsworth

Kiresuk T J, Lund S M 1978 Goal attainment scaling. In: Atkinson C (ed) Evaluation of human science programmes. Academic Press, New York

Kübler Ross E 1970 On death and dying. Social Science Paperbacks, Tavistock, London

Ley P 1988 Communicating with patients. Croom Helm, London and New York

Moos R H 1984 Context and coping: towards a unifying conceptual framework. American Journal of Community Psychology 12: 5–36

Penson J, Fisher R 1991 Palliative care for people with cancer. Edward Arnold, London

Power P W, Dell Orto A E 1980 The role of the family in the rehabilitation of the physically disabled. University Park Press, Baltimore

Trieschmann R D 1980 Spinal cord injuries. Pergamon, New York

Wilkinson S 1990 Psychological aspects of physical disability. In: Broome A (ed) Health psychology: processes and applications. Chapman and Hall, London

Wright B 1983 Physical disability, a psychological approach, 2nd edn. Harper Row, London

14. Mental handicap/learning disability

Ros Lyall

Disabled persons have the inherent right to respect for their human dignity. Disabled persons, whatever the origin, nature, and severity of their handicaps and disabilities have the same fundamental rights as their fellow citizens of the same age, which implies first and foremost the right to enjoy a decent life, as normal and full as possible.

United Nations Declaration on the Rights of Disabled Persons 1975

This chapter is intended to provide the reader with an introduction to mental handicap and an overview of the role of rehabilitation, or more appropriately, habilitation, as it applies to people who have a mental handicap. The main focus is on practice in the UK.

The additional use in the title of the alternative label learning disability is quite deliberate. Mental handicap is increasingly being referred to as learning disability and the term learning difficulty still pertains in some areas but has been found wanting by many groups. The growth of the advocacy movement over the past 10 or so years, in particular organisations such as 'People First' which promotes self-advocacy for people who have a mental handicap, has put pressure on professionals, voluntary organisations, policy makers and others involved in the field to find a less pejorative label. Some groups denounce the need for a label altogether. In the United States amongst many other countries, the term mental retardation is still current, although a move to 'intellectual disability' is gaining ground. What is clear to many people is that labels can be useful; they inform policy and planning and provide a focus for training professionals in very specialised areas. The Royal College of Psychiatrists has retained the term 'mental handicap'; the UK Government is using the term 'learning disability' as do many voluntary organisations. Many health professionals are more comfortable with learning disability than any of the other options

233

to mental handicap, e.g. learning difficulty, and therefore, in deference to the wishes of the many people to whom the term 'mentally handicapped' would previously have applied, learning disability will be used synonymously, with and where possible instead of, mental handicap.

WHAT IS A MENTAL HANDICAP/LEARNING DISABILITY

A learning disability is not just a learning difficulty: dyslexia may cause a learning difficulty but does not amount to a mental handicap or learning disability. There has to be some impairment of intellectual functioning associated with impaired adaptive behaviour and developmental delay, particularly in terms of socioemotional development.

Diagnosis of mental handicap/learning disability is no longer based purely on measurement of IQ. The DSM-III-R (American Psychiatric Association 1980) lists the criteria for diagnosis as:

1. Significant sub-average intellectual functioning—an IQ of 70 or below on an individually administered IQ test.

N.B. The IQ range for people of normal intelligence is 80–120, i.e. 2 standard deviations from the norm of 100. The total measurable range is from 20–170+.

2. Concurrent deficits or impairments in adaptive behaviour, taking the individual's age into consideration.

3. Onset of intellectual impairment before the age of 18 years.

Mental handicap is therefore clearly placed as a developmental disorder. It is not a mental illness, although the public and many professionals in other spheres find the distinctions difficult and frequently confuse the two. Neither is it an applicable term to an individual over the age of 18 who suffers intellectual impairment as the result of a disease process or injury occurring after the developmental period, e.g. brain damage after head injury, chronic psychosis.

The tools used in the diagnosis of a learning disability vary depending on the age of the individual. Babies and young children are routinely seen at developmental clinics where delay in reaching milestones will be picked up and when such delay is severe then a 'positive' diagnosis will often be made. Some will have a diagnosis made at or before birth as the inevitable associations between some inherited or genetic conditions and a learning disability are established. Older children who perhaps were regarded as slow may be picked up at school where IQ tests are commonly used. One obvious disadvantage of this is that IQ test results are not static; they can be affected by other additional difficulties, e.g. visual or auditory problems and are not a foolproof indicator of future functioning. Other features of developmental delay should also be noted.

In adults, IQ assessments are rarely performed on a routine basis. Assessment of adaptive behaviour — skills to enable an individual to live a normal life — is much more relevant, as is the history and the experienced clinician's impression. This latter part is not about a quick look and a diagnosis of 'IQ 50' as so commonly stated in notes from the 1940s and '50s, but is about an assessment of how an individual relates to you, his general understanding of concepts, his thought processes etc., outwith a formal test situation.

Correct diagnosis is very important for an individual. A positive diagnosis should mean access to a variety of specialist resources to help the individual and others involved with him to maximise his potential. However, it also, unfortunately, often means denial or difficulty of access to other relevant services which are not aimed specifically at those with a learning disability.

The pitfalls of diagnosis and the factors which may affect the 'test' results are illustrated in the following case study.

Jane is a 20-year-old young woman who comes from a Cantonese family. At the time of referral, she lived with her parents, older brother and two younger sisters. She had gone to mainstream primary school but transferred to special school (for educationally sub-normal children) at 11 years of age. She had poor language development in English (her second language), difficulty in articulating and also a mild congenital non-progressive myopathy. IQ testing at school had indicated a large discrepancy between verbal and non-verbal tests — she scored higher on non-verbal tests. Jane was regarded as a shy, passive girl who worked hard. It was known that her family found her 'handicap' difficult to comprehend and often were very disparaging about her. Because of this background and a diagnosis of learning disability she ended up being seen by professionals in mental handicap.

Jane clearly stated that she did not wish to be regarded as 'special'—all attempts to get her on to special needs training or employment schemes failed because they were for people with a learning disability. It became clear that her understanding of concepts was far greater than the majority of people diagnosed as having a learning disability.

Her general appearance and approach indicated someone with

psychological difficulties but not learning disability, although clearly she had learning difficulties in some areas and was not totally 'normal'. A further IQ assessment based on Raven's matrices—a non-verbal, non-cultural test —indicated average intellectual ability. This was substantiated to some extent by the results of the standard IQ test used for adults—Wechsler adult intelligence scale — which indicated low scores in culturally sensitive verbal sub-tests and those which would be affected by her physical and mental state. The implication was of decreased performance as a result of anxiety, lack of self-confidence and difficulty in speaking. Clearly, mental handicap was neither a viable diagnosis or a suitable specialty to be helping her. However, once labelled, it is difficult to change other people's perceptions. Jane herself seemed to feel somewhat vindicated and appears to be more confident and assertive particularly within the family.

Other definitions

Although educationalists, psychiatrists, psychologists and social policy makers have to a large extent agreed about basic components of mental handicap/learning disability definitions, there remain the legal and statutory definitions applicable to this group of people which are framed in different language and often make use of outmoded concepts.

Mental Health Act 1983. Mental Health (Scotland) Act 1984

These two British Acts (and the Mental Health (Northern Ireland) Order 1986) have retained definitions of mental handicap and therefore jurisdiction over some people with a mental handicap with regard to compulsory admission to hospital, treatment and other apparent restrictions on free choice. This is despite some very intensive lobbying by MENCAP (a voluntary organisation) and other organisations.

The definitions relevant to people with a mental handicap are as follows:

Mental impairment—a state of arrested or incomplete development of mind (not amounting to severe mental impairment) which includes **significant** impairment of intelligence and social functioning and is associated with abnormally aggressive or seriously irresponsible conduct.

Severe mental impairment—a state of arrested or incomplete development of mind which includes **severe** impairment of intelligence and social functioning and is associated with abnormally aggressive or seriously irresponsible conduct.

These definitions will continue to be used by psychiatrists to facilitate compulsory treatment in hospital whether by use of the relevant Mental Health Act or through the criminal justice procedures allied to them. In their dealings with lawyers, judges, etc., psychiatrists and psychologists will still be called upon to use IQ assessments as a definitive means of diagnosing mental handicap, and will still be faced with requests to determine an individual's mental age.

Nor does the confusion end there, with some current Acts still using definitions and terms from even earlier Mental Health Acts, e.g. mental defective, and newer ones such as the UK Personal Community Charge regulations (the poll tax) allowing exemption on the grounds of severe mental impairment, the definition of which includes those suffering from dementia or brain injury.

INCIDENCE/PREVALENCE

How many people are we describing? Studies of incidence and/or prevalence of learning disability have to be carefully read. Many have only looked at those defined as having a severe learning disability, and there is general agreement that the overall prevalence for this group is approximately 3 per 1000. Improved medical care means that the prevalence in some specific groups, e.g. children under 5, has increased over the years but whether this affects the overall incidence has not been finally determined. Studies which have looked at the prevalence of less severe learning disability have been few and far between, as have those looking at overall figures; however, quoted figures are around the 3% mark (cf. incidence of schizophrenia at 1%).

Applying this to a specific population could imply a figure of approximately 21 000 in an overall population of approximately 700 000 (the Lothian region of Scotland). The majority of these people will not require services. Estimates of need within Lothian region have quoted figures of approximately 5 000, i.e. less than 1%. The vast majority of this group will be people with moderate and severe degrees of mental handicap according to the American Association on Mental Deficiency classification. This classification is based on IQ and is shown in Table 14.2 (see p. 240).

However, it is important to remember the contribution of education, social circumstances and economic factors to individuals with mild degrees of intellectual impairment as delineated by

IQ measurement which may imply that the diagnostic criteria for mental handicap would not be filled.

CAUSES OF MENTAL HANDICAP/LEARNING DISABILITY

Many causes of learning disability are now known and identifiable. There remains, however, a sizeable minority of cases—approximately 40%—for whom no cause can be identified. Table 14.1 lists some of the better known causes.

Many of the causes listed in Table 14.1 lead to a severe degree of learning disability — they are more readily identifiable earlier in life. There are, however, considerable numbers of people for whom no organic cause can be found, whose learning disability is classified as mild, and who are lumped together under the heading of 'subcultural mental handicap'. This description assumes an interaction of genetic and environmental factors. There is considerable evidence that social factors are a substantial part of the aetiology of some form of mild learning disability. However, there is also evidence that prolonged intervention on a large scale to minimise the effects of these social factors does not produce the decrease in prevalence that would be expected. Familial and cultural responsiveness to mild learning disabilities will continue to play a major role, particularly when diagnosis of learning disability is based not solely on IQ, which as already stated is an imperfect means of diagnosis, but also on adaptive behaviour, the norms for which tend to be based on middle class, normally intelligent populations. Subcultural learning disability is most common in social class V.

Table 14.1   Some known causes of mental handicap/learning disability

Prenatal	
Maternal infection	Cytomegalovirus
Injury	Rhesus incompatibility
Chromosomal	Down's syndrome (Trisomy 21)
Genetic	Phenylketonuria
Perinatal	
Birth injury	Anoxia leading to cerebral palsy
Infection	Gastroenteritis in new born
Other	Prematurity
Postnatal	
Infection	Encephalitis
Genetic	Disorders of carbohydrate metabolism
Injury	Lead poisoning
Other	Severe uncontrolled epilepsy

PREVENTION

Identification of causes for learning disability may lead to the possibility of preventing further cases. This is exemplified by the increasing number of screening tests for pregnant women designed to detect affected fetuses and enable selective termination of pregnancy if the woman wishes. An example of such a screening test is amniocentesis offered to all pregnant women in the UK over the age of 36, who are at increasing risk of bearing a child with Down's syndrome (Trisomy 21). Other screening procedures such as the Guthrie test, performed routinely on all newborn babies to identify those at risk of learning disability because of phenylke-tonuria, have resulted in the virtual elimination of this as a cause of learning disability in the younger age groups. Affected individuals grow and develop normally provided they eat a diet low in phenyl-alanine until they reach adulthood. Should an affected woman become pregnant, it is necessary to return to the special diet to avoid damaging the fetus profoundly.

Public education has a major part to play in prevention of learning disability. Maternal health is recognised as of profound importance in bearing healthy, normal children. Recent years have seen an increase in health education directed towards giving up smoking, reducing or stopping alcohol intake, stopping illegal drug taking, etc., before and during pregnancy. The spread of HIV and AIDS and the transmission of the virus to babies born to HIV-positive mothers may also in the future give us another regrettable cause for learning disability. Public awareness has been raised, but as with so many similar programmes it appears that those who respond positively are not in the highest risk category. For instance, whilst the overall incidence of smoking is dropping, it appears to be increasing in young women, despite all the health warnings for them and any potential pregnancy.

Mental handicap/learning disability can be prevented in some cases. It cannot usually be cured, and therefore rehabilitation is perhaps the wrong term to use in describing the processes whereby people with learning disabilities are enabled to live more normal lives. Habilitation is a more accurate term since it does not carry an expectation of reinstatement of fitness and health which is inherent in the definition of rehabilitation.

Curing learning disability only refers to those situations where an individual is diagnosed as a child as having a mild learning disability, perhaps because of social and educational factors and

Table 14.2 Classification of degrees of mental handicap/learning disability

Category of mental handicap	Measured IQ range	Potential degree of support	Approximate prevalence in the population
Mild	50–70	Visiting support/ daytime staff	30/1 000
Moderate	35–49	24-hr staffing sleep in at night	3.0/1 000
Severe	20–34	24-hr waking staff	3.0/1 000
Profound	Below 20	24-hr trained staff	0.5/1 000

who, over time, improves his situation so that he can no longer be classed as learning disabled. For example, a young man of 17 from a poor social background, frequently a truant from school who, because of criminal activity and a learning disability diagnosed by IQ and other means, is sent to an institution where he is able to mature, gain social skills and remedy his education may be discharged cured of his learning disability!

Table 14.2 shows the classification of degrees of mental handicap/learning disability as defined by the American Association of Mental Deficiency classification, and gives an indication of the degree of support which may be required to enable an individual to live successfully in the community, and the approximate prevalence.

HISTORICAL ASPECTS

Historically, people who had a learning disability were stigmatised and whilst some of the balance has been redressed with the advent of normalisation (see later) and the push towards community care, there are still myths around which can hinder or prevent people with a learning disability leading as normal a life as possible. In the latter part of the 19th century and first half of this century, people such as Tredgold (Tredgold & Soddy 1970) and Fernald (1919) espoused the cause of the Eugenics Movement dedicated to preserving the purity of races. In some countries, this led to the compulsory sterilisation of people with a learning disability to prevent them producing more 'promiscuous criminals'. It was a commonly held belief that people with a learning disability were prime sources of sexual irregularities — promiscuity, prostitution and perversion, and that they were inherently criminalistic. Despite much research to try and back up these beliefs, no evidence to support them was found, indeed the opposite was found to be true and Fernald amongst others was forced to change his views. However, the damage had been done and even today, apparently intelligent professional people will still produce these arguments to try and prevent resettlement of people from institutions to more appropriate community residences.

There were some enlightened people who attempted to provide better care and training for people who had learning disabilities. Their efforts proved that with intensive training, many people thought to be incapable of learning basic self-care skills could be taught these and other skills such as communication, reading, writing and numeracy. Institutions were established to promote these ideas but as the numbers of institutions and those in them increased the emphasis switched to containment. The pressures of the Eugenics Movement and a perceived need to remove the care of people with learning disability from families to the State led to the passing of a Mental Deficiency Act (1913) to permit the compulsory institutionalisation of people with a learning disability in the UK. As noted previously even today, people with a learning disability can still be compulsorily detained in an institution under the terms of the appropriate Mental Health Acts (Mental Health Act 1983, Mental Health (Scotland) Act 1984, Mental Health (Northern Ireland) Order 1986).

In the 1950s, it was becoming clear that institutional care was not necessarily a good thing. The ideas which led to the establishment of the original institutions had long been lost. The move towards more community-based care began and the Mental Health Act 1959 placed a requirement upon local authorities to provide appropriate residential and day care. An important milestone was the passing in 1974 of the Education (Mentally Handicapped Children) (Scotland) Act which made it a duty for local authorities to provide education for all handicapped children, echoing the views of those earlier pioneers. On an international scale, the philosophy of normalisation, a principle described by Nirje in 1969 and expanded by Wolfensberger (1972), held that people with a learning disability had the right to 'as normal a life as possible'. This philosophy underpins current thought and practice in relation to people with a learning disability and is a vital part of the shift from institutional to community care.

The specific principles inherent in normalisation (Nirje 1969) are:

1. Opportunities to have a normal daily rhythm.
2. Opportunities to experience a normal weekly rhythm.
3. Experiencing the normal rhythm of the year.
4. Opportunities to undergo the normal developmental experiences of the life cycle.
5. The right to normal respect and consideration of choices, wishes and desires and the right to self-determination.
6. Living in a heterosexual world.
7. Applying normal economic standards.
8. Normal environmental standards.

In practice, what does all this mean? Examples are listed below against the relevant principle number.

1. Not being forced to go to bed at 8.00 pm when the night staff come on duty.
2. Having weekends different from weekdays.
3. Experiencing different weather conditions—going out in the rain.
4. Not being treated like the eternal child, allowed to experience bereavement and grief.
5. Being asked if you would like milk and sugar in your tea.
6. Not being segregated.
7. Having enough money, being paid appropriately for work.
8. Not having to share a room if you do not want to.

Some of this may appear trivial, but the genesis of normalisation from the institutional experiences of the 1950s where wards of 60 or more people were herded together with no personal possessions or choice gives some understanding of the importance of such matters on an individual level.

CURRENT SITUATION

The shift of care from institutions to the community has continued since the early 1960s.

In the late 1980s, a major change in the delivery of health and social care was proposed by the Government. Following the recommendations contained in the Griffiths Report (Department of Health 1988), the NHS and Community Care Act 1990 clearly laid the lead responsibility for providing services for people with learning disabilities on local authorities. This is not to say that the NHS does not continue to have a role in service provision for this client group, but that any provision should be clearly linked to health needs. The distinction between health and social care, however, is not clear cut and there is a large grey area. Under the 1990 Act, funding of community care is to be removed from the DSS (Department of Social Security), who contributed largely through the benefits system of the welfare state, and transferred to local authorities. Provision of care is, in the future, to be clearly based on assessment of need and a premise that people should remain in their own homes if they wish. Unfortunately, the funding is not to be ring-fenced for learning disability as it is for mental illness. Thus we have almost come full circle, and it is important not to allow the advances in care and training and the principles of a normal life to be lost at the expense of providing community care on a shoestring.

Habilitation and rehabilitation in learning disability may often be lifelong, and does not involve the learning disabled individual alone. In order to provide a coherent view of the role and function of habilitation in learning disability, the rest of the chapter is divided broadly into childhood, adolescence and adulthood.

CHILDHOOD AND FAMILIES

'A handicapped child means a handicapped family.'

The birth of a child who has a learning disability is a potentially traumatic event for parents and siblings. In the past, such families were often told to put their child in an institution and forget about it. Thankfully, this is not now standard advice and the vast majority of such children are cared for at home with support from appropriate education and child care resources where available.

Early counselling of families with a child who has learning disabilities is now recognised as being essential. This may be on an individual basis or in groups. It is an area of rehabilitation which has been neglected for many years and where small voluntary organisations have often filled the gap left by professionals. Examples are Nucleus, which provides trained parent and non-parent counsellors, and the Down's Syndrome Association. Parents faced with a learning disabled child will grieve for the normal child they have lost, and for the normal future that they expected. They may reject the child and/or the diagnosis.

Parenting skills which they took for granted may be lost when faced with a child whose demands are much greater than normal. Professionals should be attentive to these needs, to offer appropriate practical and supportive advice and help where necessary. Many parents complain that they get no help from professionals— perhaps it is our own feelings of inadequacy in dealing with people's grief and difficult circumstances often outwith our personal experience, but if we are to fulfil our roles we must be involved. One common complaint that parents make is that their learning disabled children will not settle and sleep at night. This can be extremely disruptive to a family. Medication often has little effect. In many cases, it is no worse than the difficulties experienced by families of normal children; the difference is in the parental response—they feel unable to leave a child to settle noisily if she is learning disabled and the child quickly learns that this is a good way to gain attention. Parents require practical advice and support to deal appropriately with these sorts of problems.

Education for learning disabled children starts at a very early age in terms of specific educational input. Early intervention techniques were heralded as a means of minimising handicap— their value overall is doubtful although children can make gains in specific areas in the short-term. Parents and others, however, feel that they are beneficial and there is no doubt that they can improve the parents' relationship with their learning disabled child. One commonly used form of early intervention is the Portage guide to early education. This is aimed at pre-school children and uses the parent as teacher under the supervision of a trained professional— often a community nurse in mental handicap, speech therapist or clinical psychologist. The programme is designed to start as soon as possible after birth and diagnosis. It concentrates on six developmental areas — motor skills, responsiveness to stimulation, cognitive ability, language development, socialisation and self-help skills. Goals are set for each area and the teaching is broken down into very small steps. It is intensive, with weekly visits from the professional. Progress is likely to be noticeable in some areas each week due to the size of the steps involved—this improves the parents' view of the child and their relationship.

School age

As noted in the introduction, education for all children was assured in Britain from the mid 1970s.

Currently, the majority of children with moderate or severe degrees of learning disability will be educated within local authority schools which cater for children with special needs. Those with mild degrees of disability may be 'mainstreamed' — attend ordinary school with the added support of specialist teachers. This is an increasing practice as there is more emphasis on integration. The move towards greater parental choice regarding schooling means that this option is likely to be extended to more disabled children. Curricula at schools catering for mild and moderate degrees of learning disability are broadly similar to mainstream schools, although with more emphasis on independent living skills. For those with more severe disability, development of communication, social and self-help skills and leisure pursuits are considered more appropriate as is practical problem solving. For specific groups of children and young people, e.g. those with autism, specialist voluntary organisations such as the Scottish Society for Autistic Children or Camphill – Rudolph Steiner schools provide special residential education.

Children with complex learning disabilities, otherwise known as profoundly mentally or multiply handicapped, pose a challenge to educational services. There are two major categories: those whose developmental delay is such that at school age they are still functioning as children of less than 1 year of age, and those whose attendant behavioural difficulties compound a slightly less severe developmental delay so that overall they are profoundly disabled. Ideally, education for these groups requires close co-operation between specialist health provision and education — many will have major medical and nursing needs because of epilepsy or serious physical problems. Innovative arrangements whereby community nurses in mental handicap work full time in special schools have demonstrated the value of this close co-operation. Education is geared to increasing awareness of the child himself and of others, and stimulation of vision, hearing, movement, smell and taste for the multiply handicapped and in areas of self-help— toileting, feeding, dressing, etc. — for those not quite so developmentally delayed.

ADOLESCENCE

Education for adolescents with learning disability can continue to 18 or 19 (or even older in some circumstances). Further education at colleges on 'extension courses' or 'life skills' courses is increasingly available for those with mild and moderate degrees of learning disability. Integration into mainstream colleges, albeit on distinct courses is also being planned for some severely and profoundly learning disabled young people—in these situations co-operation between education, social work and the health authority is again essential as specialist health care professionals such as community nurses in mental handicap, speech therapists and physiotherapists are an integral part of providing an appropriate service. College courses, where appropriate, look at independent living skills, social and interpersonal skills, vocational training and leisure activities. Many of those with normal intellectual development do not need to learn such things in an organised setting—many would probably benefit if they were enabled to attend, but for the young person with a learning disability it is a vital aspect of habilitation. It often continues into adult life with attendance at adult basic education courses which are not always aimed specifically at those with a learning disability.

Adolescents are particularly prone to overprotection. Girls may be put on the contraceptive pill or sterilised 'just in case'; both boys and girls may be referred to psychiatrists for treatment for temper tantrums when in reality this is 'normal' adolescent rebellion; and they may be prevented from travelling anywhere alone or by public transport. In some situations, it has been necessary to admit an adult to an institution to try and reverse the effects of institutionalisation in the family!

Support for families is available not just in the form of residential and day care or education. Short-term respite care for children is almost essential but not universally available. Professional support from specialist community mental handicap nurses, social workers, etc., can make a big difference to a family's ability to manage. There is a delicate balancing act to be achieved between feast and famine in support.

Attempts to achieve this balance and to facilitate access and communication for parents and professionals have resulted in the formation of multidisciplinary teams, commonly but not universally known as CMHTs (community mental handicap teams). Their role will be discussed in greater detail later in the chapter.

Self-help groups, support groups and counselling groups also provide valuable support for parents, carers and siblings. They are not universally acceptable; some parents and carers do not find them helpful, for a variety of reasons. The groups often attempt to plug the gaps in statutory services as previously noted; many do an excellent job. Whereas the focus of statutory services and professionals is often on the individual with a learning disability, self-help groups often focus on the needs of the carers — sometimes 'pressure groups' result to promote the needs and aspirations of individuals with a learning disability (e.g. Parent Pressure).

After school/college

Traditionally, social work departments have provided adult training centres (ATCs) for people with learning disabilities after they have left school or college. Inevitably, demand outstrips available places. Many of the same skill areas covered in schools or colleges are also present in ATC programmes. In some ATCs, sheltered work placements or supported placements in the open market are available. Increasingly, voluntary and statutory agencies are providing employment schemes specifically for people with a learning disability — much depends on the local employment market. These enable people to earn a 'proper wage' instead of the bonus money (often about £2–£5) that attenders at ATCs often receive for being there for 5 days.

In some areas, voluntary agencies provide day centre places. These are often 'work' based, with pottery, weaving, stained glass, bakery and joinery, etc., attempting to provide experience of producing saleable items. The underlying philosophy, in such organisations as Rudolph Steiner, of the inherent worth of each individual, plays a major part in the success of these centres in providing for those who do not fit into the ordinary ATC.

As the trend to sheltered employment and supported work placements increases, so ATCs and resource centres are providing places for people with profound multiple handicaps. Special needs places in centres require higher staff:client ratios and in some areas, community nurses in mental handicap and other specialist health care workers have been seconded or placed in ATCs on a part- or full-time basis. This has much improved the accessibility for those with significant health care needs.

Institutions

Many institutions for people with learning disability are closing or retracting considerably. It is no longer usual for people to be admitted when they reach late adolescence or adulthood. At their height, they provided a home, 'care and training' for approximately

25% of the population with learning disabilities. That percentage is now less than 4% in England and Wales, although it remains somewhat higher in Scotland (approximately 15%). Commonly placed geographically isolated from centres of population, they are trying to resettle their residents into community settings. Institutions have been blamed for many of the difficulties which individuals encounter when they move, and programmes of habilitation and resettlement involve lengthy and intensive training. That being said, some difficulties, notably those classed as behaviour disorders or challenging behaviour, are not always the result of institutionalisation; many individuals have been placed in institutional care *because* of these problems. It is accepted that the role of institutions should now be restricted to providing care and treatment for those with significant medical and nursing needs, additional behavioural or psychiatric problems. However, there are concerns that they will be called upon in the future to admit people for more social reasons because of potentially restricted access to community care.

Providing care for appropriate people does not have to take place in current institutional settings. Health care, including residential and treatment facilities, can be provided in small community-based units which are staffed by relevant health care professionals.

ADULTHOOD

The role of families in caring for their relative with learning disability often continues beyond childhood and adolescence into adulthood. Improved day care and residential facilities provided by statutory, voluntary and private agencies help to ease the burden. However, there are still families who reject all such help and devote their lives to caring for the individual concerned. Habilitation and the provision of a more normal life are often fraught with great difficulties in these situations as families overprotect and isolate the individual leading to crisis situations when one or both carers die.

Leaving home

Many people leave the parental home in their late teens, early twenties. This may be for employment, further education or emotional reasons to mention a few. This option is one which has been and remains much more difficult for people with learning disabilities to take. The availability of residential accommodation with appropriate support is limited, although expanding. The range of such accommodation from single-person supported flats supplied by housing associations to intensively staffed hostels for small numbers of people with multiple handicaps is increasing, but as in many areas of life, demand far exceeds supply. In recent years, specialist housing associations and voluntary agencies have come to the fore in attempting to fill the gaps left by statutory bodies. Many schemes have depended on DSS funding — attendance allowance, board and lodgings allowance, etc., and whilst funding is guaranteed to some extent for those set up before April 1993, the new arrangements under the Community Care Act may mean a change in the provision of residential care.

Some social service departments now recruit 'community carers' — people paid a standard rate to provide a home for one or more people with a learning disability either in the carer's home or occasionally in a self-contained part of the house. This form of 'adult fostering' has been very successful with a number of people; however, there are pitfalls, the largest being the high expectations of the carer for the person with a learning disability, particularly with regard to their emotional development and interpersonal skills — not everyone is a smiling happy person with Down's syndrome who causes no bother. Very few people, whether they have Down's syndrome or not are like that.

Innovative schemes have enabled not just people with learning disability but also the physically disabled, elderly and those with mental illness to live more independent lives. Share Housing provides well-staffed small group homes for people with severe learning disabilities and major national organisations such as MENCAP provide a range of accommodation. Family living with a difference is provided by the Rudolph Steiner organisation with communities often set in rural situations and self-contained in most aspects of their day-to-day life (enlightened institutions?). They provide a valuable resource for those for whom standard, urban provision is not appropriate, often for behavioural or emotional reasons.

Parents of people with learning disabilities usually want security of provision for their offspring. They want a home for life to provide reassurance for them as they become unable to care.

But be warned, the normalisation zealots who say that everyone should leave home may cause untold problems in situations where neither parent(s) nor their child wishes to take advantage of the offer of residential care or more independent living. Just because *most* people do it does not mean that it should be the goal of all people with a learning disability. People should have the choice.

Resettlement

The push towards community-based care has enabled many residents in long-stay institutions to leave and live in more appropriate accommodation in their local communities. For some, this has meant social services hostels or equivalent voluntary agency provision, but for others, unable to take advantage of mainstream provision, it has meant becoming involved in innovative joint projects between the Health Board and a voluntary agency. In one such venture, two staffed hostels for approximately 20 people are owned and managed by a voluntary agency and staffed by a mixture of care staff employed by the agency and specialist nursing staff seconded by the health authority. The success of these and other similar projects is underlined by the ability — 3 years on — for the seconded staff to be withdrawn. These successes are in stark contrast to the situation in some areas where resettlement has left people in bed and breakfast accommodation with no structure to their lives, vulnerable and with little or no support. The strategy which underpins all resettlement should be the provision of a quality of life at least equal to but preferably better than that which an individual enjoyed within the institution. Some may say that anything is preferable, but if care is not taken, many people will lose support, access to recreational and leisure facilities and a relatively risk-free environment. Life outside an institution can be very hard.

Leisure and recreational activities

The availability of these within the community has increased for all sections of the population. Clubs which cater specifically for people with learning disabilities are often an integral part of a voluntary organisation. However, new emphasis on integration has prompted the setting up of community resources for all groups. This has its problems as many people are wary of those with learning disabilities and they may then become isolated. An alternative is to create resources for people with a learning disability and then allow/invite the rest of the public to join in. Cafes, drop-in clubs, use of specialist facilities (ATCs, etc.) by other groups have all shown that integration can work. People who are learning disabled enjoy many of the same things as everyone else; the

Special Olympics has shown how much pleasure and self-fulfilment can be gained from participating in sporting activities, and theatre groups have done for some others what no amount of training and habilitation can do. The importance of leisure and recreation is increasingly recognised amongst all sections of the population and should be an integral part of everyone's life.

HABILITATION AND REHABILITATION

The process

It has already been said that for people with a learning disability habilitation is often an ongoing process. The concepts inherent in rehabilitation, of regaining former abilities, do not apply to the majority of those who have a learning disability, although clearly for some who develop additional difficulties such as serious mental illness, challenging behaviour or physical problems, rehabilitation does have a place.

The advent of community care policies based on the Griffiths Report has resulted in new terms and terminology for people with learning disabilities as well as other groups. We now have to refer to 'assessment and care (or case) management' and 'needs led services'. The ideas and practices embodied in these terms have been part of habilitation for a number of years.

Assessment

'People with a learning disability are not a homogeneous group.'

Assessment is an ongoing process. It enables a formulation of ideas regarding an individual's strengths and weaknesses, highlights areas of need and leads to a comprehensive package of care including treatment, which will facilitate the individual's progress in order to achieve greater personal autonomy and an improved quality of life. The package of care and the goals of the care plan(s) require regular re-assessment and re-structuring as necessary. Particularly in the area of learning disability, professionals have to be wary of making pronouncements which see too far into the future. There are many ambulant people with a severe learning disability whose parents were advised that their child would never walk.

Assessment may also concentrate on one particular aspect of an individual, e.g. communication difficulties. It would, however, be unwise to ignore all the other areas of an individual's functioning, or indeed family or environmental matters which clearly have a bearing on the individual's presentation.

Assessment, therefore, is to facilitate treatment in its widest sense and to delineate goals. Who does the assessment depends on the presenting need. Learning disability as a specialty has a considerable number of different and diverse professional groups involved in service provision. In an ideal world, all areas would have access to the appropriate professionals — in practice, psychiatrists become involved in clinical psychology matters, as do community nurses. Physiotherapists and occupational therapists fight hard to see patients/clients for treatment only and often get drawn in to providing more generalised 'occupation' or recreational sessions.

Requests for specific assessments often emanate from the multidisciplinary clinical team providing care for in-patients in hospital. The results of the assessment and an agreed care plan are discussed with the patient/client where appropriate, and the situation monitored through regular multidisciplinary meetings.

Clients living in the community may be referred by any number of people, including parents and carers. There, requests for assessment are often channelled through the local CMHT. CMHTs exist to provide a single door, easy access to a variety of professionals who can provide help for people with learning disabilities. They also provide a time-saving forum for professionals to discuss cases which may involve more than one professional or team member. In many areas, teams are supported by both major statutory agencies — health and social work, and typically comprise social worker(s), community mental handicap nurse(s), consultant psychiatrist and clinical psychologist. Additional members from the many other groups involved, e.g. speech therapists, occupational therapists, physiotherapists, GP, consultant paediatrician, housing support worker, to mention but a few, also have an important role to play, although often on a part-time client-led basis — i.e. they are not always permanent members of the team.

There has been criticism in some areas of the concept of CMHTs. Some argue against the necessity for specialist services, others regard them as time-wasting talking shops. It would appear that, under the new arrangements with social work having the lead responsibility, and the clear intention that multidisciplinary assessment and care management should be the norm when appropriate, CMHTs are ideally placed to provide an appropriate vehicle for assessment and care management for people with a learning disability, and that statutory agencies should avoid re-inventing the wheel!

Assessment then should be holistic, although it is often led by a single factor, e.g. poor communication, behavioural disturbance; it should be carried out by the minimum number of appropriate professionals, and be appropriate to the individual's intellectual ability. The results should inform the practice and thinking of those who are 'treating' the individual, and there should be regular evaluation and re-assessment as necessary.

Assessment — then what? The care plan concept

The care plan is based on a total approach to the individual. Not every single facet of the care plan requires to be informed by formal assessment. Background information is often more than adequate to direct any general habilitation process, and should also mitigate the effects of ideological zealots as illustrated below.

A young man of 25, who is perfectly capable of living independently if he would learn to budget and do simple cooking, lives with his parents and siblings in a nice area of town. He has his own room, attends an ATC, keeps all his pocket money, his mother does all his washing, ironing, etc., cooks his meals as she does for the rest of the family, he comes and goes to a large extent as he pleases. His social worker thinks he should leave home and become more independent and sets up a care plan to help him achieve this. Unfortunately, the young man has no desire to leave the comfort of his parents' house and his relatively easy life, and perhaps not surprisingly, the training programme not only fails but also has negative effects as his anxiety levels rise. Had there been a little more thought about his general circumstances a more appropriate care plan could have been implemented. Habilitation has to have, to a large extent, the co-operation of the individual concerned.

Examples of care planning currently used are: (1) the individual programme plan (IPP)—a written plan of action with realistic goals and the means of achieving them for different areas of an individual's life. The plan is reviewed and updated on a regular basis and is produced by those professionals closely involved with the person concerned. The subject of the plan is able to put his point of view independently or through an advocate; (2) shared action plan — this is similar to an IPP but with one major difference, the individual is involved right from the start and goals, etc., are set jointly and there is collaboration on planning.

Both these examples include evaluation of the process and the ability to change direction if necessary. In implementing any strategies agreed, do not try to do too much too quickly. Wherever possible, particularly if the habilitation is based on skill acquisition, e.g. learning to cook simple meals, the training should take place where the person will be expected to carry out the task routinely. Training kitchens, etc., have their place, but people with a learning disability often find it difficult to generalise learning from one setting to another. Be prepared to break the steps down to smaller segments if necessary.

Care planning therefore is the basis for any habilitation or rehabilitation in people with learning disabilities. It fulfils the criteria for a client-centred, needs-led approach which is not static and is subject to regular re-evaluation. As a concept it is ideal for use in multidisciplinary assessment and care management under the new arrangements for provision of community care.

SPECIFIC ASSESSMENTS AND AREAS OF INTERVENTION

People with a learning disability have many areas of their lives which may require intervention in terms of habilitation and progression to more independent living. There are many assessment tools which aim to delineate those areas requiring help. Two of the most widely used are the ABS—Adaptive Behaviour Scale (American Association on Mental Deficiency) and the HALO assessment—(Hampshire Assessment for Living with Others). In the former, observations by care staff and others provide information regarding adaptive and maladaptive behaviours; the latter incorporates the individual's view of how important a particular skill is for them.

Challenging behaviour

Maladaptive behaviours or challenging behaviours may have a far-reaching effect on an individual and his/her environment. They can seriously impede a person's progress and in some situations prevent a hospital resident moving out to more appropriate accommodation. The assumption that an individual's challenging behaviour was merely a response to being in an institution and that moving the person out to a small group home would ensure completely normal behaviour has been disproved on many occasions, often sadly, to the detriment of the individual concerned. Challenging behaviour can be modified; it is time-consuming and requires a rigorous approach to assessment and consistent implementation of any programme. Assessment of challenging behaviour is best done by observation in order to identify clearly triggers which may be environmental or more personal, and to clarify management strategies. This may be achieved by asking staff to record clearly each incident on an ABC model (antecedent, behaviour, consequences) or by a trained observer 'sitting in' for periods of time. In some situations, it will be clear that the means of modifying the behaviour is to respond to it in a consistent non-rewarding manner; in others improving a skill such as communication may be the answer. In yet more, some combination of approach will be necessary. Improvements in the person's quality of life (and that of their living companions) will attest to the success of the interventions. Other approaches which may be tried include 'gentle teaching' — this seems to be more successful with severely handicapped people than traditional behaviour modification techniques, particularly for self-injurious behaviour.

Mental illness

The incidence of mental illness in people with a learning disability is slightly higher than that of the normal population. This applies both to neurotic and psychotic illnesses. Diagnosis can often be more difficult and the presentation very different. Such people are doubly disadvantaged and may require habilitation and rehabilitation. Neither may be possible until the illness is under some control. People with a learning disability are now much more exposed to the stresses and strains of everyday life and are at greater risk of becoming unwell. There is also a tendency to automatically ascribe behavioural change to something other than a psychiatric illness and to proceed without excluding that possibility (in a similar fashion to physical illnesses). The following case history, considerably abridged, may help to highlight the difficulties.

Jane is a 36-year-old woman living in a local authority hostel. She has a long history of challenging behaviour — temper tantrums, aggressive outbursts, non-co-operation, running away, etc. She had been threatened with expulsion from her ATC because of her behaviour towards other trainees. Intensive work with a behaviour modification programme and a restructuring of her daily routine produced some improvement, however, staff felt that her mood was low. She became increasingly demanding, child-like and was also on the go all the time, up and down all night, collecting leaves, paper, etc., and storing them in her room. A diagnosis of mixed affective psychosis was made and she was admitted to the health authority hostel for treatment and stabilisation. The behaviour modification programme continued, having become a management plan for the clearly delineated challenging behaviours; the other behavioural disturbance resulting from her major mental illness was treated with a depot phenothiazine. She remains well some 18 months later (at the time of writing). It is likely that she has had manic depressive psychosis for many years in addition to her learning disability, which is severe, and her challenging behaviour. Staff need clear guidelines as to her management and also need to get to know her very well.

Pre-senile dementia

Increased life expectancy in people with Down's syndrome has led to an increasing incidence of pre-senile dementia. The association between Down's syndrome and dementia has been known for many years and recent work indicating the location of the gene responsible for pre-senile dementia to chromosome 21 has further strengthened the link. The emphasis here is to maintain skills as far as possible and to provide appropriate supports for the individual, parent(s) or carers.

Integration of people with mild and moderate learning disabilities into mainstream psychiatric services when they develop a mental illness is desirable but not always achievable. Whilst on the one hand they may not cope well with a busy acute psychiatric ward and be unable to participate fully in ward programmes, they have far more in common with these patients than with residents in a long-stay institution for severely learning disabled people. For these people, it is their mental illness which is the major diagnosis and not their learning disability. This is particularly relevant for those who develop psychotic illness and who may require highly staffed secure accommodation for a short period of time. Unfortunately, many after-care services, particularly those run by voluntary organisations, will not take people with a learning disability, despite the fact that many people with chronic psychosis are functioning at similar levels. The techniques of rehabilitation which are applied to this group are equally applicable to people who have a dual diagnosis.

Use of medication

Use of antipsychotic medication has been much discussed in the management of people with learning disability. There is clearly a place for it in the treatment of psychosis; what is more contentious is its use to treat challenging behaviour or hyperactivity. Indiscriminate use to control people is not acceptable. However, some benefits in terms of reducing tension and overactivity to enable learning do justify its use in certain circumstances. Drugs such as carbamazepine, principally used as an anticonvulsant, do appear to have a beneficial effect on people who have unpredictable outbursts of temper and aggression, as do antipsychotics such as haloperidol or clopenthixol. If antipsychotic drugs are to be used in the absence of clearly diagnosed mental illness their use must be regularly reviewed (as for those who are diagnosed). In general, minor tranquillisers do not have a place except in the very short-term.

Social skills and sex

People with a learning disability often have major deficits in social skills which make them noticeable. Standing too close to someone or inappropriate social touching are just a couple of examples which are dealt with during habilitation programmes. When such inappropriate behaviour appears sexual in its nature, then the problems for the individual and for carers and professionals take on a whole different quality.

A typical scenario is an adolescent man aged 16–17 years with a moderate degree of learning disability who is charged after having kissed or fondled a young girl. On the face of it, this is serious and raises all sorts of spectres in the public's mind. In practice, the young man has probably had little or no sex education, is not aware that what he is doing is against the law, and is not able to recognise sexual needs as such in himself. It is an area of education, training and habilitation that is often neglected and leaves people with a learning disability very vulnerable.

Craft & Craft (1978) have written extensively on sexuality and learning disability, and emphasised the fact that people with learning disabilities are no different in their needs and desires from anybody else. Community care means that more young people (and older people) who have a learning disability are going to be potentially vulnerable in this area. This and the increasing incidence of HIV and AIDS throughout the normal population add further weight to the argument that the best way to protect individuals is to give them information and not keep them ignorant.

Social skills training uses several methods—modelling, role-play, social re-inforcement, instruction and importantly feedback, depending on the particular skill being taught, e.g. conversation skills. As with other forms of training in people with learning disabilities, there are problems of generalising the newly learnt skills to other areas. It seems that greater success is achieved when social skills training forms part of a larger programme to increase community integration. One such programme, produced by the Open University and MENCAP (1986), is called 'Mental Handicap: Patterns for Living', which aims to support professionals and others involved in promoting and implementing positive changes in the lives of people with a learning disability. At the heart of this programme is the need for community integration and the role of social skills in achieving this.

This chapter has endeavoured to give the reader an introduction to mental handicap/learning disability, and to indicate where habilitation and rehabilitation fit in the general scheme. It is important to remember that people with a learning disability are not immune from additional psychiatric or physical problems and to stress again that their learning disability does not preclude them from benefiting from appropriate rehabilitation. Do not take the view that rehabilitation, or any other form of treatment, is not worth it 'because they're mentally handicapped'. Anything which improves an individual's quality of life is 'worth it'.

REFERENCES AND FURTHER READING

American Psychiatric Association 1980 Diagnostic and statistical manual of mental disorders, 3rd edn. American Psychiatric Association, Washington DC
Craft A, Craft M 1978 Sex and the mentally handicapped. Routledge & Kegan Paul, London
Department of Health 1988 Community care agenda for action. London
Fernald W E 1919 A state program for the care of the mentally retarded. Mental Hygiene 3: 566–574
Fraser W I, McGillivray R C, Green A M (eds) 1991 Hallas' caring for people with mental handicaps, 8th edn. Butterworth Heinemann, Oxford
Nirje B 1969 The normalisation principle and its human management implications. In Kugel R, Wolfensberger W (eds.) 1972 Changing patterns in residential services for the mentally retarded. President's Committee On Mental Retardation, Washington DC
Open University in collaboration with Mencap 1986 Mental handicap Patterns for living. Open University Press, p. 555
Tredgold R F, Soddy K 1970 Tredgold's mental retardation, 11th edn. Baillière Tindall and Cassell, London
Wolfensberger W 1972 The principle of normalisation In Human Services. National Institute on Mental Retardation, Toronto

15. The future

Clephane Hume   Ian Pullen

You cannot fight against the future.
                    W E Gladstone 1866 (Speech on the Reform Bill)

Rehabilitation is a relatively young branch of psychiatry. Within its short life there have been many changes, including the introduction and scientific evaluation of effective drug and social therapies, the move of former long-stay patients into the community and the closure of some large mental hospitals. This would not have been possible without the development of a range of complementary services provided by other agencies working in the mental health field. But what about the future? Some changes are inevitable and easy to predict: others are more speculative. The pace of change continues to accelerate, bringing in its wake many fresh challenges for all of those working in the field.

THE CHALLENGE FOR POLITICIANS

In most countries, services for people with chronic mental health problems are funded, almost entirely, from the public purse. This makes them vulnerable to political dogma and economic pressures. The increase in the numbers of people with serious mental health problems being returned to the community coincides with a prolonged period of economic recession, rising unemployment and homelessness. There is real concern that these vulnerable individuals may be denied access to the services they need and deserve.

The advent of 'consumerism' in all service industries places the onus on individuals to demand the services they require and to use complex complaints procedures if the service is poor or unavailable. Unfortunately, people with chronic and severe mental health problems, because of their handicaps, will be unable to make full use of 'consumer power'. It is necessary for others to lobby on their behalf and to raise political awareness of these issues. Unsightly homelessness in city centres will not be cured by the short-term provision of hostel places alone. The needs of this disparate group will vary and individuals' needs must be assessed. The political challenge is to provide appropriate levels of funding for rehabilitation.

THE CHALLENGE OF EQUALITY

Changes in rehabilitation are of great importance to women. The move to community care has increased the burden on family carers, most of whom are women. The increasing numbers of the elderly (set to rise into the next century), mean an increase in the number of people with dementia, and the majority of very old people are women. Mental health problems of most sorts are more likely to be experienced by women. Yet those who plan and manage mental health services, and the politicians responsible for funding (local or national) are more likely to be men.

Living in a multicultural society brings the challenge of providing appropriate services that are accessible to all, respecting cultural, social and religious differences. This will only be successfully achieved when those employed on the planning and managing of services reflect the cultural and sexual mix of society.

THE CHALLENGE OF EVALUATION

Great progress has been made in evaluating the effectiveness of specific drug and social interventions. These rigorous evaluations have been based on scientific principles using control groups and 'blind' rating. How will the whole range of new services be evaluated? The danger is that in the enthusiasm for 'consumerism' market research will replace real evaluation. The challenge for the next decade is to develop evaluation procedures that take into account client preference, as well as cost, efficacy and quality.

THE CHALLENGE OF PREVENTION

The UK government publication 'The Health of the Nation' (1992) sets health targets including: the more effective management of stress in people presenting to their general practitioner; a reduction of alcohol- and tobacco-related disorders; a reduction in the rising suicide rate. Simple counselling and relaxation techniques, together with the use of Eastern skills, such as yoga and meditation, may achieve the first target. The level of alcohol and tobacco consumption in a society is related to the real cost of these commodities. Government taxation policies are likely to have far greater impact than any advice from doctors.

The causes of suicide are many and complex. Yet we know that over half of those who commit suicide in Britain have been treated for a mental health problem at some stage in their life, and of those, the majority will have been seen by the mental health services within the two months prior to their death. The link between community care and suicide has already been raised. The challenge will be to ensure that in the move to the community individuals do not fall through gaps between the different services.

THE CHALLENGE OF CHANGE

The accelerating rate of change presents, perhaps, the greatest challenge to those working in the field of mental health. New patterns of funding, management and training may be perceived as threats by many. Working in new environments with new colleagues from different professional backgrounds requires a flexibility that not everyone will possess. Staff support is too important to leave to managers; it should be the responsibility of all of us.

Gladstone's quotation at the head of this chapter is apposite. Opposition to progress will never succeed for long. The future should be viewed as a challenge, ripe with opportunities if only we can spot them.

REFERENCES

Department of Health 1992 The Health of the Nation: a strategy for health in England, HMSO, London

Index

ABC (antecedent: behaviour: consequence) analysis in challenging behaviour, 255
ABS (Adaptive Behaviour Scale) (American Association on Mental Deficiency), 254
Accommodation, provision of, 39, 105, 248–289, 250
Acquired immune deficiency syndrome (AIDS), 160, 173,176–177, 209, 218 (Table 13.1), 227
  people with learning disability, vulnerability, 257
  risk in babies of HIV-positive mothers, 239
  see also Human immunodeficiency virus (HIV)
Acute confusional states (delirium), 196–197
Adaptive Behaviour Scale (ABS) (American Association on Mental Deficiency), 254
Adult Training Centres (ATCs), 247, 250
Advisory Committee on Alcoholism: 'The pattern and range of services for problem drinkers' (1978), 168
Advisory Council on the Misuse of Drugs, 163, 165, 175
Advocacy movement/advocacy support, 70, 233
  see also Self-help/self-advocacy, organisations for
Age Concern, 202
Ageing see Old age
AIDS see Acquired immune deficiency syndrome (AIDS)
Alcohol abuse, 159–166, 218 (Table 13.1), 221
  'new chronic patients' in hospital, 31

services for alcohol abusers, 166–168, 177
  community alcohol teams, 168
  counselling and education, role of, 172–174
  detoxification, 167, 168
  in-patient services, 31, 167, 168
  out-patient care, 167–168
  support groups, 174–175
  voluntary organisations, 174–175
  see also Substance abuse
Alcoholics Anonymous, 174
Alzheimer's disease, 188, 209
Alzheimer's Disease Association, 194, 202
American Association on Mental Deficiency
  Adaptive Behaviour Scale, 254
  classification of degrees of mental handicap, 237, 240 including Table 14.2
American Psychiatric Association
  Diagnostic and Statistical Manuals (DSM), 28–29, 162
  mental handicap/learning disability, criteria for diagnosis (DSM-III-R: 1980), 234
  schizophrenia, classification and diagnosis (DSM-III-R: 1987), 23, 85 including Table 6.3
Amitriptyline, 81, 82 (Table 6.2)
Anorexia nervosa, 26, 220
Antidepressants, 38, 81, 82 (Table 6.2), 195
Antipsychiatric movement, 20–21, 39
Anxiety, 25, 26, 29, 77
  old people, 187
  physical conditions giving rise to, 214, 218 including Table 13.1, 220

Assessment, 61, 75–76, 97, 99, 102
  dementia, 190–192
  learning disability, 251–253, 254
  methods of, 61–66
    assessment forms, designing of,
      63–64
    check lists, inventories,
      questionnaires, rating scales,
      schedules, 62–66, 73
    disadvantages of different types of
      assessment, 65–66
    observation and behavioural
      analysis, 64
    recording of information, 64–65,
      66
  of need, 69, 70–71, 102–106,
    107–108, 109, 113
    medical and psychological needs,
      103–105
    resource–based needs, 105–106
  skills, 61, 63, 64, 67–69
  purpose of, 61
  timing of
    people in hospital, 67–68
    people in the community, 68–69
  topics for assessment, 69–71
  transcultural aspects, 149–150
Asylums
  historical aspects, 35–37, 38, 42
  see also Hospitals
Audit Commission report: 'Making a
  reality of community care'
  (1986), 41
Audit in health care, 73, 81, 126–127

Bereavement, 19, 199–202
'Better Services for the Mentally Ill'
  (DHSS 1975), 40
Blurring of roles in professionals, 70,
  119, 121–123, 128, 129
Bulimia, 220

Camberwell Family Interview, and
  assessment of expressed
  emotion, 87
Camphill-Rudolph Steiner schools, 245
Cancer, 209, 211, 219, 227
Capgras syndrome, 194, 195
Carbamazepine, 257
'Care Management and Assessment'
  (SSI 1991), 70
Care packages 75–76, 97, 111, 113, 251
  'Care Management and Assessment'
    (SSI 1991), 70
  community care, 76, 102–103,
    108–111

assessment of needs, 69, 70–71,
  102–106, 107–108, 113
co-ordination of care package,
  106–107
dilemmas in planning of services,
  107–108
hospital care, 97–102
  aims, 97, 98, 99
  goals, 97, 98, 99, 102
  objectives, 97–98
  priorities, establishing of, 99, 100
  recording treatment plans, 99–100
  treatment planning and
    implementation, 97–98 including
    Fig. 7.1, 100–101
  treatment termination, 102
mental handicap, care plan concept
  253–254
'Caring for People: Community Care
  in the Next Decade and Beyond'
  (DHSS 1989), 41, 123–124
Case management, 106–107, 113, 115,
  124–125, 251
  'Care Management and Assessment'
    (SSI 1991), 70
CBR (community-based rehabilitation)
  see Community care
Challenging behaviour in people with
  learning disabilities, 254–255,
  257
Chlordiazepoxide (Librium), 37–38
Chlorpromazine, 37, 82 (Table 6.2)
  schizophrenia treatment, 89, 92,
    93
Chronic brain failure see Dementia
City Roads Project, London (for drug
  abusers), 169
Classification of psychiatric disorders,
  21, 25–28, 28–29, 32
Clifton assessment procedures for the
  elderly (CAPE), 192
Clinical audit, 73, 81, 126–127
  see also Institutionalisation
Clopenthixol, 257
Clozapine, 82 (Table 6.2)
  schizophrenia treatment, 90, 93
Cognitive-behavioural theory, and
  mental illness, 77
Communication, 6, 12–13, 43
  families of mentally ill persons, 140,
    141–142
  listening to the client, 7
  transcultural aspects, 146
Community alcohol teams, 168
Community-based rehabilitation
  (CBR) see Community care

Community care, 108–111, 135–137, 143
  assessment of people, timing of, 68–69
  attempts to treat chronic patients in the community, 55–56
  cost: comparison with hospital-based care, 58
  daily living programme (DLP), 54, 58
  development of, 35–40, 241
    changes in recent years, 41–42
    learning from the past, 42–43
  hazards of, 57
  home versus hospital, 45–46, 58
  knowledge of the community important for rehabilitation team, 7, 101, 230
  limitations of experimental evaluation studies, 57–58
  mental handicap, 248–251
  normalisation, 55, 78, 240, 241–242
  stages in rehabilitation, 4–6
  substance abusers see Substance abuse
  teamwork, problems arising in, from movement towards community care, 127–128
  theory of community psychiatry, 46–47
  see also Care packages, community care; Families, and rehabilitation
'Community Care: A Reappraisal' (GAP 1983), 40
'Community Care – an Agenda for Action' (Griffiths Report 1988), 41, 242, 251
Community carers (adult fostering scheme), 249
Community drug teams, 169
Community mental handicap teams (CMHTs), 246, 252–253
Community psychiatric nurses (CPNs), 4, 39, 169
Computers, use of
  in assessment, 62, 64, 66
  in research, 73
Crisis intervention service, applied to families, 140, 142
  Family Crisis Therapy (FCT) teams, 37, 53–54 including Table 4.1, 58
Critical psychiatry, 21

Daily living programme (DLP), 54, 58
Day care, 49, 104, 106, 167–168, 241
Day centres, 104, 107, 167–168, 187, 247
Day hospitals see under Hospitals

Death
  bereavement, grief, and thoughts on death, 19, 199–202
  dying persons, grief of: and counselling, 201
  impact on professional carers of death of patient, 201–202
Deinstitutionalisation, 4–6, 35, 36–43, 45–46, 55–58, 135–137
  see also Community care, development of; Normalisation
Delirium, 196–197
Delusions, 26
  hospital admissions, decisions on, 46–47
  old people, 195, 196, 197
  schizophrenia, 85 (Table 6.3), 86, 92, 93
  self-harm carried out in response to, 221
Dementia, 26, 28, 32, 187, 188, 209
  management, 190–192
  'new chronic patients' in hospital, 31
  physical conditions related to, 190, 218 (Table 13.1), 221
  pre-senile, 188
    in people with learning disability, 256
  symptoms, 188–190
Dementia praecox, 22
  see also Schizophrenia
Depression, 26, 29, 77, 82, 218 (Table 13.1)
  old people, 187, 192, 195–196, 196
  physical conditions giving rise to, 214–215, 218 (Table 13.1), 219
  post-natal, 20
  suicide association, 198, 221
  see also Manic-depressive disorder
Diagnosis, 21, 23–25, 32, 75–76
  advantages and disadvantages, 24
  reliability of, 28–29
Diagnostic and Statistical Manuals (DSM) (American Psychiatric Association), 28–29, 162
  mental handicap/learning disability, criteria for diagnosis (DSM-III-R: 1980), 234
  schizophrenia, classification and diagnosis (DSM-III-R: 1987), 23, 85 including Table 6.3
Disability, meaning of, 2–3
Disability Assessment Schedule (WHO DAS) (World Health Organisation 1988), 62

Disabled Income Group (DIG), 230
Disabled persons, rights of, 3, 233
DLP (daily living programme), 54, 58
Douglas House, Manchester (hostel), 55
Down's syndrome 238 (Table 14.1), 239, 249
  Down's Syndrome Association, 243
  pre-senile dementia association, 256
Droperidol, 81, 82 (Table 6.2)
  schizophrenia treatment, 93
Drug abuse, 159–166, 221
  HIV infection *see under* Human immunodeficiency virus (HIV) infection
  psychiatric symptoms, 218 (Table 13.1)
  services for drug abusers, 168–172, 177
    community drug teams, 169
    counselling and education, role of, 172–174
    detoxification, 169
    hostels, 170–171
    in-patient units, 169
    needle and syringe exchange schemes, 171–172, 173
    outreach programmes, 171
    support groups, 174–175
    therapeutic communities, 170
    voluntary organisations, 165, 174–175
  training of professionals in rehabilitation, 175–177
  see also Substance abuse
Drugs used in therapy
  adverse effects, 94–95
    tardive dyskinesia, 76, 81, 94–95
  attitude of clients and patients to medication, 11
  introduction of (1952–1962), 37–38
  learning disability, 256–257
  psychotropic drugs, 79–82
  classification, 82 (Table 6.2)
  supervision of medication, 104
  see also specifically named drugs

ECT (electroconvulsive therapy), 83–84, 90, 195–196
Education (Mentally Handicapped Children) (Scotland) Act (1974), 241
EE (expressed emotion)
  HEE (high expressed emotion), 141
  schizophrenia association, 87, 91, 94
Elderly people *see* Old age

Electroconvulsive therapy (ECT), 83–84, 90, 195–196
Employment opportunities
  people with learning disabilities, 247
  people with mental health problems, 105
Ethnic minorities *see* Transcultural aspects of rehabilitation
Eugenics Movement, 240–241
Evaluation, 61, 71–73, 97, 98 (Fig. 7.1), 102, 110–111
  programme evaluation, 71–72, 73
  quality assurance, 71, 102
  transcultural aspects, 152–153
Expressed emotion (EE)
  high expressed emotion (HEE), 141
  schizophrenia association, 87, 91, 94

Families, and rehabilitation, 133–135
  crisis periods, 140, 142
    see also Family Crisis Therapy (FCT) teams
  future of rehabilitation, 143
  meaning of 'family', 134
  meaning of 'rehabilitation', 134–135
  mental handicap (learning disability) of child, 243–244
    of adult, 248
  mentally ill persons (two groups) concerned in rehabilitation process, 135–137
  old people's families, 193–194, 195
  physical disability of a member of the family, 213, 216
  respite care, 142
  support for families as carers, 104–105, 140–143, 193–194, 195
    needs, 137–140
  transcultural aspects, 153–154
  see also Expressed emotion
Family Crisis Therapy (FCT) teams, 37, 53–54 *including* Table 4.1, 58
FCT *see* Family Crisis Therapy (FCT) teams
Flupenthixol decanoate, 82 (Table 6.2)
  schizophrenia management, 94
Future challenges in rehabilitation, 259–261

Gentle teaching in challenging behaviour therapy, 255
Geriatric Health Scale (GHS), 192
GHQ 30 (General Health Questionnaire 30), 73
Grief, 19, 199–202

Griffiths Report: 'Community Care – an Agenda for Action' (1988), 41, 242, 251
Group for the Advancement of Psychiatry (GAP), 39, 40, 45, 46, 202

Half-way houses, 4, 55, 161
  see also Hostels
Hallucinations, 26, 46, 221
  acute confusional state (delirium) in old people, 196
  hospital admissions, decisions on, 46–47
  schizophrenia, 85 including Table 6.3, 86, 92, 93
  self-harm carried out in response to, 221
HALO (Hampshire Assessment for Living with Others) assessment in learning disability, 254
Haloperidol, 81, 82 (Table 6.2), 257
Haloperidol decanoate, 82 (Table 6.2)
  in schizophrenia management, 94
Handicap
  derived from mental illness, 20
  meaning of, 2–3, 206
Head injury, 209, 226, 229
  psychiatric symptoms produced by, 218 (Table 13.1), 219, 220
Headway (self-help group for head injury patients), 220, 229
Headway Halfway House (substance abuse treatment centre), 175
'Health of the Nation, The' (Government report 1991), 160, 166–167, 260
HEE (high expressed emotion), 141
  see also EE (expressed emotion)
High expressed emotion (HEE), 141
  see also Expressed emotion (EE)
HIV see Human immunodeficiency virus (HIV) infection
'Hospital Services for the Mentally Ill' (DHSS 1971), 39
Hospitals
  adverse effects on patient of admission to, 47, 49, 51–52, 135–136
    see also Institutionalisation
  alcohol abuse, treatment, 167–168
  assessment of patients, timing of, 67–68
  attempts to manage without admission to, 53–55, 57

'capital charging' of, 42
closure of mental hospitals, 56, 58
cost of care: comparison with community care, 58
day hospitals, 37, 54, 167
day versus in-patient care, 54–55
development of rehabilitation in: and development of community care, 36–43
factors affecting decision to admit patient (historical aspect) 46–47
'graduate patients', 31–32
home versus hospital, in psychiatric care concepts, 45–46, 58
length of stay, attempts to reduce, 52–53, 57
mental handicap, institutions, 247–248
'new chronic patients', 31
stages in rehabilitation in, 3–5
transcultural aspects of admission, 148–149
ward rounds, teamwork and leadership aspects, 120
  see also Asylums; Care packages, hospital care
Hostels, 4, 37, 40, 54, 55, 250
  drug abuse rehabilitation, 170–171
Human immunodeficiency virus (HIV) infection
  drug abusers, 160, 165, 171–172, 173–174, 174, 221
    training of professionals in rehabilitation, 176–177
  people with learning disability, vulnerability, 257
  risk in babies of HIV-positive mothers, 239
  psychiatric symptoms, 218 (Table 13.1)
Huntington's chorea, 209

Individual programme plan (IPP) in care planning for learning disability, 253–254
Informant Questionnaire of Cognitive Decline in the Elderly (IQCODE), 192
Informed consent to treatment, 83
Institutionalisation, 20, 45, 47, 248
  attempts to manage without hospital admission, 53–55
  attempts to reduce length of hospital stay, 52–53
  institutional syndrome, 47–52

Institutionalisation (*contd*)
  attempts to combat the syndrome, 50–51
Intelligence Quotient measurements, 63, 234–238, 240
International Classification of Diseases (ICD) (World Health Organisation), 28, 29
  schizophrenia, diagnosis of, 85

Key workers, 69, 70, 106, 107, 115, 123
  goal planning in physical disability rehabilitation, 222
  transcultural aspects, 151
  ward rounds in hospitals, 120

Learning disability *see* Mental handicap (learning disability)
Learning theory on behaviour, 77
Leucotomy, 84
Lofepramine, 81, 82 (Table 6.2)
Lunacy Acts, 36
Lunch clubs, 5, 105, 187

'Making a reality of community care' (Audit Commission Report 1986), 41
Management Advisory Service report (MAS 1989): role of clinical psychology, 117, 122–123
Management in rehabilitation
  challenges, 76
  models of mental illness, 76–78
  planning, 75–76
  see also Assessment; Care packages; Case management; Evaluation; Treatment
Manic-depressive disorder, 23, 26, 28, 30, 83
  see also Depression
Maudsley Hospital, 36
  daily living programme (DLP) studies, 54, 58
  schizophrenia treatment trial, 89–90
Medication *see* Drugs used in therapy
MENCAP (Royal Society for Mentally Handicapped Children and Adults), 57, 236, 249, 258
Mental Deficiency Act (1913), 241
Mental handicap (learning disability), 233, 258
  adolescents with learning disability, 245–248
    after school/college, 247
    adulthood, 248–251

leaving home, 248–250
  leisure and recreational activities, 250–251
  resettlement: change from institution-based to community-based care, 250
  causes, 238 *including* Table 14.1
  challenging behaviour in, 254–255, 257
  children with learning disabilities, 243–245
    school age, 244–245
  classification of degrees of, 237, 240 *including* Table 14.2
  current situation on service provision, 242–243
  definitions, 28, 234–237
  diagnosis, 234–237
  drugs used in therapy, 256–257
  families of people with learning disabilities
    children with disabilities, 243–245
    adults with disabilities, 248
  habilitation and rehabilitation, 239, 242–243, 251–254
    assessment, 251–253, 254
    care plan, 253–254
  historical aspects, 240–242
  incidence and prevalence, 237–238, 240 (Table 14.2)
  institutions, 247–248
  mental illness in people with learning disability, 255–257
    pre-senile dementia, 256
  normalisation, 240, 241–242
  prevention, 239–240
  sexuality, 257
  social skills, deficits in, 257–258
'Mental Handicap: Patterns for Living': (Open University and MENCAP 1986), 258
Mental Health Act (1959), 38, 241
Mental Health Act (1983), 40, 134, 241
  mental handicap, definitions of, 236–237
Mental Health (Northern Ireland) Order (1986), 241
  mental handicap, definitions of, 236–237
Mental Health (Scotland) Act (1960), 38
Mental Health (Scotland) Act (1984), 40, 134, 241
  mental handicap, definitions of, 236–237
Mental illness *see* Psychiatric disorders
Mental Treatment Act (1930), 36

MIND (National Association for Mental Health), 39
Mini-Mental State Examination (MMSE), 192
Minnesota method (substance abuse treatment method), 174–175
Morningside Rehabilitation Status Scale (MRSS), 62
Multidisciplinary teamwork see Teamwork
Multiple sclerosis, 208, 209, 211, 218 (Table 13.1), 219, 224
    Multiple Sclerosis Society, 229
Myalgic encephalomyelitis (ME), 218 (Table 13.1), 219

Narcotics Anonymous, 174
National Alliance for the Mentally Ill (NAMI), 142
National Health Service, 37–42
National Health Service and Community Care Act (1990), 41, 70, 102, 163, 165
    people with learning disabilities, 242–243, 249
National Schizophrenia Fellowship (NSF), 40, 57, 142
Needs
    assessment and management, 69, 70–71, 102–106, 107–108, 109, 113
        medical and psychological needs, 103–105
        resource-based needs, 105–106
        skills see Skills
    dilemmas in planning of services, 107–108
    families' needs, 137–140
Neuroleptic malignant syndrome complicating antipsychotic medication, 95
Neurosis, 28, 78, 82
    definition, 25–26, 26–27
    outcome, 30
    see also Depression; Obsessional neurosis; Phobic neurosis
Normalisation, 55, 78, 240, 241–242
Nucleus (voluntary organisation providing counselling of families with learning disabled children), 243

Obsessional neurosis, 26, 77, 82, 195
Occupational therapy, 36, 40, 52, 117, 126, 187
Old age, 181, 202–203

abnormal ageing, 188
    acute confusional state (delirium), 196–197
    delusions, 195, 196, 197
    dementia (chronic brain failure) see Dementia
    depression, 187, 192, 195–196, 196
    family of elderly person, problems of, 193–194, 195
    paraphrenia, 197
    physical changes, 190
    problem behaviour, 194–195
    pseudo-dementia, 196
    relatives' groups, 194
    therapies for elderly people, 193
    unidentified physical illness, 197
abuse of the elderly, 197–198
bereavement and thoughts on death, 199–201
challenges of working with the elderly, 202–203
enduring power of attorney, 199
grief, 199–201
incapacity in managing affairs, 198–199
myths of, 181–182
normal ageing, 182
    future aspects, 186
    management of, 185–186
    physical changes, 182–183
    psychological changes, 183
    social changes, 184–185
    support for old people, 186–187
suicide and suicidal behaviour, 194, 198
testamentary capacity, 199

Paraphrenia, 197
Parents see Families, and rehabilitation
People First organisation, 233
Personality, definition of, 27
Personality disorder, definition of, 27
PHAB (Physically Handicapped and Able Bodied) (club), 220
Phenothiazines 82 (Table 6.2)
    schizophrenia treatment, 89, 90
    see also Chlorpromazine
Phenylketonuria, 238 (Table 14.1), 239
Phobic neurosis, 26, 77, 82
Phoenix House (therapeutic community for drug abusers), 170
Physical disability, 205–206
    barriers to integration of disabled person, 215–216
    coping with the disability, 207
        adaptation, theories of, 207–208

Physical disability (*contd*)
  disability, nature of, 210–211
  loss associated with disability,
    211–213
  onset of disability, nature of,
    208–210
  psychological issues in, 213–215
  psychiatric problems contributing to
    physical illness, 220–222
  psychiatric symptoms produced by
    physical conditions, 214–215,
    217–220
  psychological issues, 206–207,
    213–215
  psychosocial problems, 216–217
  rehabilitation in - psychological
    perspective, 206–207, 229–230
  goal planning, 222–223
  information to, and education of,
    patient, 224–225
  privacy of patient, 225
  social skills, 227–229
  suicidal feelings of patient, 226–227
  taking time with patients to discuss
    their feelings, 225–226
Pick's disease, 188
Portage guide to early education
    (learning disabled children), 244
Present State Examination (PSE), 18,
    25, 28, 62, 73, 91
Pressure sores, 224
'Problem Drug Use: A Review of
    Training' (report by the
    Advisory Council on the Misuse
    of Drugs 1990), 175–176
Problem-oriented medical records
    (POMRs), 99–100 *including*
    Fig. 7.2
Procyclidine: schizophrenia
    management, 92, 93
Pseudo-dementia, 196
Psychiatric disorders
  aetiological factors, 29
  classification, 21, 25–28, 28–29, 32
  diagnosis, 21, 23–25, 32, 75–76
    advantages, 24
    disadvantages, 24
    reliability of, 28–29
  'graduate patients' in hospital, 31–32
  handicap resulting from, 20
  'illness', interpretation of, in mental
    illness, 20–21
  models of mental illness, 76–78
    behavioural model, 77
    conspiratorial model, 77
    crisis model, 77

    family interaction model, 77
    medical model, 78
    moral model, 77
    organic model, 77
    psychotherapeutic model, 77–78
    social model, 78
  'new chronic patients' in hospital, 31
  outcome, 29–30
  pathways to psychiatric care, 18–19
  people with learning disabilities,
    psychiatric disorders in, 255–257
  prevalence, 17–18
  prevention
    primary, 19
    secondary, 19–20
    tertiary, 20
  recurrent illness, problems of, 30–31
  *see also specifically named psychiatric
    disorders*
Psychologists, role of, 117, 122–123, 126
Psychosis
  definition, 26–27
  drug nomenclature, 81–82
  hospital admission: historical aspect
    46–47
Psychosurgery, 84
Psychotherapy, 77–78, 82
  schizophrenia treatment, 82, 90

Quality assurance, 71, 102

Reality orientation (in therapy for
    elderly people), 193
Recording of information, 62–66, 73,
    99–100
REHAB (rating scale, for assessment), 62
Rehabilitation
  aims of, 2–3
  definitions and nature of, 1, 16,
    134–135
  factors influencing process of, 12–16
    client, 13
    communication, 12–13
    social, economic and other
      external influences, 15–16
    staff, 14–15
  principles of, 6–12
    application of, 11–12
  stages of
    community context, 4–6
    hospital context, 3–5
Rehabilitation of Metropolitan Addicts
    (ROMA) drug project, 171
Reminiscence therapy (for elderly
    people), 193

Remoxipride, 82 (Table 6.2)
schizophrenia treatment, 90
'Requirement for mourning model' in
adaptation to physical disability,
207–208, 214
Research in rehabilitation, 73
hospital environment evaluation,
51–52
Reserpine, 37
Resources, for rehabilitation, 101, 103,
106, 109
knowledge of, importance for
rehabilitation team, 7, 101, 230
resource-based needs of mentally ill
people, 105–106
Respite care for families, 142
'Restitution' in psychiatric illness, 30
Richmond Fellowship (for community
mental health), 40
Rights of disabled persons, 3, 233
Role blurring in professionals, 70, 119,
121–123, 128, 129
Role expansion in professionals, 119
see also Role blurring in professionals
Role-play, 227, 258
ROMA (Rehabilitation of Metropolitan
Addicts) drug project, 171
Rudolph Steiner organisations, 247, 249
Camphill-Rudolph Steiner schools,
245

Schizophrenia
aetiology, 83, 86–89
antipsychiatry movement, 20–21
development of concept of, 21–23
diagnosis, 21–23, 28, 32, 85–86
including Table 6.3
electroconvulsive therapy
(contentious role of), 83
hospitals
admission, historical aspect, 46–47
effect of hospital environment,
research evidence, 51–52
'new chronic patients' in, 31
short stay and normal stay
compared, 52–53
incidence, prevalence and
distribution, 36, 84–85, 86, 137
management and treatment
acute management, 92–93
assessment, 91–92
failure to respond to treatment, 93
long-term management, 93–94
physical treatment, 89–90
psychosocial interventions, 90–91
psychotherapy, 82, 90

serious side-effects and
complications in antipsychotic
medication, 94–95
very disturbed patient, 93
National Schizophrenia Fellowship
(NSF), 40, 57, 142
prognosis, 30, 93–94 including
Table 6.4
schizophrenogenic families, concept
of, 88
self-harm carried out in response to
delusions, 221
symptoms, 22–23, 26, 85–86, 92
treatment see management and
treatment
Schneider's symptoms of the first rank
(schizophrenia), 22–23, 86
SCODA (Standing Conference on
Drug Abuse), 175
Scottish Association for Mental Health
(SAMH), 39
Scottish Society for Autistic Children,
245
Seebohm Committee Report (1968), 39
Selective serotonin re-uptake inhibitors
(SSRIs), 82 (Table 6.2), 195
Self-help/self-advocacy, organisations for
families, 143
mental handicap, 233, 246–247
physical handicap, 220, 229–230, 230
substance abuse, 174
Sexuality
old people, 182–183
people with learning disability, 257
people with physical disability, 217,
228
Shared action plan: in care planning in
learning disability, 253–254
Short Report (report from Social
Services Committee of House of
Commons 1985), 41
Skills, 105
assessment, 61, 63, 64, 67–69
people with physical disability, 224,
227–229
professional carers, 14, 62, 121–123,
128, 129
social skills, 63, 69, 227–229,
257–258
substance abusers, 166
Smoking, and mental and physical
health, 160, 224, 239
Social treatment of psychiatric
conditions, 83, 103–104
social skills training, 227–229,
257–258

Social workers, 36, 39, 40, 126, 187
    in community drug teams, 169
Sodium amytal interview, 196
Spinal injury, 209, 211, 224, 226
    Spinal Injuries Association, 229
Staff
    attitude of, to rehabilitation work
        and to patients, 10, 15, 50
    knowledge possessed by, 14
    skills of, 14, 62, 121–123, 128, 129
Standing Conference on Drug Abuse
    (SCODA), 175
Stress
    schizophrenia associated with, 83,
        86, 87
    social treatment of, 83
Stroke, 209, 211, 215
Substance abuse, 159–162, 220
    rehabilitation, 162–164, 177
        community reinforcement, 166
        counselling and education, role of,
            172–174
        facilities of, 164–166
        multidisciplinary teamwork, 164
        relapse prevention, 166
        skill training, 166
        support groups, 174–175
        training in, 175–177
        voluntary organisations, 165,
            174–175
    see also Alcohol abuse; Drug abuse
Suicide: and suicidal behaviour and
        feelings
    community care involvement, 57, 261
    old people, 194, 198
    physical disability: suicidal feelings
        resulting from, 226–227
    physical injury due to unsuccessful
        suicide attempts, 221, 226
    schizophrenia, association, 92

TAPS (Team for the Assessment of
        Psychiatric Studies), 56, 58
Tardive dyskinesia as adverse effect of
        drugs used in therapy, 76, 81,
        94–95
Teamwork, 6, 14–15, 113–115,
        128–129
    case management, 106–107, 113,
        115, 124–125, 251
    'Care Management and
        Assessment' (SSI 1991), 70
    collaboration between team
        members, 126–127
    definitions of, 115–116

    key workers, 69, 70, 106, 107, 115,
        123
    goal planning in physical disability
        rehabilitation, 222
    transcultural aspects, 151
    ward rounds in hospitals, 120
    multi-racial teams, 156
    need for, 116–117
    patient involvement, 125–126
    problems and conflicts, 117–123
        blurring of roles, 70, 119,
            121–123, 128, 129
        leadership, 119–120
        movement towards community
            care, 127–128
        ward rounds, 120
    substance abusers, 164
Thurston House (substance abuse
        treatment centre), 175
Transcultural aspects of rehabilitation,
        7, 145, 156, 230
    adaptation by migrants, 147–148
    culture
        definition and significance, 145
        difficulties arising from cultural
            differences, 147
    ethical and political issues, 155
    language problems, 146
    migration into Britain in recent
        years, 145–146
    multi-racial health teams, 156
    recruitment of professionals from
        ethnic minorities, 155
    rehabilitation process
        referrals, 148
        admission to rehabilitation unit,
            148–149
        assessment, 149–150
        rehabilitation planning, 150–151
        implementation of rehabilitation
            plan, 151–152
        evaluation, 152–153
        discharge/placement, 153–154
    separate facilities or integrated
        service?, 154–155
Transcultural Psychiatry Unit
        (Bradford), 146–148, 151, 152,
        155
    programme of Unit's study days
        adaptation of migrants, 147–148
        culture, 147
        language problems, 146
Treatment, 95
    choice of, 76–78, 79 including
        Table 6.1
    informed consent to, 83

Treatment (*contd*)
  physical methods of, 79–84
  range of, 79
  see also Care packages; Management
    in rehabilitation
'Treatment and Rehabilitation' (Report
    of the Advisory Council on the
    Misuse of Drugs 1982), 163
Trethowan Report (DHSS 1977),
    117
Tricyclic antidepressants, 38, 81, 82
    (Table 6.2)
Trifluoperazine: schizophrenia
    management, 94
Tunbridge Report on rehabilitation
    (DHSS 1973), 117

United Nations Declaration on the
    Rights of Disabled Persons
    (1975), 3, 233

Valpar Battery for occupational skills
    assessment, 63
Viruses
  psychiatric problems arising from
    infections, 218 (Table 13.1),
    219, 219–220
  schizophrenia, is it caused by
    infection?, 87

Voluntary organisations, 39–40,
    106–107, 229–230
  for elderly people, 194, 202
  for families, 142, 143
  for people with learning disabilities,
    243, 246, 247, 249, 250
  for substance abusers, 165, 174–175
  *see also specifically named voluntary
    organisations*

Wagner Report (1988), 55
Work, opportunities for
  people with learning disabilities,
    247
  people with mental health problems,
    105
'Working for Patients' (DHSS 1989),
    41–42
World Health Organisation
  Disability Assessment Schedule
    developed by, 62
  International Classification of
    Diseases (ICD) produced by,
    28, 29, 85
Worthing Experiment (1958), 38

Younghusband Report (1959), 116